Will Pop Eat Itself?

WILL POP EAT ITSELF?

Jeremy J. Beadle

faber and faber

LONDON · BOSTON

First published in Great Britain in 1993
by Faber and Faber Limited
3 Queen Square
London WCIN 3AU

Photoset by Cambridge Composing (UK) Ltd, Cambridge
Printed by Clays Ltd, St Ives Plc.

A CIP record for this book is available from the British Library

ISBN 0-571-16241-X

10 9 8 7 6 5 4 3 2 1

Contents

Acknowledgements

Many people have contributed ideas and thoughts which have fed into my creative process. Amongst those I should single out are: Anthony Sellors, who commissioned the radio talk which started it all; Ben Rich and Gerard Hurley, for valuable comments and for challenging my tendency to glib generalization; Pascal Gabriel, for insights into producing; Colin Howes and Alexis Grouwer for legal thoughts; Boyd Steemson, for views on management in the music business; and Tracey Scoffield at Faber and Faber, for endless patience and putting much into perspective.

The largest debts of gratitude are due to: Rex Brough, a good producer and a good friend, whose enthusiasm saw me through some moments of extreme lassitude; and, of course, to Chris Barstow, who helped conceive the book and then had to nurse me practically every step of the way and never once complained about the fact.

I also owe a vast amount to my father, who died in December 1992. Despite having little or no sympathy with the subject, he gave me unflagging practical and moral support which I could never hope to repay. I wish he could have seen the end result.

All these people have done their best to put this book on the right track; if it has gone off the rails, it has done so entirely under my own steam.

Introduction

'Give me Big Mac, fries to go'
Pop Will Eat Itself,
'Def Con One', 1989

As opening quotations go, this must seem spectacularly crass and superficial. But context is all.

'Def Con One' is one of the best tracks on the album *This is the Day . . . This is the Hour . . . This is This!*, an album on which the band Pop Will Eat Itself took their practice of making 'songs' by collage, using bits of other people's records, to a neurotically humorous extreme. The album was very much a reaction to what was going on around the band, both in their own profession and in the 'real world' beyond pop music. Starting from the premise 'Astley's in the noose' – it was popular in 1988 and 1989 to pillory poor old Rick Astley for being the ultimate in plastic manufactured pop – and encompassing such music-business social events as James Brown's arrest and imprisonment, *This is the Day* drew in images and sounds like a radio antenna restlessly trying to tune in to about seventy stations at once. Much of the impact lay in the collision of these disparate elements. 'Def Con One' managed to cram together into the space of one four-minute track snatches of The Osmonds, Lipps Inc. (a Giorgio Moroder synthesizer disco invention), The Creatures (half of Siouxsie and the Banshees),

The Isley Brothers and the theme from *The Twilight Zone*, to name about one-twentieth of what's going on, all at 118 beats per minute, and all gathered around a lyric about nuclear warfare in the age of designer consumerism – 'Def Con One' is one of the stages in a nuclear alert.

That all this material can be fitted on to a single pop record is due almost entirely to the digital sampler, a piece of hardware which allows the user to take pre-recorded sound, edit it, change it, distort it and remould it. When the sampler first appeared in the early 1980s, few people imagined it would have much effect – another new toy, a nine-days' wonder, which would soon be put aside, a Mellotron for the digital age. Except that somewhere in the mid-1980s, the sampler's potential collided with the cutting and scratching techniques popular in the music of New York's hip-hop scene, and a whole range of pop musicians were inspired to create a different kind of music, a music which raided pop's past and put it in a new and modern – and sometimes quite unnerving – context.

There comes a time in all artistic fields when the tradition of the past weighs so heavily that the only way forward seems to be to 'rip it up and start again'. Sometimes the ripping up can be of the most basic constituent elements – a return to the twelve notes outside any context of key signatures, the use of underlying geometric figures like cubes. Sometimes the way forward seems to lie in cannibalizing that weight of tradition which lies so heavy. That's certainly something of the impetus behind the music of Pop Will Eat Itself and The Justified Ancients of Mu Mu. In a literary context a similar inspiration had led T. S. Eliot, under Ezra Pound's guidance, to produce *The Waste Land* in 1922, that neurotic reflection of Eliot's private disasters and the post-Great War landscape of desolation. *The Waste Land* too is a work of collage, relying at least in part on the dislocation and the relocation of the familiar in a bleak and novel context, where Cleopatra floats into a world peopled by

2

pub chatterers keen to 'get the beauty of it hot' (food again). A Sunday roast speaks as many volumes about the social pretensions and hopes of Eliot's characters, their desire to cling to class values and an economic stability which the Great War had shot to pieces, as the Big Mac and fries say about the consumerist attitudes which Pop Will Eat Itself seek to mirror so neurotically. There's truth in the grim joke that technicians stage-managing the end of the world by ballistics would be quite likely to send out to the nearest McDonald's.

If you really want to know what's going on in a society, look at its popular culture. Recently an American economist suggested that the best source of economic indicators was the pop singles chart, citing the presence of Martika's essentially pessimistic (in so far as it means anything at all) single 'Toy Soldiers' at Number 1 in the summer of 1989 as an indication that the public had lost faith in the 'economic miracle' of the 1980s. This was, in its way, an extension of the old 1960s and 1970s 'hemline theory' – the idea that the length of women's skirts went up and down with economic confidence – and was perhaps a little over-simplistically expressed. Sometimes popular taste will appear to contradict the events of the 'real world'. The UK charts of the second half of 1989 offer a salutary example: as the economy slithered into recession and the Thatcher government inflicted more and more wounds on itself, the British public rushed out to buy . . . Jive Bunny and the Mastermixers and their packaged nostalgia medley records. Again, in 1991, as economic confidence remained stubbornly at rock bottom, despite 'expert' promises of recovery, the UK public turned on their TVs in huge numbers to watch not some caustic, satirical reflection of their plight but a re-creation of the never-never world of H. E. Bates's *The Darling Buds of May*, the first series ever to have all of the episodes of its first run at Number 1 in the ratings. I don't think the presence of a tax-man among the characters has much significance in this context. But setting the popularity of this TV series against the films the UK public flocked to see argues for some deeply disturbing schizophrenia in the British soul. The top three box-office movies for 1991 were *Robin Hood, Prince of Thieves, Terminator 2* and *Silence of the Lambs* – designer violence and psychopathy past, future and present.

Popular taste is obviously prey to the marketing profession and the hype machines, perhaps to a greater extent than ever before. But popular culture is a more subtle and fickle beast than marketing executives will sometimes allow. It's easier to draw conclusions with hindsight than to try and plot graphs of popular taste in advance. There's always something that makes all the would-be pundits shake their heads and ask themselves 'Why?' It's relatively understandable that *The Country Diary of an Edwardian Lady* should spend almost four years on the best-seller lists – nostalgia again. But where did the great thirst for the complex mathematics of Stephen Hawking's *A Brief History of Time* originate? The tragic romance of Hawking's motor neurone condition is scarcely sufficient explanation. That Benny Hill should have had a comedy record at Number 1 in the charts is pretty understandable, but why did the public once flock out seemingly *en masse* for the music-hall Italianisms of Joe Dolce's 'Shaddup You Face'? They all came from 'left-field' – an element of popular taste which makes pop music what it is.

One thing which has always been part of pop music, since the 1960s, is a sense of nostalgia for a lost golden age, and a belief that the successful music of the day isn't 'as good' as what went before. Pop has always looked to its own past, even to the days before pop as we know it was 'invented'. Opinions vary about when exactly that was. American statistical volumes tend to date the 'rock era' from the date in 1955 when Bill Haley and his Comets reached Number 1 with 'Rock around the Clock'. Yet in retrospect, and for all its use in the vandal-provoking film *The Blackboard Jungle*, 'Rock around the Clock' is just another tin-pan alley song, not markedly different from 'Shake, Rattle and Roll', an earlier Hayley hit which was quite happily performed by BBC showbands in the musical interludes of Light Programme comedies (there's a particularly good version of 'Shake, Rattle and Roll' somewhere in the BBC archives performed by Ray Ellington and his band during an edition of *The Goon Show*). However, one thing everyone can agree on is that the first pop star in the modern sense was Elvis Presley. He was the first to have a serious career employing all the marketing and all the technology available, the first star of 'rock 'n' roll'. And Presley recorded cover versions. Even that early in the game, stars looked to the past. From the word go, the cover version (the re-recording of someone else's song) has been part of the game. In the 1950s and early 1960s, it was expected that a big American hit by a relative unknown (or even by a big star) would be covered by a British 'name' (the process happened in reverse too). This was still going on sporadically in 1965, as those who remember Cilla Black's assault on 'You've Lost That Lovin' Feelin'' can testify. However, cover versions were not necessarily the key to success by this time, as The Who's early career shows; it was only when they started writing their own material that they achieved success.

But to some extent pop has always been eating itself. There have always been cover versions, and cover versions have always been present in the charts. This need not automatically be a sign of stagnation, yet by the mid-1980s it was easier to get a hit single in the UK if you were dead or retired or a TV personality than if you were a clever or inventive pop musician. It was at this point that the underground techniques of hip hop and rap collided with the imaginations of various people and the digital sampler, changing the face of pop music as we know it. But the advent of the sampler also coincided with the arrival of the 'sound bite' approach to politics and public life – an approach espoused by both the media and astute politicians who saw which way the wind was blowing – as well as with the arrival of the great consumer boom which gave the 1980s its definitive style. This may have been an accident, but such accidents are quite instructive about society.

And, at the musical level, that's partly what this book is about. It isn't exhaustive by any means, and it is highly subjective and idiosyncratic. All critical opinions are in fact subjective and idiosyncratic, but there's less pretentious objectivity about the criticism of popular culture, and rightly so too, than there is about 'serious' music criticism or literary analysis. Some people might object that I've tended to concentrate too much on what achieved a high profile, on what got into the charts. But love them or loathe them, the charts are the barometer of popular taste and ultimately, whatever they might pretend, anyone who makes a pop record does so in the hope that they'll end up in the charts (and on *Top of the Pops*). The charts tend to make sometimes for a rather train-spotterish approach to the subject, especially for anyone cursed with a statistically organized memory, but they also have their own sense of humour, even when they're being subjected to ruthless manipulation. For example, did EMI realize the sublime joke in ensuring that Cliff Richard's Christmas Number 1 of 1990, the slickly religious 'Saviour's Day', was deposed the week after Christmas by Iron Maiden's 'Bring Your Daughter . . . to the Slaughter'? Probably not, I suspect.

Part of the argument of this book, in its early chapters at any rate, is that the 'crisis' of stagnation which threw mainstream pop on to its new track has happened before at a much 'loftier' level. 'Pop' as we understand it was – whether you date it from Haley, Presley or some other more recondite marker of your own devising – born around 1955 or 1956, and reached a point where it seemed exhausted about thirty years later. The digital sampler proved the ideal tool for pop to take itself apart, thus arriving at modernism and post-modernism simultaneously. If this seems far-fetched, remember that in most 'higher' art both modernism and post-modernism took the basic constituents of the form and placed it in a new context. Context is all. The major difference is that modernism in 'high' art drove the public away in vast numbers. Clearly that didn't happen with pop music: the consumer took to 'Pump up the Volume' and other symptoms of the new music with enthusiasm. In fact, the modernist tendency staked out a pretty fair share of the market. But for how long? And is there any future in this kind of auto-cannibalism? Or is the idea that pop will eat itself a much older one than we realize?

Jeremy J. Beadle
London, February 1992

1 · Things Fall Apart

By their ephemera shall ye know them. It's worth restating that you can learn a lot about a society from its popular culture, and that if you want to get to grips with any period in history, you need to understand what was being consumed – in every conceivable sense – at the time. Even coprology (the study of faeces) can tell us a great deal about everyday life.

So the question 'Will Pop Eat Itself?' is about more than pop. This isn't merely a defence mechanism, born of the fear that it's shameful for adults who can string polysyllabic words together even to be listening to this stuff, let alone taking it seriously. Pop music is an interesting microcosm of all popular culture, of all culture. It has managed to cram into thirty years of frenetic activity and wildly swinging moods a progress from naïvety, through the 'Golden Age' (as people still like to think of the 1960s) into doubt, despair and decadence up to a point where even great pop students and enthusiasts have been heard to declare that it has come to a 'dead end'. Other art forms usually take centuries to go through the same cycle. But popular music will always find some way forward, and has always tended in moments of weakness to feed off itself. Digital technology has simply given a new twist to this perennial tendency.

But how can popular culture be enlightening? Popular culture existed long before pop music as we know it. Every artefact in some way reeks of the period of its creation, but some provide more focused snapshots of their time than others. Take, as a random example, a few key works form the 1930s. Students of 'serious' English literature will tell you that the 1930s is the decade of Auden, Spender and Isherwood; of T. S. Eliot; of James Joyce labouring over *Finnegans Wake*. But in this decade there was an English writer working who has been of no interest to literary critics, yet this same man introduced two concepts which have gained mythological status in the imagination. The constructs were 'Mr Chips', definitive stereotype of the devoted English schoolmaster and 'Shangri-La', the lost Paradise of Eternal Wisdom. The author who dreamt up these ideals was James Hilton, a man who seemed to have the rare knack of writing 'filmable' novels. Not only were *Goodbye Mr Chips* and *Lost Horizon* big box-office successes when given the Hollywood treatment, but Hilton also created the smash hit 1940s weepie with the ludicrous plot, *Random Harvest*. Social and educational trends may perhaps wish Mr Chips a permanent goodbye in the not too distant future, but both he and Shangri-La are ideas which still roam through the imaginations of people who haven't encountered either in book or film form.

Of course Hilton wasn't a 'better' writer than Auden, Eliot or Joyce. If this ability to create 'mythological constructs' were the sole criterion by which you rated authors, then the great twentieth-century writers in English would be Agatha Christie, Margaret Mitchell and Edgar Rice Burroughs. But the ability to strike some chord in the popular imagination – in a way that Auden, Eliot and Joyce could never hope to achieve – is worthy of admiration; and the chords struck by such artists can tell us something about the audience for which they catered. Both Hilton's celebrated creations are ideals beyond any possible reality and are – especially in their Hollywood incarnations – dripping with wishful escapist nostalgia. The film of *Goodbye Mr Chips* hit exactly the right Hiltonian tone. It was a love letter to 'Middle England', drafted in the belief that somehow a decent middle-brow minor public school embodied all that was best about Western liberal culture. The film actually took the book's implicit politics further with a panegyric to rural Austria and by playing up the role of the good German as a crucial agent of the plot. This would scarcely have been lost on anyone with any remote awareness of world events in 1939, the year of the film's release. Shangri-La, the Tibetan paradise of *Lost Horizon*, was a dream of a mystic orientalism which the shabby militarism of the regimes in the Far East had banished from reality. Hilton tapped exactly the right elements to strike a chord in 1930s Britain of nostalgia and escape, above all the sense that somewhere in the world (or even somewhere in the English public-school system) there are elders with a repository of wisdom and understanding.

There's something similar about the obsessive way that *Gone with the Wind* seized the popular imagination – a lost, beautiful and above all chivalrous world, crammed full of glamorous parties, heroism and grand passions, where even the slaves were content and the Ku-Klux-Klan were just a bunch of right-minded vigilantes, seems a lot more attractive than most people's everyday lives. It depicted a war, true, and all the UK audiences were experiencing war in some way as they watched the movie on its original release; but the personal, face-to-face nature of even the carnage of the American Civil War represented an ideal dream world when contrasted with the threat of an impersonal death in a mass air raid. Many great popular successes involve large doses of escapism and sanitized nostalgia. Indeed *The Sound of Music*, one of the most remarkable popular cultural phenomena of the 1960s, offers an interesting example of a double-edged retreat. For those who hated the social changes, the transformations in sexual behaviour and the supremacy of the avant-garde it represented a marvellous assertion of old values, even positing the extreme sexual image of a convent against the 'real world'. But it's also the story of how feminine, matriarchal values assert their superiority over nasty

11

macho militarism, implying that the world would be a better place if the family got together and sang 'Edelweiss' a few times.

There's a book to be written about the impact on the popular imagination of Rodgers and Hammerstein's fake Tyrolean idyll. Certainly it had enough of a hold to find its way into a few digital samplers. 'The Lonely Goatherd' turned up at the end of the short edit of the Justified Ancients of Mu Mu's 'All You Need is Love' and it's hard to imagine that 'Bring Me Edelweiss', Edelweiss's bizarre retread of Abba's 'SOS', was innocent of *The Sound of Music* associations. Such is the iconic power of *The Sound of Music*, that for a vast number of people merely the word 'edelweiss' evokes images of Julie Andrews renouncing her wimple for a dress made out of curtains to spend a life watching Christopher Plummer lip-synching.

The successful pop record is many people's idea of the ultimate in ephemera, and perhaps no form is more rooted in its exact historical moment than the popular song. Hence the 'potency of cheap music' despised by Elyot and Amanda in Noel Coward's *Private Lives* (although the play itself rather celebrates this power). The persistent success of reissued singles and the raiding of the back catalogue by artists using the digital sampler may seem to imply that some popular music is 'timeless', but in almost every case there is some new contemporary association undreamt of at the original moment of manufacture. Take two successful reissues of 1990. 'Unchained Melody' by the Righteous Brothers was itself a cover version of a song already a decade old when first released in 1965. It was reissued to become the best-selling single of 1990, but for most people who bought it in this incarnation it was the love song from the romantic film *Ghost* (the biggest-grossing movie of 1990). The song began life as a highly successful song from an unmemorable 1955 film called *Unchained*. The movie died, but the song took on a life of its own, was recorded by all and sundry over a couple of decades, and returned – in one of these cover versions – to its screen function thirty-five years later. This time the film was successful.

Bobby Vinton's 'Blue Velvet' was also, when it first appeared in 1963, a cover version of a decade-old song, and has also enjoyed a lease of life in a film – the title song of David Lynch's weird and wonderful cult success of 1986. But as with many of the successful reissues in the late 1980s and early 1990s, it was TV advertising which propelled it into the Top 3. I can't imagine that Bobby Vinton had Nivea Cream in mind when he recorded the song. In fact, originally it was part of an early 1960s ancestor of a concept album bringing together a number of songs with the word 'blue' in the title. And it is not very likely that people who bought 'Blue Velvet' in 1990, or hadn't encountered it before then, will automatically think 'Ah, Nivea' when they hear it in future. It would be tempting to make a totally erroneous sociological leap from the Vinton success and its commercial origins and assume that Great Britain in 1990 was obsessed with skin cream – these are the dangers of reading indicators from popular success. What the presence of 'Blue Velvet' near the top of the charts does show, however, is that for many viewers the product pushed by an advertisement and the style and content of the 'advert as film' could be seen as discrete elements.

In both of these cases – which are typical of many others – the recording had been divorced from its original context and married to a completely different context, a context in which the people who bought the record in 1990 will place it in perpetuity. In some ways each song had been cut out of its original picture and pasted into a new one.

The 'cut-and-paste' mentality – working on smaller units – was central to early essays in sampling in pop music. Pop Will Eat Itself's first pieces were very little more than freaky, witty juxtapositions. While the Justified Ancients of Mu Mu's early releases all aimed at having some over-riding integral unity of statement – clashing AIDS fears with samples of the ultimate Page 3 pin-up Samantha Fox in 'All You Need is Love' to great political point – a narrative like that of 'Whitney Joins the JAMs' is little more than an amusing pretext for some very effective cut-and-paste work. But then you don't sign a pledge to be profound when you buy or use a sampler.

Changing the context of artistic artefacts or their constituent fragments happened long before pop music was born. Bits and pieces is what modernism and post-modernism are all about. Both, especially the latter, are terms that get bandied around the rock media rather a lot these days. Both are essentially twentieth-century ideas, but can only really be understood by appreciating what came before, what the certainties were whose loss led to the doubt, irony and cynicism which are the hallmark of the modern and the post-modern. After all, the twentieth century has been the era in which all the old humanist certainties crumbled to dust, bringing conventional, straightforward artistic modes of expression to a crisis from which most are still trying to recover.

The last ninety or so years haven't been too kind to cultural certainty in any manifestation. This period has seen the rapid disintegration of those cultural hegemonies which have formed the basis of the ebb and flow in human affairs since historians started writing. None of the empires which flourished in 1900 is in working order in 1993. Meanwhile the twentieth century's empires have a poor track record: the Soviet Union died before its seventy-fifth birthday, and the American economic empire is in deep financial trouble, irredeemably mortgaged to the Japanese.

European empire-building began on a large scale in the Renaissance, at a time when the philosophical centre of the Western world shifted significantly. Humanism, based broadly on classical precepts, asserted the centrality of man and his ability to control the world around him. This faith in humanity and human reason meant that the art of the period was basically representational and faithful to the outer, anthropocentric world. The modal music, allegorical literature and stylized painting, which were all elements of the theocentric Middle Ages, were gradually transmuted into the forms generally familiar today, the forms which have dominated culture over the past three and more centuries. The Middle Ages had created for itself an elaborate system of forms and formality, of stylization, based on concepts such as chivalry, courtly love and bounded by a powerful, if venal, church establishment which ensured that mortality and pessimism were predominant in human thought. Indeed, if you read a great deal of late medieval literature, it seems to speak straight through to the twentieth century in a way that the triumphalists of the nineteenth century – Kipling when he was crass, the abysmal Alfred Austin, Tennyson in his role as public poet – never approach. And parts of Johan Huizinga's highly influential *The Waning of the Middle Ages*, written in 1924 when the old certainties had suffered a horrific rebuff in the mire of Flanders during the Great War, read like a commentary on Europe in the late 1980s and early 1990s.

From the early sixteenth century, music evolved away from the more oriental, supposedly Greek-based sounds of the old modes (with their Greek names, Phrygian, Dorian, Ionian, etc.) to the diatonic tonality and key systems faithfully taught in music-theory lessons to this day. It was three centuries before anyone openly challenged the supremacy of this tonality. Even composers who found it stifling, like Wagner, Mahler and Richard Strauss, still found elaborate ways of working within its confines. Mahler even applied 'key' labels to his more mature symphonies, but to see his Sixth Symphony described as 'in A minor' or his Ninth 'in D major' doesn't give any sense of the tonal tensions and resolutions which will form part of the works in the way that knowing a Mozart symphony is 'in E flat' will. However, Mahler's successors knew the old ways were no way forward and – to varying degrees and with vastly varying enthusiasm – Schoenberg, Berg and Webern wrenched Western music away from the old diatonic tonality and started again from the basic twelve notes, using them outside a system of key signatures which rely on the traditional euphonious harmony.

The great works of medieval English literature are all, at root, allegorical. *Sir Gawain and the Green Knight*, *Pearl* and *Piers Plowman* are all works which reveal their meaning through a contemporary referential framework and, in the case of *Gawain*, some elaborate colour-coding at whose exact significance we can only make educated and scholarly guesses. While the anonymous poet (or poets) of the first two and William Langland may have been making precise points about human nature and its deficiencies, none of these works were intended primarily as 'mirrors to nature' giving an accurate reflection of everyday life as enjoyed by their authors or any of their authors' contemporaries. *Piers Plowman*, it's true, contains quite a lot of detail about ordinary medieval life, but this is always subsumed by some great allegorical collision with symbolic figures. And if there was such a thing as popular medieval literature, it consisted of the endless stream of romances about chivalry and derring-do derring-done by handsome, brave knights, usually with an Arthurian connection and lots of religious overtones. So many were churned out that a comparison with Mills and Boon isn't entirely inapt, except that God and the Grail tend to do service for the virginal nurses of twentieth-century romances.

But Sir Philip Sidney's treatise *A Defence of Poetry* spoke against the concept of literature as elaborate allegory. This may have something to do with Sidney's Protestantism and the fundamentally Catholic nature of most medieval literature, even the tackiest. The role of literature, as Sidney defined it, was to hold a mirror to nature. He wasn't anticipating Zolaesque realism, of course; his interest was in truths about human nature. Admittedly there's little realism in any sense in the strange crucible of incest, murder and transvestism which is Sidney's *Arcadia*, but in his lyric poetry, especially his sonnet sequence *Astrophel and Stella*, Sidney went a long way towards defining a realistic personal literature which spoke of individual experience while carrying universal resonances. The desire to describe human nature and human emotions in this way marked the literary way forward. No one would call Shakespeare's plots 'realistic', but his greatness lies (verbal dexterity apart) in his delineation of human nature.

The appearance of the novel (whether you want to locate it in seventeenth-century Spain, with Cervantes' *Don Quixote*, or eighteenth-century England, with Richardson's *Pamela*) sig-nalled the existence of a form which was to become dominant in all Western countries in the nineteenth century, and whose hallmark was, above all else, representational realism.

Above all, whatever the written medium or style, up to a certain point in the nineteenth century writers aspired to main-tain the illusion of omniscience within their own work. The great allegories of the Middle Ages threw observations at the reader, who then had to decipher it all. This is particularly true of Chaucer, as Terry Jones's book deciphering the real truth of the 'verray parfit gentil Knight' shows. What you are told at surface level in *The Canterbury Tales* is by no means the whole truth, whereas the story Fielding or George Eliot tells you is a fully rounded picture which doesn't ask you to question the status or reliability of the narrative voice.

The breakdown of authorial certainty and omniscience is traditionally a hallmark of modernism. Convention might place this breakdown somewhere in the early twentieth century, marking the Great War as the historical episode which made its advance to centre stage inevitable. By this reading *The Waste Land* and *Ulysses* (or possibly *A Portrait of the Artist as a Young*

Man) become the seminal modernist works. Slightly more sophisticated readings seize on the works of Pound, Wyndham Lewis and the Vorticists, with Conrad and late Henry James thrown in for good measure as immediate forebears. I'd suggest that one of the great signposts that the old conventional author was on his way out comes with Dickens's *Great Expectations*, in which a good three-quarters of the action is given to the reader by a completely deluded (and not especially sympathetic) narrator. If you can't trust your narrator, who can you trust? You've got to do the work yourself, of course, and when that happens the 'author' becomes less important, because the centre is placed by the reader and not by some authoritative body. This is seen in a much more sophisticated and recognizably modernist fragmentary manner in the works of Henry James, especially in the short story 'In the Cage', which, with its heavily loaded use of fragmentary words and phrases in the form of telegram messages, is at times like a design for a deconstructionist's playground.

'In the Cage' is a story of upper-class adultery and treachery seen entirely through the eyes of a lower-middle-class young woman working at the post office counter in a general store in Mayfair. Her main task is to count the words on telegram forms, and for her words are simply objects, disjointed and without significance, to be judged only according to their quantity. It's a tedious task – words, you might say, are her life sentence. She becomes interested in the telegrams of a handsome captain staying with a family nearby and begins to construct an elaborate fantasy about his life and emotional situation based on the fragmentary – and eminently misleading – evidence he puts over the counter. Descriptive signals offered to the reader indicate that the Captain is not to be trusted, as few sexually active and attractive men are in James's work. The telegram clerk tries to make some sense of these words, but lacking any sense of the 'true' context, she creates her own background and reorders events to suit the story she'd like to write. Of course, she's hopelessly wrong: once again, context is all.

In the end the reader of 'In the Cage' has to decide what's really going on. There's a very funny scene when the woman accosts the Captain in a park in the early evening and, on my reading, he clearly thinks she's supplementing her income with a little prostitution. But the narrator isn't present to tell you what to think, as he very rarely is from this point on in James's fiction. Indeed when an apparently omniscient narrator returns to the scene again, in *The Golden Bowl*, it's something of a shock to realize that this narrator is just as inadequate an interpreter as one of the partial and prejudiced characters, and one of the narrator's main functions is to comment upon the author's metaphors and similes, pointing out their severe limitations, their extravagance. The old narrative certainties are reduced to fragments. And while of course the old narrative certainties lived on in the works of Wells, Bennett and Galsworthy, the intellectual currents of the times were running with James and subsequently Conrad, whose great novels abandon conventional chronological time sequence and are as much about the accretion of myth which gathers around a narrative as about that basic narrative itself.

To point out that Eliot had been well anticipated in the reduction of the world – particularly the word-world – to fragmentary verbal molecules is not to attempt to undermine the vast impact of *The Waste Land*, a work whose resemblance to the later phenomenon of sampling in pop music was mentioned in the Introduction. After Ezra Pound had run his metaphorical blue pencil through Eliot's gentler, more romantic mock-Augustan passages and made the juxtapositions in *The Waste Land* all the more severe and harsh, more confrontational, what was left was a work which seems to be made up almost exclusively of lines from other people's work, or at least distorted echoes of other works.

Obviously, *The Waste Land* wouldn't have exercised the influence it clearly has over Western literature if it had simply been an anthology of odd lines from earlier authors. What the jagged confrontations of styles – from contemporary popular song through Wagnerian reference, Baudelaire and Hindu mysticism to Shakespeare and the anthropology of medieval romance literature – created was more than merely the sum of many disparate parts. It was a statement of the age, of how the age refracted all the old ideals and ideas, how these had, for a human race exposed to the crushing experience of the Great War and shocked out of its comfortable suppositions about progress, taken on new and darker overtones.

After all, the Great War seemed to have been foreshadowed by the growing doubts which had been encroaching on intellectual certainty since the late nineteenth century. The advent of Freud had turned the great imperial exploratory tendency more inward. Conrad's influential novella *Heart of Darkness* explicitly used colonial exploration and (would-be) development as a metaphor for the journey to the 'heart of darkness' and 'horror' in the heart of every person. There'd been so much social unrest and division in most European countries between 1880 and 1914 that the war was, as we all are too well aware, greeted with extraordinary enthusiasm. It wasn't so much the 'innocence' or 'naïvety' that the popular myth has given us to believe in; simply the sense that here, at last, was something unifying, something worth doing, something better than potential civil war, unrest, bad labour relations, violent demonstrations about women's suffrage and so on. 'Swimmers into cleanness leaping' was Rupert Brooke's optimistic metaphor, and Brooke's popularly acclaimed naïvety about the war must always be put into the context of his appallingly cynical and pessimistic poetry written before the sonnet sequence '1914'. There's not much evidence of an abiding belief in heroism in a work like 'Menelaus and Helen'. The war was, for the French as well as the British, for the Russians and the Austrians too, the last great attempt to patch things up and avoid cataclysm. So when that went wrong, every old certainty really was shot to pieces and things really had to fall apart. And that's what *The Waste Land* brilliantly encapsulates.

It's the sense too at the back of *Ulysses*, another monstrous rag-bag, this time attempting to incorporate the whole History of Western Prose into one minutely – neurotically – observed day in the life of nobody in particular, but certainly not Everyman. Leopold Bloom is the ultimate displaced person, a Jew in Ireland with a Middle European name (redolent in Joyce's day of Belgium, which had sent over many refugees in 1914, the most notable example being a fictional one, namely Agatha Christie's Hercule Poirot).

In the same way that the reliable omniscient narrator was something of a lost cause, so the concept of representational art took something of a knock. The old idea, predominant since the fifteenth and sixteenth centuries, that a painting should aim for realistic, life-like portrayal fell in the face of first the impressionists, who sought to destroy the clarity of outline and then the cubists, who looked to reduce all forms to their basic geometry. Once again the way ahead seemed to be through taking structures apart and presenting them in pieces. The more successful representational artists, like Stanley Spencer, took refuge in a kind of neo-medieval stylized method, and later painters like Francis Bacon seemed to seek only the distortion and ugliness in their subjects. The old aesthetics were shot to pieces. In fact, after the appalling discoveries at Auschwitz, Dachau and similar establishments, old aesthetic ideals seemed based upon an appallingly naïve view of human nature. 'No poetry after Auschwitz' is one famous judgement; the critic George Steiner has described these places as the Bluebeard's Castles of our century.

Responding to this spiritual crisis was a necessary artistic task, given that art is a means by which humans try to assimilate the world around them, but this wasn't necessarily what the public wanted. As the arts began tearing themselves apart, reducing themselves to basic constituents, be it twelve tones, cubes, or simply ransacking the back catalogue of previous writing, they ascended out of the popular domain. Comfortable escapist ideas – Mr Chips and Shangri-La again – were much more palatable, much more in keeping with what was needed. In an age of developing technology and mass production, first there was the cinema, and then there was television, and somewhere between the two came the gramophone record.

The vicissitudes in the early history of the gramophone record have been well documented elsewhere. But by late 1952 it was a sufficiently established artefact in Britain for someone to bother compiling a weekly list of popularity according to sales and thus the charts, the whole basis of the commercial end of the record industry, were born. It seems odd today to conceive of the pre-rock-era charts, but the dominance of record sales by Vera Lynn, Al Martino, Kay Stafford and Mantovani is there as a matter of public record. Really, though, it was with the arrival of rock 'n' roll in late 1955 – traditionally associated with the success of 'Rock Around the Clock', a fairly staid, typical tin-pan alley number sung by the pudgy, unthreatening Bill Haley – and above all with the rise of Elvis Presley in 1956–7, that the record companies and those associated with them began to see where the real potential of their property lay. There had been heart-throb stars before Presley of course – Al Bowlly in the 1930s, Frank Sinatra in the 1940s, Johnny Ray in the mid-1950s (for a couple of years contemporaneously with Presley) – but Presley was irrevocably different for two significant reasons. First there was the overt sexuality of his performing style, something which tapped into the same youth-orientated appeal as James Dean and which promoted the new concept of the 'teenager'. Second was the increasing prosperity in both

America and Europe in the late 1950s. Not only had 'teenagers' been invented but quite a few of them had disposable income to spend on records and artefacts related to the stars whose records they bought. 'Disposable income' earned by the mass market (soon to be 'consumers') was itself a novel concept. Presley's career, brilliantly managed by Colonel Tom Parker, arguably one of the greatest Svengalis of all time (Brian Epstein and Malcolm McLaren should also appear on that list, although neither had Parker's flair for sustaining a career over decades), set a benchmark which all who followed sought to imitate. The late 1950s search for a 'British Elvis' was frenetic and, in retrospect, not a little absurd if one looks at the 'sexy' posturings of such latterly cosy figures as Cliff Richard and Tommy Steele. Although Presley became a 'showbiz figure', and despite his extreme corpulence he was never entirely cuddly; the early air of sleaze and sexual debauchery was never completely dissipated.

The pop-star business was the child of two peculiarly twentieth-century phenomena: the technology of recording and mass marketing. Since 1956 the nature of recording technology has changed rapidly and beyond recognition. The death of the vinyl record seems, as I write, imminent and inevitable. The phenomenon of sampling in its present form would have been unimaginable in the early days of popular music, yet sampling, or something like it, would have been inevitable. Pop music is after all a necessarily limited form – a simple, memorable melody, which requires a relatively simple tonality and series of tonal relations, usually over a regular four-in-a-bar beat. There is only a limited number of permutations through which these basic requirements can be met. And when forms are exhausted the tendency is to turn inwards.

But the sense of exhaustion and the desperate search for some new 'phenomenon' – a demand which sampling was designed in part to meet – were due also to the pressures placed on popular music by its corporate business side, by its life in the market. By the middle of the 1980s, the public appetite for sensations had become insatiable, but each new 'sensation' seemed to have a shorter and shorter shelf life. What ever happened to King, the 'new' stars of early 1985? The teen idols of early 1987, Curiosity Killed the Cat, were in 1992 booked for cabaret at a Butlin's holiday camp. It was a precarious and doubtful business forever seeking novelty, and therefore no different from any other market in the late twentieth century. Popular music – like most popular culture and like that eternally potent 'cheap music' – has its unique place in defining contemporary *Zeitgeist*, and can tell us as much about its period as James Hilton's novels can tell us about the 1930s.

The wilful acts of disintegration necessary in sampling are, like cubism, designed to find a way ahead by taking the whole business to pieces, reducing it to its constituent components. But it's more than that. It's also an attempt to look to a past tradition and to try and move forward by placing that tradition in a new context. And then, on the other hand, much more trivial at first sight but of equal importance, sampling represents the necessary search for distraction in a neurotic age. It has been described as a reaction against 'the well-crafted song'. It's also proved to be a way into music-making for non-musicians, like punk in the 1970s and skiffle in the 1950s. But sampling also illustrates the old story, the story this lengthy preamble has tried to tell. When the road ahead is blocked, then rip it up and start again with the pieces at your disposal. Just like *The Waste Land*, like Schoenberg, like cubism.

Except you can't dance to cubism.

2 · Bricks in the Wall of Sound

When pop music reached the point where it needed to take itself apart, it was clear that pop was about more than just the 'music'. More, that is, than just the melody and harmonics of a song (or whatever) which could be represented on a page by traditional musical notation. Pop music was about recording, about the production of recorded sound, and when pop modernists wanted to take everything to pieces, it was recorded sound which they identified as the basic element to be reduced to fragments and cheerfully cannibalized. The arrival of sampling, which allowed previously made recordings to be subjected to this 'indignity', shifted the balance of artistic power from singers, songwriters and instrumentalists to producers. Every recording made has to be produced, and so musicians who want to record have to have a producer (or learn how to produce themselves). With the sampler, a producer could construct new artefacts from 'real' (i.e. non-synthesized) performances without having to endure the presence of musicians. Producers could emerge as artists in their own right.

Actually, this wasn't such a novelty. The 'producer as artist' was a concept which had existed in recording circles for several decades, although it wasn't pop music which provided the first examples. For all that we know now, that much early rock 'n' roll and beat music of the 1960s owed probably more to the session men and pioneering producers, the first producer to realize just how great the potential of the recording studio was, just how greatly it differed and what a potentially good thing that difference was, worked in classical music.

Originally, the idea of recording was to preserve exact replicas of live events for posterity. Musical recordings were praised for their fidelity to 'the real thing', incredible though this may seem listening to them now. The earliest recording star, Italian operatic tenor Enrico Caruso, couldn't at first come near to reproducing 'the real thing' – the technology for making a decent recording of a full orchestra didn't exist. It's hard to imagine now why recordings like Caruso's 1902 performance of 'Veste la giubba', the famous tear-jerking aria from *I Pagliacci*, Leoncavallo's melodramatic tale of love and revenge among circus folk, should have caused a sensation. The piano reduction of the score is feeble, and to modern taste, Caruso's endless gulps and sobs are extremely off-putting. But above all, the whole thing sounds exceptionally thin and nothing like a live performance. Yet it was, for many, the nearest they'd ever get to the 'real thing', and as such it was accepted as a substitute. Lying behind the idea of the record was the concept of a live performance taking place.

This remained the case with recordings of both classical and popular music for something like half a century. In fact, the gramophone record itself remained a novelty item until some point during the 1930s, when the American jukebox resuscitated the flagging career of the 'pop' record. Records recreated the instrumental and vocal performances of your favourite dance bands. Initially they had something of a struggle in out-selling sheet music. As always, availability of the basic technology had something to do with it; availability of disposable income was also a significant factor. In a consumerist society such as our own, where the record business itself is a carefully organized beast with consummate marketing skills, promoting a radical change demanding lots of expensive new hardware has proved relatively easy. Hence the rapid shrinkage of the market for vinyl records and the rise of the compact disc over the past decade. The initial breakthrough in the market for any kind of recorded sound took much longer – not too surprising against the economic backdrop of the 1930s.

The change in attitude to recording didn't emanate from the pop field. Pop recordings went on, give or take the occasional novelty record, being reproductions of some notional live event until the early 1960s. Standards of production sound continued to improve, and producers wielded some influence over the artistes they worked with, pushing the country-music-based Elvis Presley towards a more up-tempo blues sound – to take a relatively significant example at random – but records were still intended to create a sound which could and would be reproduced as part of the promotional treadmill in the star machinery which was now getting into its stride.

But, over half a decade before Presley became a phenomenon, a British producer of classical-music recordings, Walter Legge, was introducing a brand new – and highly portentous – attitude to recording. Legge was very much the disciple of an American producer called Fred Gaisberg, who was active in the early twentieth century in studios all over the world (political situations permitting). Gaisberg was intimately involved in the career of Caruso, and also instrumental in promoting the great Russian bass Chaliapin on record and developing the early career of Yehudi Menuhin. Gaisberg's attitude to recording was to produce in the studio some kind of snapshot of the kind of performance each artist would normally give in public venues. Legge acknowledged Gaisberg as his 'forerunner', but saw greater possibilities in recording. He saw the studio as a place in which conditions and recording techniques allowed for the creation of sounds better than those normally achieved in places of public performance. In fact, he recognized the artificiality of recording, and may have been the first record producer fully to appreciate the possibilities this artificiality offered.

On his 1951 version of Wagner's *Tristan und Isolde* Legge perpetrated one of the first pieces of 'dishonest dubbing' in recording history. His Isolde was Kirsten Flagstad, by common consent one of the finest Wagnerian sopranos ever to tackle the epic mythic roles. However, by 1951 her voice was, for all its heroism, on the wane and the upper register couldn't cope with the highest note in the great love duets between the two central characters. There are two versions of what happened as a result of this. One is that Flagstad requested and named a deputy to sing these notes for her and that this was all done without manipulation of tape within the recording sessions. This may well be true and is certainly EMI's authorized version. But the fact that the chosen deputy was none other than Elisabeth Schwarzkopf, Walter Legge's wife, has given rise to an alternative tradition, that Legge foisted his wife (and protégée's) voice on to Flagstad's after the event much to Flagstad's annoyance. In this version Flagstad vented as much of her spleen on conductor Wilhelm Furtwängler as on Legge, refusing to record Wagner with Furtwängler again on the two opportunities which subsequently arose during the last three years of the conductor's life.

It's unclear – and questioning experts or those 'in the know' serves only to obfuscate rather than elucidate – which version is accurate. What really matters is that on the resulting recording it takes a fantastically trained and alert ear to tell when Schwarzkopf's interpolations take place. Generally the deception works, and by common consent the Furtwängler *Tristan* – which is a testament simultaneously to the conductor's vision of the work and the producer's vision of what studio recording can achieve – remains the finest available on record even forty years later. And it couldn't be reproduced on stage. On stage even the most heroic and suitably Wagnerian voices will tire and wilt at some juncture during the four hours or so that the average *Tristan* lasts. In Legge's studio such unfortunate things need never happen. Not only that, the traditional distractions of attending a live performance were all removed. No irritating fidgets gossiping or eating chocolates in the row behind; no unfortunate seats behind a pillar or placed distressingly close to one section of the orchestra, thus destroying any sense of balance. A record could bring you the best possible singers in the best possible conditions to be enjoyed on sound-enhancing equipment. Strategic microphone placement could ensure that every word and every vocal nuance could be clearly heard, and how often is that the case in theatre, opera house or concert hall? Legge went on to deliver several more 'definitive' recordings to the world (in so far as any classical recording can be definitive) and many critics in the 1990s consider some of his 1950s recordings to be unsurpassed.

One project Legge never attempted was a complete recording of Wagner's Ring Cycle in studio conditions. This cycle – consisting of one 'short' prelude (*Das Rheingold*) and three immense three-act operas (*Die Walküre, Siegfried,* and *Götterdämmerung*) – might seem to a creative record producer to cry out for studio presentation. The Ring is an enormous and demanding work drawn from traditional northern mythology and Germanic medieval literature. Even without the extraordinary demands on both singers and orchestra (and conductor) made by the complex score of the cycle, the staging presents almost insuperable problems. Over the course of four productions, a designer and director must find a way to represent the creation of a world and, ultimately, its destruction. Characters fly around on winged horses, change shape from dwarf to dragon (and back), summon up impenetrable rings of magic fire, walk through said magic fire, and perform other feats of similar everyday proportion. A visual challenge, to say the least. Equally challenging for designers and directors is the fact that the best Wagnerian singers rarely look right for their parts, thus making it inevitable that the public might feel a certain let-down seeing dwarves towering over the Aryan role model Siegfried. A studio recording, particularly one directed (the word 'produced' seems somehow deficient) by someone as alive to the possibilities of the studio as Walter Legge, would not only circumvent all the visual problems inherent in The Ring, but it would also overcome all those problems of stamina of balancing the noise of sound effects against the efforts of performers. It wasn't Legge, though, who produced the first complete studio Ring issued to the public; it was the producer whom he saw as his natural successor, a man prepared to take Legge's vision of the best possible performance in the best possible conditions a logical step further. Legge appreciated the studio for its essentially antiseptic qualities and for the chance it offered to perform and record until something was – in his view and, if the artists wanted in at the cutting and mixing stage, the view of the performers – exactly right. John Culshaw agreed with this view, but saw the studio as something more. It was a box of tricks, a place where effects could be created to add to the drama, where a kind of cinema of sound could be produced. Legge's recordings are pure, carefully placed, accurate, but very short on sound effects. Culshaw created a furore in the classical world by introducing extraneous noises, by using every effect the studio could afford to create a sense of theatre over and above that achieved by the performers. And where better to lay out one's manifesto and show off one's capabilities than in the spectacular sound world of Richard Wagner?

To this day critics are severely divided about the merits of the Ring Cycle produced by Culshaw for Decca with Georg Solti as conductor. Defenders of the set point out that it has won many listeners to Wagner simply for its sheer excitement. After all the first issue, *Das Rheingold* (1959), actually reached the Top 10 of the American album charts. Whatever their artistic shortcomings, the four recordings that make up the Culshaw/Solti Ring Cycle have a sound quality that you can't argue with, a sound quality born of the producer's commitment to studio recording as not merely a tool, but an art form in itself. Many of the versions of Wagner more highly prized by 'serious' Wagnerians make pretty wretched listening if you don't already know the music (a lot are, in fact, more or less pirate recordings sneaked out of live Bayreuth performances or taken from radio relays of live versions in unlikely Italian locations). It may be ironic that, despite the seemingly insurmountable problems he set producers, designers and directors Wagner was a composer who thought clearly and irrevocably in terms of the live event, of the actual opera house, to the extent that he even designed his own and imposed a new set of standards of behaviour on audiences and theatre managers.

Whether you consider it irony or not, John Culshaw saw Wagner as a perfect vehicle for his attempts to perfect his studio artistry. He and Legge both saw recording techniques as offering a new kind of artistry to someone interested in music – the artistry of the producer. Culshaw didn't see himself as a creator of new 'talent' in quite the same way that Legge did when he force-fed his wife a diet of other people's recorded interpretations of vocal music before recording her, but both were passionately committed to the studio as a place where legitimate perfection could be achieved.

And so classical music had spawned 'producer artists' long before pop music approached its adolescence. This perhaps emphasizes that what happens in popular culture usually has its corollary somewhere in 'high culture'. Admittedly when producers began to dominate popular culture it was more overt and somehow more to be expected. Pop stars are, traditionally, putty in the hands of the scheming Machiavellis who surround them – agents, managers and producers; classical musicians are, traditionally, inspirational geniuses who play from the soul. In fact, classical musicians – especially the successful ones – have their agents, managers and so on, who are likely to be every bit as manipulative as their pop counterparts. A market-place is a market-place. The similarities should never be ignored.

As distinctive in her way as Schwarzkopf, another singer who married her producer was Ronnie Spector. Comparisons between the Spectors and Legge and Schwarzkopf may seem like blasphemy to some, but the story is basically the same. From the earlier days of rock 'n' roll, Phil Spector had seen the studio as a place where more could be achieved than simply the recording of songs performed in roughly the same manner they would be sung live. Spector had a vision of a 'total sound world', which would advertise not the singers of the songs, but their creator. And he didn't mean the songwriters. Of course, he had a hand in writing the material too – that was vital. But for Spector the real point of a song was the sound which enveloped the melody and lyrics.

The Spector effect quickly became labelled the 'wall of sound', but it's rather difficult to describe the noise to anyone who hasn't heard it. Basically it derived its effect from an extravagance of instrumentation, at a time when much rock and pop music steered clear of too lush and rich a sound. Most Spector productions would involve prominent orchestral strings and, where appropriate, blazing brass. But however much orchestral instrumental noise there was, Spector would always make the rhythm underpinning the song insistent; sometimes, as in 'Da Doo Ron Ron', it would be a driving rhythm, but on slower songs, like 'Baby I Love You' or 'You've Lost that Lovin' Feelin'', the pulse would be steady and equally evident. Spector was as generous with his percussion as with melodic instruments, and a fast Spector production in full cry would seem to feature armies of tambourines and similar percussive effects. This was all bathed in an echoing atmosphere which could, on occasion, make a track sound as if it was coming from the bottom of a well or out of a very large bathroom. But the 'wall' effect was mainly achieved by the fact that the mix of most Spector productions placed equal value on every disparate element that had gone into it. The voice was another instrument, equal in value with the third tambourine, not lost in the mix, but not placed far in front of everything else.

A lot of the most famous songs to come out of the brilliant yet egocentric organization called 'Philles' – even the record label's name testified to its creator – were, divorced from their sound world, banal to the point of absurdity. This was almost part of the point. The two biggest UK hits of The Crystals, 'Then He Kissed Me' and 'Da Doo Ron Ron' – among Spector's best-known songs – have some of the simplest chord sequences possible and lyrics of almost sterile conventionality (rhyming 'dance' and 'chance', 'bride' and 'cried', even 'had' and 'Dad' in the former, making an obsessive refrain of the nonsense title in the latter). As surprisingly successful cover versions by Cilla Black and, later, Daryl Hall and John Oates showed, 'You've Lost that Lovin' Feelin'' is completely hollow without the echoing atmospherics which bathe the contrasting high–low voices of Bill Medley and Bobby Hatfield (The Righteous Brothers). Spector waves banality under the listener's nose, underlining its triteness precisely by the grandiosity and pomp of the surrounding production. And why not? He knew that the staple diet of the pop song was the idealistic, happy-ending, boy-meets-girl song. These were lyrics that didn't need an interpreter, didn't require you to be aware of more than the fundamentals of life, set to music you didn't need a specially trained ear to appreciate the subtleties of, given a big pseudo-operatic treatment, because they were songs about situations which were the nearest the majority of pop-music consumers would ever come to grand opera. Spector's greatest works were products of a glorious bygone naïve age enshrined in all the luxury the technology of the day could afford. This conscious celebration of naïvety explains why for many listeners Phil Spector's abiding masterpiece remains his *Christmas Album*. It's nominally a Various Artists album, but who cares whether The Ronettes or The Crystals or whoever else are performing on 'Frosty the Snowman' and 'Winter Wonderland'? The point is that these are Phil Spector productions, and Spector captured something in the *Zeitgeist*, something combining youth, naïvety and the exuberance that can go with both, to produce a unique document. In this cynical age, no one can make a Christmas album without seeming either manipulatively over-commerical or ridiculous. (Alexander O'Neal's 1989 attempt managed the rare double of seeming both.)

Spector was above all a perfectionist and his studio quest to create his 'perfect' wall of sound may have contributed to his famed breakdown. He cultivated the role of 'monster', of egocentric tyrant, and was prepared by all accounts to steam-roller over all opposition. In recording 'River Deep, Mountain High', he's said to have paid Ike Turner – who's still credited on the record – just to stay away from the recording sessions. His treatment of his wife's voice – as just another brick in his wall of sound – consistently underrated her ability. Ronnie Spector may not have been Aretha Franklin or even Dusty Springfield, but her distinctive timbre was vital for the pleading tone of The Ronettes' most famous songs, 'Be My Baby' and 'Baby I Love You'. But as time moved on, Spector didn't and to an increasingly 'sophisticated' audience the matter – and the musical manner – of his songs remained firmly rooted in the early 1960s. The great Spector heyday was, really, 1962–3, the final days of the great Kennedy and Camelot myth. By 1966, when Spector produced 'River Deep', the American public had lost interest, although the single was still a sizable hit in the UK. But from this point on, Spector had been left behind and reduced to an element of nostalgia. True, he worked with The Beatles in their final days and with individual Beatles after the group's break-up, managing in the process to create one more great Christmas single (John Lennon's 'Happy Xmas (War is

Over)'), but this was never a particularly happy marriage of talents and certainly not a lasting one. Too many egos were involved.

Spector's own great work may have been a symptomatic part of the 'youth' of popular music, but at least two significant figures in the genre's adolescence showed signs of either direct or indirect influence. The figure most obviously and umbilically linked to Spector was, of course, Brian Wilson, manic genius in charge of The Beach Boys. Spector was such an important influence on Wilson that the Beach Boy seems to have felt obliged to imitate his idol to the extreme and have a complete breakdown. Once Wilson's mind disintegrated, one of his most vivid recurring hallucinations was that he was being persecuted by a vengeful Phil Spector. Spector as spectre, as it were. Wilson's debt was very openly acknowledged in such loving and careful recreations of key Spector works as 'And Then He Kissed Me' (carefully transposed to 'And Then I Kissed Her') and 'I Can Hear Music'. Wilson was so keen for these to be accurate reconstructions that they were recorded in mono, at a time when mono recording was disappearing. The latter single (released in 1969) is arguably one of the most successful attempts to recreate the Spector sound, showing up later essays like those of Roy Wood in the 1970s for the confused messes they were. Wood's mistake was to try for too much complex noise over too complex a melodic and harmonic progression. There was too much pastiche, too much self-consciously camp glam-rock parody about Wizzard, the 'group' Roy Wood created as his vehicle for these neo-Spector experiments, for the imitation (intended, one suspects, as sincere flattery) to be anything other than seventh rate. This doesn't alter the fact that the Wizzard hit singles – especially 'See My Baby Jive', 'Angel Fingers' (the closest to a success in Wood's own artistic terms) and 'I Wish It Could Be Christmas Every Day' – are some of the most enduringly (and endearingly) funny pop records ever made.

Brian Wilson was able to get close to Spector's heart because he began his career in the same optimistically naïve atmosphere. Early Beach Boys songs are as basic and simple in both musical and lyrical content as all the great Spector works. Somewhere along the line, though, Brian Wilson grew up. Perhaps it started with the preoccupation with harmony. Close harmony represents an 'honest naïve' strand in the American musical tradition; the traditional close harmonies of the middle-American barber's shop quartet hark back to an honest, decent and uncomplicated past. What better image of simple, honest, decent, middle America than the close harmonies of a barber's shop quartet going at full throat into 'Wait Till the Sun Shines Nelly'? Indeed, in 1957, the supposedly sophisticated New York theatre establishment found a way of celebrating that lost innocence. The musical *The Music Man*, set in a small Midwest town at the turn of the century, was a stage representation of that good old-fashioned barber's shop-centric musical tradition. The New York establishment had no hesitation in awarding *The Music Man* almost every Tony Award going, in preference to that show's rival: the jazzy, cross-rhythmic, modern celebration of urban deprivation and racial violence – Leonard Bernstein's *West Side Story*. Yet it was Bernstein's music which ultimately gripped the popular imagination, precisely because it looked forward out of the naïvety to which neither America nor Britain could hope to cling for much longer.

And in some parallel manner The Beach Boys developed from their early surfing origins, their simple close harmonies like those of the world of *The Music Man* and their playful, very 1950s teen-rebel stances. In fact, as a 'rebel' song 'Fun, Fun, Fun', with its story of an inept teenage girl driving her T-Bird and rebelliously forgetting about homework, seems more innocent than Eddie Cochran's 'Summertime Blues'. As The Beach Boys – and the USA – grew up, the complexity of the harmonies developed correspondingly. And as the harmonies became more complex, so did the structure of the songs.

Of course, Wilson's developing sense of harmony soon passed the point where the requisite sound could be made by five voices alone. Multi-tracking became an absolute necessity, and The Beach Boys thus became a group whose real genius lay in studio recording, and whose essential 'sound', like Spector's, was truly achievable only within the confines of the studio. Wilson was driven by an ambition to create, again like Spector, a complete self-enclosed sound world readily identifiable and identifying the author. It was with the album *Pet Sounds* (1966) that Brian Wilson came closest to defining his artistic vision. In some ways, that album charts the progression of The Beach Boys to that point: it opens with the happy, boy-meets-girl story of 'Wouldn't It Be Nice' and closes with the cynical and disillusioned 'Caroline No'.

Pet Sounds was followed almost immediately by the single 'Good Vibrations', almost certainly The Beach Boys' best-known and best-loved song. This perfected the combination of fresh vocals (heavily multi-tracked) and studio effects, relying heavily on electronic keyboard noises for the motor rhythm underpinning the vocals. For a successful single there's also a remarkable variation in tempo, even in style, and at the time the record was hailed as a breakthrough in production. Spector's sound had been a solid slab of luxuriant mono; Wilson inevitably made voices more prominent in the final mix. The Beach Boys were, after all, first and foremost a vocal harmonic group. Wilson's productions also didn't sound as though every musical resource available had been thrown into the mixing pot.

Unfortunately, the success of 'Good Vibrations' only helped to inspire Brian Wilson to more manic extremes in his quest for perfection. Whether he could ever have defined this 'perfection' – or recognized it if he'd achieved it – is a moot point. The immediate casualties in this process were the internal relationships within the group, Wilson's own mental health, almost an entire album and the next single, 'Heroes and Villains'. The first two casualties have been well documented, as has the eventual loss of the *Smile* album, designed to top even *Pet Sounds*. The fate of 'Heroes and Villains', though, shows how the obsession with studio effects could at times mar a creator's ability to see the wood for the trees. The Beach Boys were, after all, wedded to the basic concept of the song, but Brian Wilson's obsessive editing and re-editing of various takes of 'Heroes and Villains', seemed in the eyes of all the other group members and Tony Asher (his collaborator at that juncture) to destroy the structure and fluency of the song itself, leaving the final version (with which no one, including Wilson, was satisfied) rather like a collage of effects and disjointed extracts. The public verdict was relatively negative, too. Even in the UK, where The Beach Boys had had much more success with *Pet Sounds*, the single managed one week in the Top 10 (at Number 8), a disappointment after their previous three singles had all reached the Top 3. From that point onwards, The Beach Boys found their career in a decline, which was halted briefly over the next three years by the simple expedient of going back to their roots with less effect-based songs such as 'Do It Again' and a version of the old traditional song 'Cottonfields' (an inferior reworking when set against 'Sloop John B').

Brian Wilson's ambitions as producer didn't exist in isolation from the rest of the music business. Quite the contrary. *Pet Sounds* was a statement of his own artistic ability, but he has also in recent years quite openly stated that his work on the album was provoked by hearing The Beatles' *Rubber Soul*. The actual process of recording *Pet Sounds* took place while The Beatles' *Revolver* album (regarded by some critics as their most successful integrated offering to the market) was prepared and released. And Paul McCartney has stated that the initial reaction of the British group to *Pet Sounds* was one of jealously depressed admiration – 'How can we follow this?' The answer to this apparently rhetorical question was, of course, one of those pieces of vinyl which has become a cultural icon, *Sergeant Pepper's Lonely Hearts Club Band*, now seen as the quintessence of the summer of 1967 – the hippy, flower-power, San Francisco summer, the Summer of Love.

So much has been written and said about *Sergeant Pepper* that it's hard to find anything to add, particularly given that I don't share the general adulation of it common among people of my own age. To me it seems firmly planted in the tradition of good old-fashioned British music hall, full of comic regional accents, silly sound effects, with a few overblown and pretentious lyrical ideas thrown in (to say nothing of the toe-curling embarrass-ment of George Harrison's sitar-obsessed 'Within You, Without You'). As a technical achievement, though, it's remarkable and the credit – as with so much of The Beatles' output – belongs to the producer, George Martin. The twenty years or so since the break-up of the group has seen Martin's role in their develop-ment more honestly admitted. And while I wouldn't wish to take much away from the obviously astonishing song-writing talents of John Lennon and Paul McCartney, it's now clear that without George Martin there wouldn't have been such a distinc-tive sound framework in which to place Lennon and McCartney's songs. Obviously as the group developed, their own ideas about sound developed correspondingly; and, like The Beach Boys, there's the same sense of fresh, exuberant innocence growing into something more sophisticated. In this, Brian Wilson was right to hail *Rubber Soul* as the landmark – it represented a giant step forward on the basic beat-group sound evident right up to the soundtrack of *Help!* and it also coincided with the group's decision not to play any more live dates. From the middle of 1965 onwards, The Beatles' sole *raison d'être* was as a studio recording group, and George Martin helped them to realize this ambition. It was a significant moment in the devel-opment of popular music as an art form with all the ambitions that phrase implies. It was also a significant moment in recording history. Whatever Walter Legge may have tried to do in the studio, no artist had ever felt that a recording career could be a complete and entire substitute for live performance. Recording had come a long way from the tool Caruso had used to reach people who would never otherwise hear him.

George Martin was neither a Phil Spector, nor a Brian Wilson. Spector wanted to be credited over and above every act he groomed, even invented, like a cinema *auteur*. Wilson had no noticeable ambitions to create a stable of Brian Wilson protégés but he had a single creation, The Beach Boys, which was the vehicle for his ideas. George Martin, on the other hand, was (like Walter Legge) first and foremost an EMI studio producer, with such products as the *Beyond the Fringe* cast album to his credit, and not ambitious to promote his own name or to act as a Svengali. In fact, a lot of what Martin achieved technically has had a more direct bearing on the development of today's technologically orientated pop culture than many more self-publicizing, 'ground-breaking' producers. You could argue that the splicing of fairground organ noises and other sound effects into 'Being for the Benefit of Mister Kite' on *Sergeant Pepper* was an early (and highly successful, as well as relatively sophisticated) form of sampling, well in advance of any of the multi-track noise effects of Spector and Wilson. One wonders whether in the 1990s George Martin wouldn't have insisted on record-label credits reading 'George Martin featuring John and Paul', so immense was his influence and bearing upon the whole artistic (and commercial) project of The Beatles. In the 1960s, even in the wake of Spector, the idea of a producer taking the lion's share of the credit was still inconceivable. Thus other great producers, who again contributed much to the development of key sounds in pop music, happily took a back seat, settling for power within the record company and in the studio.

I'm thinking here especially of the great producers of soul

music. In Detroit at the Motown Studios, Eddie Holland, Lamont Dozier and Brian Holland created their own sound 'idea' within the generally homogenized Motown sound around a series of groups from the stable. The Isley Brothers, The Supremes (before Diana Ross's ego insisted on the separate credit) and above all The Four Tops all gained from the HDH touch. Indeed, The Four Tops were more or less an HDH creation. The team wrote the songs and produced the records – very much the Stock, Aitken and Waterman of the 1960s. Like SAW – incredible though it may now seem to a culture which worships dance music (even if the record companies still don't like it) – HDH were exposed to criticism: all their songs sounded alike; the individuality of the artists wasn't allowed to come through; it all sounded like a production line. Motown *was* a production line, of course, but a phenomenally high-quality product was rolling off it. Like SAW twenty-odd years later, HDH (and the other great Motown teams, those large corporate committee groups of writers and producers operating under group pseudonyms like The Clan and The Corporation) replied by continuing to be successful. Particularly entertaining was their response to the criticism that all Four Tops songs sounded alike – a single by The Four Tops called 'It's the Same Old Song'. When the Motown sound began to develop a new 'psychedelic' sophistication, HDH went off and had some (sadly brief) success running their own record label, Invictus. Although the enterprise was short-lived as the market was by this time (1970–1) entering a new, tougher phase which had no place for heartfelt emotional out-pourings to a dance beat, Invictus gave the pop world two unforgettable singles – Chairmen of the Board's 'Give Me Just a Little More Time' and, best of all, Freda Payne's 'Band of Gold'. And HDH drum rolls live on in a whole host of sampled records. As do the more 'sophisticated' noises of their immediate successor at Motown, Norman Whitfield, the man who turned The Temptations from another besuited soul group into a 'serious' act turning out mini-epics such as 'Cloud Nine', 'Ball of Confusion' and 'Papa Was a Rollin' Stone'.

Other great soul-based producers of the time were to be found in the Atlantic studios. Jerry Wexler and Arif Mardin more or less discovered Aretha Franklin's real potential as a singer. They 'gave' her a sound by which the public could identify her; they found a framework within which her voice could perform its own equivalent of pyrotechnics. Their achievement is hailed now, but at the time the idea of giving public acclaim to record producers and technicians was unheard of. Arif Mardin went on turning this trick through the middle 1970s. First he put Daryl Hall and John Oates inside a soul sound on their first big hit 'She's Gone' (1974) and set them off on a path highly unfashionable at that time for white singers, with the result that in the US Hall and Oates became one of the most successful duos in pop history. Next he co-produced the *Main Course* album (1975) with The Bee Gees and helped change that group's direction, thus spawning one of the most successful soundtrack albums ever – *Saturday Night Fever*. Incidentally, in thus relaunching the career of The Bee Gees and helping them to find this new sound, Mardin was instrumental in setting up the great production Svengalis of the late 1970s and 1980s. In the wake of *Saturday Night Fever*, a Bee Gees production was instantly identifiable, whether the artist was a total unknown (like Samantha Sang), a great soul singer (Diana Ross or Dionne Warwick), or even a pair of country stars (Kenny Rogers and Dolly Parton).

By the time The Bee Gees assisted in the recuperation of the chart career of Diana Ross (resurrecting her from cabaret death for a new generation) with the 1986 hit 'Chain Reaction', the idea of Svengali producers whose name was more memorable was well established – the concept didn't merely provoke nostalgic thoughts of Phil Spector. To begin with, the UK had

seen in early 1970 a whole run of hit records featuring basically
the same personnel, all studio session performers, under a
succession of different names. Vocalist Tony Burrows briefly
hit the public eye in 1967 as part of the custom-built 'Summer
of Love' group (complete with close harmonies) The Flowerpot
Men, successful with their all-British totally non-authentic 'Let's
Go to San Francisco'. Just under three years later, Burrows
became a staple of the weekly chart show *Top of the Pops* as lead
singer of Edison Lighthouse ('Love Grows'), White Plains, the
original Brotherhood of Man, even novelty performers The
Pipkins. The releases in question were as disposable as Burrows's identities, but they briefly threatened the record companies cherished idea of band and star identity. But Burrows
was not the representative of a single producer, or a production
team. It was over the next two years that the first great British
production team emerged.

The British success story of the 1970s was the Chinn–
Chapman stable. Nicky Chinn and Mike Chapman began as
producers of almost absurd bubble-gum music: The Sweet's
'Co-Co' and 'Poppa Joe' were early examples, as was the
execrable 'Chop Chop', written for DJ Tony Blackburn (still
then deluding himself with the prospect of a successful singing
career). Along came glam rock, heralded by T. Rex's switch
from hippy underground group, full of love and metaphysics,
to a pop-song based rock 'n' roll band centred on a flamboyant,
effeminately dressed personality (Marc Bolan), and the
resurgent David Bowie in his androgynous Ziggy Stardust
persona. Down market there was Gary Glitter, and Chinn and
Chapman saw a new craze starting. The Sweet's 'Little Willy',
a sort of rockish bubble-gum song charted at the same time as
Gary Glitter's first hit, 'Rock and Roll'; by the time The Sweet
brought out a new single, 'Wig-Wam Bam', Chinn and Chapman had decked them in provocatively glamorous garb and
given the bassist a camp task to perform straight to camera

(where applicable). Chinn and Chapman understood – like no songwriting/producing team before them – the power of TV, above all the power of one show, *Top of the Pops*, in selling singles in the UK. Every group or singer they took on was given a definite TV act. It was a bit hit-and-miss to start with. Mud's original image, for their first Chinn-Chapman singles 'Crazy' and 'Hypnosis', was as pseudo-Latin tango champions, capes and all. This gave way to a more nostalgic, teddy-boy look (again with one member of the band detailed to camp it up on camera) which helped to shift enough copies of 'Tiger Feet' to make it the UK's top-selling single of 1974. Chinn and Chapman created Suzi Quatro, pretending to sell her as a tough bass-player, singing tough-woman, go-getting, sexy songs. In fact, the leather-clad image was straight out of a (pretty dreary and trite) macho fantasy. But it sold records. For each act, Chinn and Chapman tailored a particular sound, but everyone knew the real creative force behind each act. Many of these discs have become kitsch classics of that peculiarly kitsch-laden era, although underlying all the camp of the tailor-made image, the songs are remarkably banal. Chinn and Chapman almost had their own record label in that most of their acts were signed to Mickie Most's RAK label.

As with all Svengali producers, eventually the market moved away from them, but Chapman came back as the *éminence grise* behind American new-wave band Blondie. Once Mike Chapman had Blondie thoroughly in hand, he transformed them into a record-selling force of almost frightening power, this time having a favourable situation from which to help his creation sell albums as well as singles, in the US as well as the UK. *Parallel Lines*, Blondie's third album, was one of the best-selling albums of the late 1970s, and spawned that rare beast, a single which actually passed the million sales mark in the UK alone ('Heart of Glass'). With his work with Blondie, Chapman even wrote himself into critical respectability. The man behind previously despised chart rubbish acts like The Sweet and Mud was now helping to produce 'classic pop' like 'Sunday Girl'. The man who had helped create a male fantasy stereotype like Suzi Quatro was redeemed by the no less stereotypical fantasy figure of Debbie Harry. Eventually, of course, the whole concept of Blondie and anyone associated with them was subsumed in the public imagination by the figure of Debbie Harry. Chapman was ultimately eaten – in terms of public profile – by one of his own creations.

One producer-guru who had his own record label to play with and definite ideas about a sound he wished to create was Trevor Horn. Horn's career as a musician zigzagged around with some peculiarity. In 1980, only three years before he launched his new, stylish label, ZTT, on the public, he joined Yes, perhaps the quintessential ghastly pompous 1970s rock band. But before that, in 1979, he formed a techno-duo, The Buggles, who hit immediate chart success with the irritatingly and brilliantly catchy 'Video Killed the Radio Star'. Horn ensured that the promotional video accompanying the song was suitably memorable (by this point of pop history, this element was proving vital – The Boomtown Rats' earlier 1979 hit 'I Don't Like Mondays' had been boosted by a very striking video) and the song itself dealt with technological matters of popular culture with a suitably 'technological' sound (lots of sound effects and electronic instruments). Horn's interest was always primarily in sound and the potential of recording rather than in simply 'music', and it was no surprise that when he formed the ZTT label (under the auspices of the then still independent company Island) one of the groups he signed was The Art of Noise. ZTT was very much a 'hands on' operation for Horn and he conceived of his label in terms of corporate identity both for sound and for image. To the latter end he hired rock journalist Paul Morley, darling of the *NME* and *Face* set. Horn's idea of 'noise' was in some ways directly descended from Spector's: a vast, intricate wall of sound. And in 1984 Horn hit paydirt with a vengeance. By the end of January he had simultaneous Number 1 singles in the UK ('Relax' by Frankie Goes to Hollywood) and the US ('Owner of a Lonely Heart' by Yes). Between Frankie – style rebels of the mid-1980s – and Yes – progressive pomp rockers of the mid-1970s – an unbridgeable gulf would seem set, but original identity was no bar to the Horn technique. In fact the sound he achieved for Yes is closer to that subsequently associated with The Art of Noise (the references to Yes's *Close to the Edge* in Art of Noise's 'Close (to the Edit)' are fairly overt), and both group's work is recognizable as from the same stable, as was the Propaganda album release *A Secret Wish* the next year.

By the time that Horn was busy on the ZTT sound, the concept of sampling in some form or other already existed. There was the Fairlight Computer Musical Instrument, which included sampling among its armoury, and early machines dedicated purely to sampling had been developed and put to use. Also by this stage the principle of using other people's discs – or scratched snatches of them – as backing for rap tracks was well established. Trevor Horn attempted to create an 'unsample-able' sound, something so dense and complex that it was useless to other producers, who tend to prefer to sample single elements of a track – a drumbeat, a bass line, a solo voice – rather than a whole slab of variegated sound. In fact, the longer mixes of the Frankie singles were quite happy to pirate from other sources in spirit if not in fact, employing an actor to read government civil defence warnings in the event of a nuclear attack on the first twelve-inch mix of 'Two Tribes', for instance. The ZTT project rather rose and fell with Frankie, but that didn't materially affect Horn's career. Of all recent British producers he has shown a remarkable ability to adapt to new consumer demands and yet retain some form of distinctive sound. In 1991 his work with Seal – very much the recording industry's flavour of that year – helped him to another heap of production awards. And the recognizable Horn sound lived on in the lush extravagance of Marc Almond's *Tenement Symphony*.

With all respect, however, to Chinn and Chapman and Trevor Horn, the nearest Britain has ever come to producing a Phil Spector or a Holland–Dozier–Holland team is, unquestionably, the three-man writing, production and management team of Stock, Aitken and Waterman. Like all whose primary aim is to sell records, they've had more than their fair share of flak, but as the dust begins to settle (the signs in 1991 were that the market had moved away from them after half a decade in which they managed to lead and even, between 1987 and 1989, dominate it), it becomes clear that they combined the efficient production-line writing and producing skills of Holland–Dozier–Holland with Spector's ability to place anybody whatsoever, regardless of actual talent, within the context of their sound-world. They belong to the age of sampling, and at least part of what has gone on in that age has been either in reaction to them or actually done by them. And the thought of 'artistic ambition' never crossed their minds.

What SAW wanted to do – and manifestly did with great success – was to latch on to trends of the time and exploit them (in a non-pejorative sense). Their initial assault on the market was through that brand of dance music called high energy (or Hi-N-R-G), a fairly fast, upbeat, brash disco noise most associated in the mid-1980s with gay clubs. High energy owed a great deal to European disco influences, seen in the 1970s in such classics of tack as La Belle Epoque's 'Black is Black', Baccara's 'Yes Sir, I Can Boogie' and the entire *oeuvre* of Boney M. There was a high-energy base to a lot of successful disco music of the late 1970s – Amii Stewart's 'Knock on Wood' and Stephanie Mills's version of the standard 'Gonna Get Along Without You Now'. A lot of high-energy records of this period were simply reworkings of older songs over a fast (somewhere around 120 bpm) beat. Champions of this were probably The Boystown Gang, whose name indicated fairly clearly where the primary constituency for this kind of music lay. Suddenly, around 1984, and partly on the back of the overtly gay image of Frankie Goes to Hollywood (perhaps even that of Culture Club before them), the sound which had primarily been the preserve of the gay clubs crossed over into the charts, heralded first by Ryan Paris's Euro-tack classic 'Dolce Vita' in the autumn of 1983, and then by the more recognizably authentic high-energy anthems 'Searchin' (I've Gotta Find Me a Man)' by Hazell Dean and 'High Energy' by Evelyn Thomas. Indeed, the beat of the two biggest Frankie hits was to some extent a high-energy beat.

It was in this high-energy cauldron that SAW found their first major success, the provocatively androgynous Liverpudlian Pete Burns, who liked to make his near-transvestite image as threatening as Boy George's was designed to reassure and console. Burns's group, Dead Or Alive, had been playing a kind of Gothic, fast-beat high-energy for several years with only limited success. Stock, Aitken and Waterman placed the Dead Or Alive sound within a more disciplined, more 'produced' sound and managed to create, in the process, possibly the definitive high-energy record. 'You Spin Me Round (Like a Record)' was very much a 'sleeper' in an age where big chart success tends to be instantaneous or not at all, but once it began to move in early 1985 it cut an inevitable swathe through the charts. Although it took another two years for SAW to establish themselves as chart regulars, by adapting the Dead Or Alive sound, disciplining it within the 'mainstream' of high energy, the team had found what would be the basis for their greatest successes. With Mel and Kim, for instance, the sparseness of house music was grafted on to the fast beat of high energy; about 90 per cent of Kylie Minogue's greatest hits to date have been straightforward high-energy records.

One man had more reason than most to resent the huge

success of Stock, Aitken and Waterman. This man has been hitherto an unsung British hero in the development of not only high-profile producers but also high-profile DJ record creators. This double role was to become so crucial in the first flush of successful records using the sampler, but the man who got there first, who made the records, created his 'stars' (more or less out of clods of earth) and then mixed and remixed them endlessly in night clubs, was Ian Levine. One of the principal DJs at the London club Heaven, Levine had his own stable of 'artists' before SAW had ever got off the ground, all artists whose own vocal contribution (it was never more than a vocal contribution) was secondary to the highly produced, up-tempo packaging around the voice. The wonder is that, given the strong melodies he and collaborator Fiachra Trench usually came up with, Levine's Nightmare label didn't manage to cross into the mainstream charts. The formula was quite simple: take some personable girl or boy, have them record a Levine song – almost inevitably a love song along one of about four different lyrical-content lines – and then release the record with a highly appealing photo of the artist on the cover. Usually, the less talented the artist, the more appealing the photo. Thus records by formerly established artists fallen from favour whose careers Levine was trying to resuscitate – like Archie Bell and the Drells – wouldn't need a photo of any great note. Whereas releases by pretty boys like Scott Stryker, Rob Keane and the ever-changing line-up of Seventh Avenue would always have highly tempting, touched-up covers. Seventh Avenue, in particular, would always be wearing very tight, revealing clothes or very few clothes. On at least one occasion Levine's stable was in trouble when performers turned up who bore little or no resemblance to the figure on the record sleeve. The fact that the artist who appeared could actually sing was no compensation to an audience who expected a talent somewhat different from a good voice to come out of Scott Stryker. I would hesitate to state directly that Stock, Aitken and Waterman would ever have been so cynical as to provide photogenic front men for session voices, yet it's interesting that at least one line-up of Seventh Avenue provided two of the members for SAW's short-lived teen heart-throbs Big Fun.

A relatively small operation like Levine's, catering for a specialist market, faced distribution problems. The same would be true of much of the early 1990s rave-orientated dance music, were it not for the fact that record companies have by now reluctantly accepted that dance music actually sells records (indeed, without dance music the seven-inch and twelve-inch singles would arguably be dead). Although major record companies and distributors were willing to accept in the mid-1980s that a club-orientated twelve-inch remix could be a useful sales tool with the right single (there was evidence for this in the sales of the endless remixes of Frankie singles), dance music itself was still regarded with suspicion – especially anything smelling too much of a specialist audience. The gay club music which crossed over usually was sung by presentably glamorous females (Laura Branigan and Hazell Dean just about fell into this category), comfortable divas like Gloria Gaynor or camp vamp-stars of yesteryear (the inimitable Eartha Kitt). The idea of aiming such music at the teen market was something which didn't seem to occur to any marketing executives until Stock, Aitken and Waterman came along. Levine still goes strong, however, and in 1991 was up to his old tricks, resuscitating careers of former stars, putting Frances Nero back into the charts with 'Footsteps Following Me'. In early 1992 he achieved his highest profile since remixing The Pet Shop Boys' 'It's a Sin', providing production for The Pasadenas' revamp of the 1973 New York City hit 'I'm Doing Fine Now'.

The development of DJs as artists in their own right was inextricably bound up with the rise of rap; Chapter 4 considers this context. Indeed, as the producer as artist increased his profile in the late 1980s, the concept of the DJ-producer became more and more common. But by then it was possible for the producer to dwarf the 'artist' on a record's credits, meaning that a star-struck DJ no longer had to emulate 1960s DJs and turn to singing if he wanted a chart career. By 1987, a producer credit could help to sell a record, particularly a twelve-inch remix. The words 'Shep Pettibone remix' or 'Julian Mendelsohn remix' on a twelve-inch single meant something to the purchaser. Very few producers of the 1960s and 1970s could make that claim.

3 · Stars on 45

The last boom year for singles sales in the UK was 1984. At the top end of the sales charts it was arguably the greatest boom year ever. It's generally assumed that the story of the single in the 1980s was a consistent downwards slide, but 1984 rather ruined the pattern. There were six million-plus sellers, with several other singles making a respectable assault on the million barrier. For a short while it seemed that the dying single might have been rescued by a strange combination of the calculated, cynical and marketable sleaze of Frankie Goes to Hollywood and their innocent although equally consumerist counterparts Wham! Good old-fashioned pop groups with a following, who seemed to know how to lead the market – the music business had been waiting for something like this since The Beatles had gone their separate ways in 1970. However interesting and accomplished record producers might be, no major record company executive believed in the early 1980s that you could sell a record entirely on its producer. What you needed was either a craze, a novelty hook, or a marketable star.

Pop music has often tended to lurch around rather drunkenly from fad to fad. The story of the post-punk era – in terms of records that actually sold and achieved a high public profile – is of a very uncertain market looking for a direction and finding little in the way of continuity, while the public seemed less and less interested in buying the product. It was this loss of confidence which prepared the way for the fragmentary music of the sampling era, and this chapter sets out to describe – in a suitably idiosyncratic and opinionated manner – the state of the art leading up to 'Pump up the Volume' and all that followed.

In fact, at the start of the 1980s the three-minute 'well-crafted song' – the staple diet of popular music – looked in pretty fine fettle. Talk about a 'crisis in pop' had receded with the arrival of punk in 1976 and the emergence of a new wave with its face set firmly against the meandering, pompous extravagances of the supergroups who had dominated the first half of the 1970s – a time when the pop single was regarded with derision and considered inferior to the album track.

That, at any rate, is the conventional shorthand wisdom, although it conveniently ignores the triumphant survival of that quintessential 1970s child, heavy metal. It also requires a hefty suspension of hindsight or sense of irony. The adulatory music-press treatment accorded to the standard-bearers of the 'well-crafted new pop' seems implausible now if you actually look at the names involved. The Police and Sting, U2, Simple Minds, The Undertones with their feisty lead singer Feargal Sharkey . . . all names now associated with the dreaded 'Adult-Orientated Rock'.

The 'crisis in pop' that punk and new wave had come along to resolve was, like all 'crises in pop', a universal confession that no one could see where the market was going or what it wanted. This made it difficult for the money men to know how the market could be profitably exploited. The retreat and dissolution of The Beatles seemed to encapsulate the souring of the 1960s' dreams of love and freedom and peace. More important, the absence of The Beatles meant that there was no one out there to give a clear directional lead to the market. Presley's role in the late 1950s and early 1960s was taken over by The Beatles, under the tutelage of their managerial genius Brian Epstein, from 1963. They made their mark as a happy-go-lucky beat group, playing music that sounded fresh and direct, and immediately the market on both sides of the Atlantic was crowded with imitators. Round about 1965 they began to be more musically ambitious and in a series of albums beginning with *Rubber Soul* concentrated on creating an essentially studio sound not designed to be reproduced in live performance. At this point, the idea of The Beatles as a live band simply disappeared, and the original cheerful image of the group was given its final outing in the film *Help!*

A useful indicator of The Beatles' influence on the rest of the music business is always the response of their nearest competitors, The Beach Boys and, to a lesser extent, The Rolling Stones. The Beach Boys had in Brian Wilson one ingredient The Beatles didn't have – a producer of skill among their own number. Wilson's manic desire to top whatever the British group did has already been touched on. It was this urge which led to the creation of *Pet Sounds*, and to The Beach Boys' imitative dashes to India in search of gurus (perhaps more accurately described as fakirs with the emphasis on the 'fake'). Similarly, in 1968, when The Beatles suddenly turned their back on elaborate production sounds and produced a simple rock 'n' roll song, 'Lady Madonna', The Beach Boys issued a single, 'Do It Again', within four months which had the same 'return to roots' hallmark; as did The Rolling Stones' most successful release from that year, 'Jumpin' Jack Flash'.

The Beatles had immense influence, even over their nearest creative rivals, as 'market leaders' and without the clear signal of their lead to follow, the money men couldn't spot the trends and know where to put their investments. Punk seemed to offer the first sure thing in almost a decade, and its explosion into the market-place was not dissimilar to what had happened with the explosion of the 'beat groups' in the early 1960s; and since lack of musical competence seemed *de rigueur* in punk, every kid with a guitar could dream of stardom again. Also, female punk stars like Siouxsie and Polly Styrene offered a more liberated role-model to would-be women performers than the entirely showbiz female figures who had made their mark in the 1960s. Above all, punk established a small economic revolution in the music business and suddenly the British music scene was crammed with independent record companies. The now well-established concept of the 'indie' scene was born out of the fragmentation punk demanded – notwithstanding the fact that the quintessential emblems of punk, The Sex Pistols, had absolutely no interest in the small-fry end of the market. Dropped by EMI, they were immediately scooped up by Virgin. The business magazine which voted them and their manager/guru Malcolm McLaren as Businessmen of the Year for 1977 hit the nail firmly and precisely on the head.

Because of the absolute contempt expressed by most punk artists for the lengthy, pseudo-classical concept music of the established heavy rockers – like Yes's *Tales from Topographic Oceans* or Rick Wakeman's various keyboard extravaganzas – there was a grand return to that old staple of the pop business, the three- (or less) minute song. A good punk song would be short, loud and fast. Good short songs make good singles, which, with talented marketing, make for hits. Suddenly the single was respectable again, and the weekly editions of *Top of the Pops* featured acts like The Sex Pistols, The Stranglers, The Adverts and The Boomtown Rats alongside Showaddywaddy and Boney M. Thus one of punk's great achievements was to make the hit single, the traditional unit of 1960s pop, respectable again, and to relegate endless quadruple albums with unintelligible, uninteresting sub-metaphysics to the junk heaps. After punk, no one could come up with *Further Tales from Topographic Oceans*, and that's probably just as well. Some non-punk pop groups also became respectable. Music papers like *NME* – self-appointed style gurus – no longer sneered at chart acts like Abba, who, with nine Number 1 singles between 1974 and 1980 (and several multi-platinum albums) amassed some of the most

impressive sales figures of the time. Getting into the charts wa
respectable again. Media darlings The Buzzcocks devoted the
lives to producing memorable singles, as did, for the most par
The Jam.

Somewhere in the midst of all this, dance music, heavi
sneered at in the 1970s, also became respectable. This was part
to do with the strong rhythmic element the new mus
employed, and the ludicrous 'pogo' dance associated with it
the early days. Punk wasn't to be danced to in the same way
1970s disco; a more nihilistic, overtly redundant jumping up
and down was encouraged instead of all the elegant footwork
you'd associated with quintessential 1970s dancer Tony Manero
(John Travolta's character in *Saturday Night Fever*). But there
was also a side to punk and new wave which led to a rediscovery
of 1960s soul music.

Although the definitive punk front men The Sex Pistols
espoused a creed (if that isn't rather over-dignifying it) of
anarchy and indifference to establishment politics, many of the
leading musicians who rose to prominence on the new wave
had a less nihilistic political outlook. About eighteen months
after The Pistols first hit the headlines by abusing Bill Grundy
on TV, a second wave of new stars like Tom Robinson moved
to the centre of the action, and used their publicity to promote
the aims of organizations like the Anti-Nazi League and the
Anti-Apartheid Movement. There wasn't any great voice, as
there would be in the 1980s, speaking from pop music on behalf
of the Labour Party. Labour were at that point the party in
power, and they seemed, to many of those concerned about the
rise of racism and the supposed increase in support for the neo-
Fascist National Front, too weak and ill-equipped a government
to defend the rights of minorities. And so there was, as part of
this political corollary of punk, a revival of interest in reggae
music because it seemed like a symbol of a repressed people.
Your susceptibility to its influence was proof of your anti-racist

credentials. It was in this way that punk and new wave helped to nurture the ska revival, the 2-Tone record label and such genuinely energetic chart fixtures of the early 1980s as The Specials, Madness and The Beat.

In addition to which, groups like The Jam (not initially given to political pronouncements, except for their assertion that they would vote for Margaret Thatcher's Conservative Party), headed a Mod revival; Mods had always championed soul music. Old Motown records became trendy again, and a lot of the 'dance stigma' surrounding black music was removed, absolved by the patronage of the likes of Paul Weller. In retrospect, this may only have laid the ground for the Levi's advertising campaigns of the 1980s, but there was a definite upgrading of a certain kind of dance music with the arrival of the new wave. That dance music didn't have a great deal of credibility is at least partly illustrated by the nose-dive David Bowie's image and record sales took in the UK when he suddenly espoused the cause of the disco sound of Philadelphia on his 1975 album *Young Americans*. The UK public were quite happy to rush out and buy the re-released 'Space Oddity' in vast quantities, but *Young Americans* (both as album and single) and 'Fame' (which opened up Bowie's career in the US) remained ignored, providing Bowie's first relative failure for three years. *Young Americans* was simply – like much of Bowie's 1970s output – ahead of its time.

But it wasn't simply a question of black music becoming credible and transforming dance music into something you could admit to liking in polite company. There were two distinct types of dance music, and the respectable one certainly wasn't supposed to be disco in any *Saturday Night Fever* sense. Despite the cross-over success of Blondie's 'Heart of Glass' in 1979, the word 'disco' in 1980 still evoked images of white suits with flares, hairy chests and medallions. The ineffably tacky image of dance music was reinforced by that year's big

Euro-holiday hit in the UK, Ottawan's 'D.I.S.C.O.'. But the very professional and stylish work of Chic had, to some extent, begun a subtle groundshift in the popular conception of the word. And around this time, in late 1979, the first sign that rap could be commercially successful in chart terms appeared in the UK: the Sugarhill Gang's tiresomely egocentric (but very danceable) description of their sexual prowess, 'Rapper's Delight', reached the Top 3 in three weeks. This single gave, although no one realized it at the time, a foretaste of what the charts might be like a decade later, in that the words of the rap might have been original, but the backing track was simply Chic's 'Good Times', not sampled but simply replayed over and over again.

One definitely respectable aspect of dance music was that which was loosely labelled 'funk'. A lot of funk music of the 1970s was to provide the hunting ground for many rapacious samplers in the late 1980s. Defining funk is like assessing how long the proverbial piece of string is, and a fair slice of the story of funk belongs to the history of rap music; but it was in the late 1970s that white mainstream chart artists began to utilize the driving and sophisticated beat patterns which were the hallmark of James Brown, Isaac Hayes, George Clinton's various outfits (including Parliament and Funkadelic), and a great deal of Sly and the Family Stone's music.

So when media darlings Talking Heads, whose *Fear of Music* was voted album of 1979 by the *NME* (always the barometer of British trendy taste), employed Parliament-inspired funk rhythms on their 1980 album *Remain in Light*, it was clear that even 1970s dance music was returning to the fold of credibility. And separating 'funk' from much 1970s 'disco' wasn't easy; after all, the trademark of 1970s disco was the guitar sound Isaac Hayes had patented on his 1971 'Theme from *Shaft*'.

However, the great catch in all this was that once the exciting, spontaneous new wave wholeheartedly accepted dance music, it became much easier for the marketing executives to see what was coming, where it was coming from and how they could manipulate its arrival and departure. After all, the marketing executives' ultimate ambition for any new and unpredictable trend in such a consumer-dominated business as the pop industry must be to incorporate it into the mainstream and sell it in the same way as everything else.

A good indicator of the state of popular music's health is the success rate of novelty records and, to a lesser extent, re-releases. A rash of novelty records is usually a symptom of a market debilitated by more than measles. For example, 1975 was clearly a year in which pop music was floundering. The evidence is the presence at the top of the singles chart of: Telly Savalas growling his way through 'If'; TV sitcom 'stars' Windsor Davies and Don Estelle doing a not very good impression of the Ink Spots singing 'Whispering Grass', complete with sitcom catch-phrase; Tammy Wynette's seven-year-old country ballad 'Stand by Your Man'; David Bowie's six-year-old 'Space Oddity'; Billy Connolly's thoroughly unamusing parody of Ms Wynette's 'D.I.V.O.R.C.E.'. Three novelties and two re-releases, to which can be added several remakes: The Bay City Rollers destroying The Four Seasons' 'Bye Bye Baby', Mud's unlovely pseudo-acappella assault on Buddy Holly's 'Oh Boy', and Art Garfunkel's sleepwalk through a 1930s standard 'I Only Have Eyes for You'. And annoying pieces of whimsy which verge on the novelty, such as David Essex's 'cute cockney' number 'Hold Me Close', Barbados's 'Typically Tropical', The Tymes' 'Ms Grace' (a 'witty' sideswipe at radical feminism) and, of course, the most successful piece of pomp rock ever (arguably the most comic record of all time), Queen's 'Bohemian Rhapsody'. It's curious that two of the poorest chart years ever should both conclude with 'Bohemian Rhapsody' at Number 1. These are merely the Number 1s, tactfully ignoring near misses like the vengeful return of Bobby Goldsboro's 'Honey', or the meteor-like rise of Laurel and Hardy's 'The

Trail of the Lonesome Pine'. What this all adds up to is a lousy year by anyone's standards.

It's dangerous, though, to generalize too much about the glorious rag-bag of tack and coincidence that makes up chart pop music for most of the time. Any mid-1970s chart suggests that this epoch was a spectacular and unrepeatable low-point in popular musical taste. But although the early 1980s may have been supposedly the time of 'pure pop' and the Indian summer of the traditional single, the records which actually sold scarcely stand as testimony to the taste of the Great British public. A similar survey of 1980 would encompass such unlikely figures as Barbra Streisand (in her Barry Gibb phase), gay-disco queen Kelly Marie, Kenny Rogers, Eurovision stalwart Johnny Logan, the St Winifred's School Choir and The MASH (responsible for the 'Theme from M*A*S*H (Suicide is Painless)') and a fair smattering of cover versions. These are scarcely proof of some definitive trend in public taste.

But 1981 was different. Two of the top three singles of the year came from Adam and the Ants, as much a visual image as a pop group. The promo video was coming into its own and Adam and the Ants were very much a symptom of this. After years of trying, Shakin' Stevens made the big time and refused to go away, eventually winding up as the most consistently successful chart act of the 1980s. But 1981 also saw a trend which now looks dangerously – almost sinisterly – familiar, a foretaste of the sampling era.

Why the world was suddenly ready for a three-and-a-half-minute medley of ten Beatles songs, 'Sugar, Sugar' and the Dutch hit song 'Venus' over a persistent handclap is unclear. In fact, such a disc had originally existed as a Dutch bootleg and had simply used sophisticated splicings of the original recordings. It fell to Jaap Eggermont, drummer of one-song wonders Golden Earring turned producer, to produce a legally acceptable version. This was the genesis of the disc known in the UK as

'Stars on 45', which was a world-wide barnstorming success, not least in the USA where for legal reasons 'Stars on 45' was the designation of the group and the record was simply entitled 'Medley', followed by a precise list of its songs (giving it an almost unassailable place in the record books as the American Number 1 single with the longest title). This official version was no shopping-mall muzak medley, sung by anonymous, sweetly bland voices. The selling point was that the session singers employed did a passable impression – from a marketing viewpoint, at any rate – of the Fab Four. Obviously buying the rights to recycle the original recordings of the ten songs in question would have been far too much trouble and very expensive, but by having singers with some talent for imperson-ation, you could almost believe that what you were hearing were extracts from the original versions, seamlessly woven over the synthesized handclap-punctuated beat. The instrumental sound was as painstakingly recreated as the voices (to my ears, with a great deal more success, in fact), and the world fell for it.

Part of the reason for the success of 'Stars on 45' (to use the British title for convenience) was that for all their 'classic' status, Beatles songs remained stubbornly outside the disco experience of the late 1970s and early 1980s. As the idea of specially produced records, with extended mixes on the technically clearer-sounding twelve-inch single, came to dominate the disco DJ's way of thinking, so the idea of bunging old 1960s records in their pristine form into the middle of a carefully calculated programme of dance records woven together by the beats-per-minute factor with a homogenizing beat – allowing the DJ to mix out of one record into another without intruding – came to seem ridiculously unprofessional. The club DJ was quickly ceasing to be an intrusive presence who announced, 'And a happy birthday to Tracey from all her mates and here's that great old number "Hi-Ho Silver Lining" and I want to see you all get down to this one' and was becoming instead a kind of producer interested in creating effects through his records and his turntables and any other technological equipment at his disposal. Coincidentally, of course, this was the time at which the role of the DJ was being significantly changed by the advent of scratch-mixing in rap music, again expanding the DJ's creative aspect and giving 'playing records' a whole new meaning. The rap DJ's development – at this point, despite the 1979 success of 'Rapper's Delight', still very much an underground minority phenomenon – will be covered in more detail in Chapter 4.

'Stars on 45', of course, wasn't aimed at either trendy DJs or trendy consumers. But it very shrewdly caught hold of a market somewhere in the middle, young enough to enjoy discos, but old enough to feel a nostalgic yearning for old Beatles songs. One should never underestimate the impact of nostalgia. And then there were enough people for whom the tunes were 'new', for whom this was a 'sound-bite' introduction to The Beatles, an instantly packaged nostalgia. The concept of the sound bite wasn't yet current, although by the end of the decade it was to be the basic currency of political dialogue, the brief quotable extract designed to be used in news headlines and highlights. Margaret Thatcher's use of highly professional advertising was still regarded with amazement in the early 1980s; the sound bite is a very useful element in political advertising. Her speeches of this time were almost all constructed with the sound bite (by whatever name it may have been known then) in mind, built to climax at key phrases like 'The lady's not for turning'. Extracted, canned phrases were a novelty then; had anyone realized, this was a glimpse of the future.

Although the US market tired of the craze after the first 'Stars on 45' disc, medley records saturated the UK market over the months which followed. It was a cheap, bankable formula, and as such not to be sneezed at by record companies ever alert for definite trends in enthusiasm. The original perpetrators quickly came up with 'Stars on 45 Vol. 2' (a not very convincing Abba impersonation) and the wittily titled 'Stars on 45 Vol. 3', which offered a medley of passably impersonated introductions from various hit singles, thus saving money on employing vocalists. A sort of Volume 4 was a tribute to Stevie Wonder entitled 'Stars on Stevie'; but by the time Volume 3 rose and fell like a Standard Fireworks rocket on a stick, the days of the medley record were numbered. Or so it seemed until 1989 and the arrival of Jive Bunny.

Imitations included some strange hybrids. The most successful was possibly the least likely – the Royal Philharmonic Orchestra's 'Hooked on Classics'. This took several famous thematic moments from classical music – such as the beginning of Tchaikovsky's First Piano Concerto, the opening of Mozart's Fortieth Symphony, the main theme of Gershwin's *Rhapsody in Blue*, the 'March of the Toreadors' from Bizet's *Carmen*, famous classical pops all – and strung them together over the inevitable handclap. The adaptation was wonderfully seamless, the RPO did it all with great panache, but even so the success of 'Hooked on Classics' was as surprising as it was prodigious. The medley record certainly seemed like an admission of sterility, particularly when a previously successful group like The Hollies happily administered the medley handclap treatment to their own hit canon (to produce the immortal 'Holliedaze').

Medley records ran riot. There was 'Back to the Sixties', 'Beach Boys Gold' and – possibly even more mystifying than 'Hooked on Classics', where at least the original tunes had some merit – 'The Caribbean Disco Show', a compound of old Harry Belafonte and sub-Harry Belafonte songs. It was the summer craze of 1981, more omnipresent even than Adam and the Ants, and like all such crazes was well advanced into self-parody before it evaporated. There were, of course, Christmas medley records and novelty medley records ('Stars on 45 [Pints]' – a highly strained joke about pub medleys).

Technologically, of course, all this was nothing like sampling and the music of the late 1980s and early 1990s – although Jaap Eggermont felt that the 'Stars on 45' series used extremely sophisticated techniques for their day. It was almost entirely created from scratch in a studio using session musicians working on specially adapted medley versions of the songs in question. In most cases, too, the extracts from songs were to fit into some kind of homogenized theme – usually a simple 'Greatest Hits' concept. There was none of the conscious dislocation or collision of genres that the best uses of 'sound bite' would aim for later in the decade. There was no attempt to turn these songs into something else, or to extract elements from them for surreptitious use in a completely different work. In one way these medley records were throwbacks to the 1950s and the honky-tonk piano 'Party Pops' of Winifred Atwell. But this appropriation of snippets served as an indication that the market was interested, in a big way, in fragmentary songs.

Certainly some of the most successful records after sampling and fragmentation had taken over the market in the late 1980s had much in common with the medley records of 1981. The phenomenally successful Jive Bunny singles of 1989 certainly sounded like they shared more common ground with 'Stars on 45' than with 'Pump up the Volume'. The Hollies' inability to find success with new material in 1981 finds immediate reflection in acts like Alexander O'Neal, Bobby Brown, Snap and Technotronic, who maintained a chart presence without recourse to invention by releasing greatest-hits medleys under the stylish heading of 'megamix'. No doubt for the record companies the megamix was an excellent way of milking the cow bone dry. And often megamixes would have started life, like the first 'Stars on 45', as DJ bootlegs circulating the clubs. But no amount of high-tech noises and attempted modish references to the MC could redeem the Top 5 single 'Thunderbirds Are Go' – selected themes from old children's TV programmes over a

1990s dance beat – from being identified as anything other than a novelty record. It's as though the medley record simply foresaw the worst, least inventive edges of what would be trendy six years later. Which all goes to show how the pop-music business runs round in circles.

The medley-record boom came right in the middle of what was supposed to be a new golden age for the short pop song. The Jam, The Police, Soft Cell, Human League, even the last days of Abba – all were still around and receiving generous critical attention in 1981 as well as attracting large(ish) record sales. Indeed, Soft Cell's 'Tainted Love' and Human League's 'Don't You Want Me', 1981 single releases both, each clocked up over 1 million units sold. But the dominance of the chart by medley records alongside Adam and the Ants (an act relying on visual image backed up by records of little musical or intelligible lyrical content) and the uninspired re-treads of Shakin' Stevens, didn't bode well for the 'inventive' end of the market. And when a former member of punk revolutionaries The Damned appeared at the top of the charts in 1982 singing Rodgers and Hammerstein's 'Happy Talk', in a good-time version devoid of any irony whatsoever (Rodgers and Hammerstein are, in any case, probably impervious to all irony), you might well have said that the 'new wave' was well dead. Simon Reynolds, the *Melody Maker* journalist, likes to read that significance from Fine Young Cannibals' 'Ever Fallen in Love' – a style-laden, dance-able and ultimately heartless 1987 reworking of the Buzzcocks' 'Ever Fallen in Love (With Someone You Shouldn't've?)'. I can see exactly what he means, but the writing was on the wall half a decade before that.

It was this broad pattern of decline that the sales boom of 1984 interrupted. Even if you take out the 3-million-plus sale of the Band Aid record as a seasonal novelty freak you're still left with five million-sellers which accurately sum up the tenor of the year. The five are: 'Relax' and 'Two Tribes' by Frankie Goes to Hollywood, 'I Just Called to Say I Love You' by Stevie Wonder, and 'Careless Whisper' and 'Last Christmas', both George Michael compositions (the former released under his own name, the latter credited to his group Wham!). The teen heart-throbs of the year, George Michael and Andrew Ridgeley; a sentimental song from an established black singer; and of course the marketing phenomenon of the year – a representation of pop music in 1984, indeed of pop music in most years. An established 'elder statesman' singing a ballad will always draw back the older record buyers; there's always a teen heart-throb (usually male) around somewhere, however unlikely or short-lived their career; and there's always a marketing phenomenon which gives any year, even a totally duff one, its particular flavour, and usually won't travel well beyond the confines of that calendar. In 1984, the flavour was Frankie Goes to Hollywood.

The Frankie phenomenon is inseparable, really, from Trevor Horn's career. The sound of the Frankie records was entirely his and was very much part of the distinctive ZTT-label noise which also found less prominent outlets in the early work of The Art of Noise and German group Propaganda (whose excellent album *A Secret Wish* remains one of the highest pop achievements of the mid-1980s). On top of the sound, though, Frankie had three remarkable assets: a genuinely impressive pop song, 'Relax', with lyrics sufficiently controversial to merit a BBC ban (although only after about three months' Radio One airplay and a *Top of the Pops* appearance); Holly Johnson; and Paul Rutherford. These two group members had superbly complementary appearances and personalities, and both exuded an essentially gay sexual aura: Johnson's that of the camp, more flamboyantly theatrical queen; Rutherford's of the macho, leather-clad, moustachioed clone. Johnson's voice also had a distinctive timbre, and the whole ensemble added up to an immediately identifiable image – something to latch on to and sell. With a publicist like Paul Morley, former arbiter of public taste for *NME*, ZTT was, for a glorious twelve-month period, brilliantly adept at catching the public mood. Frankie's blatant consumerism (coinciding neatly with the upsurge of the 1980s optimism inextricably linked in the British public's mind with the premiership of Margaret Thatcher) also had a stylishly rebellious edge as embodied in all the 'Frankie Says . . .' T-shirts. The consciously aggressive stances of Frankie fitted well with the sense of conflict generated at home by the miners' strike, presenting increasingly unpleasant spectacles of violence on TV screens and in newspapers every day, and in foreign affairs by the belligerent noises of Ronald Reagan, at odds with the equally gerontocratic rulers of the USSR. This latter image was well exploited in Godley and Creme's otherwise indifferent promo video for Frankie's second single, 'Two Tribes'. Essentially Frankie gave a face to the early, don't-give-a-fuck consumer days of the booming 1980s.

Wham! were their innocent counterparts – equally consumerist, singing lyrics with overt references to both Doris Day and credit cards. George and Andrew, though, were 'nice boys', the antithesis to the dangerous outsiders of Frankie. The image makers had been looking for several years for a group or an artist like this: easily consumed music with no message and nice-looking people to put it over. Nick Heyward and Haircut 100 had been an early dry run, but the songs weren't strong enough. Duran Duran had proved a shrewder investment, but their songs had such wilfully obscure lyrics and their sound was so limited that it was hard for the audience to carry on identifying with them. It was no good for a group whose main purpose was to look pretty to start getting grandiose ideas about artistic intentions. With George Michael in his Wham! days they seemed to be on safer ground. Wham! had stated a very clear manifesto on their arrival on the scene in late 1982. It was about fun, 'Young Guns' having fun on the dole. When George used

the word 'dole' it was as a rhyme for 'soul' and not to go off
into some Jerry Dammers-style rant about the evils of the
Conservative Party. Even though *NME* at first saw Wham! as
some symptom of radicalism – well, they were such 'Bad Boys'
– George Michael's songs were instantly intelligible ditties about
girls and fun and teenage romance, and George and Andrew
became the apostles of the artificial tan. Selling these two was
easy. In fact, George Michael was a very good writer of light
pop songs and almost managed that near impossible feat –
writing a half-way decent Christmas song.

In 1980s terms Wham! had a remarkably long run for their
(and the marketing executives') money. They maintained a
presence around the top of the charts for almost five years and
managed to bow out still at the top of the tree. Maintaining
such a continuous and persistent impact has proved beyond
almost every act who sprang to prominence in the UK during
the 1980s. Except, of course, one – the inevitable Madonna.

Overshadowing the global pop market throughout the 1980s
have been Michael Jackson and Madonna, and it's significant
that, as record sales generally have declined, two artists whose
music is essentially dance-based have continuously out-sold
everyone else on record and dominated consumer awareness by
sheer volume of publicity. Others have, when you look at the
figures, sold as many records at individual moments – Dire
Straits, Phil Collins and Whitney Houston spring to mind, as
do Prince and Bruce Springsteen – but the inches of newsprint
devoted consistently over most of the decade to Madonna and
Jackson put everyone else in the shade. Both are first and
foremost purveyors of dance music and that is remarkable
enough in itself, but of almost equal importance is the fact that
both have more or less dictated their own image-making for the
larger part of their careers.

To what extent Jackson's image of studied peculiarity –
reclusive lunatic genius, as it were – is contrived and to what

extent accidental is a moot point, and any solution I might suggest would largely be amateur psychoanalytical speculation. Suffice to say that even when *Thriller* was released in 1982, he was far too large a star for the image makers to dominate him, and every style he's deliberately presented to the public has been a carefully scripted and dressed persona. The 1991 release of a new Jackson album, *Dangerous*, was so much a media-circus event that really the music it contained was irrelevant. In fact, the first 'new' images suggested that Jackson's personae now look several years out of date, but that didn't stop the carnival. And when the 'Dangerous' tour came around, the musical content only formed a small part of the interest. The light show, the make-up and the costumes were just as important. Equally a new Jackson single has now become an event more because of the cost of the accompanying video than for any merit in the recording available in the shops. The majority of the songs on *Bad* are fairly negligible once the production is stripped away, and *Dangerous* seems overblown, uninteresting and devoid of melody, with lyrical content which would make an adolescent wince ('Black and White' makes Blue Mink's 'Melting Pot' look both sophisticated and radical).

Jackson has a series of personae, largely self-created, which he chooses to present to the world. Unfortunately he's also, by some choice eccentric behaviour, managed to give the press the 'Wacko Jacko' label, something one suspects isn't entirely willed. Madonna, on the other hand, probably calculates every single little item concerning her which appears anywhere in public, even the apparently unflattering stuff. Her achievement as a publicist is remarkable, even if her music is formulaic to the point of cynicism. But now, as with Michael Jackson, the music is scarcely relevant, compared with the cinema, the theatre, the press conferences. And formula or no, several of the singles are, in their way, small classics: 'Borderline', 'Vogue', 'Papa Don't Preach', 'Like a Prayer', 'Express Yourself' are all good memorable songs encompassing a variety of styles – and, inevitably, visual images. As with Jackson, every new song merits a new visual style for the singer, for the supporting cast and the design. Although to my mind, Madonna shows a much surer grasp of contemporary taste in the early 1990s than Jackson. Frequently the visual image has remained more memorable than the song, even when the song itself has been relatively strong, as with the stylized black and white pseudo-1930s imagery of 'Vogue', or the calculatedly controversial mixture of eroticism and religion in 'Like a Prayer'.

Whatever one's personal opinion of their musical product, astute image-making has taken Madonna and Jackson into a hyper-star world beyond ordinary critical value judgements and cynicism gives rise to the suspicion that if either chose to freewheel and produce third-rate musical goods in the customary sophisticated packaging then the devoted public, addicted to the style and image as much as to the music, would – initially, at any rate – devour the product with as much appetite as before. And to be fair, both are painstaking and particular about the musical quality of their output within the terms they set themselves. Only Prince and Springsteen of the 'World Mega-stars' probably put more conscious effort into their actual music; but they are both driven by artistic ambition as much as the desire to promote their career, and both have taken unprofitable, anti-lucrative turns away from styles and routes which might have led them towards the Jackson and Madonna peaks.

But these twin phenomena aside, the mid-1980s after the *annus mirabilis* of 1984 saw a resumption of the slide away from a coherent sense of identity in the market. This loss of coherence heralded the return of the truly appalling, until the British charts in 1986 and 1987 were dominated by the same mishmash of novelty records, retreads and reissues – sometimes unholy amalgams of all three elements – as 1975 and 1976. The best-selling single of 1986 was a disco-aimed remake of a 1970s soul song, 'Don't Leave Me this Way'; its close runner-up an instantly forgettable ballad sung by a TV soap heart-throb, Nick Berry's 'Every Loser Wins'. The Number 1 position was successively occupied by Falco's 'Rock Me Amadeus' (Austrian novelty rap), Spitting Image's 'The Chicken Song' (TV-promoted supposed parody of summer novelty records which managed to be as ghastly as the real thing) and Doctor and the Medics' remake of 'Spirit in the Sky' (a spoof glam-rock remake of a 1970 synthesizer-based song). People also rushed out in their thousands to buy 'Snooker Loopy', a musical homage to the giants of the green baize masterminded by 'lovable cockneys' Chas 'n' Dave. The market was so open and undefined that at Christmas Jackie Wilson's 'Reet Petite', a record almost thirty years old, took the charts by storm and stayed at the top of the pile for a month. Some would argue that Christmas is always a time for unpredictable hits, but the inevitable increase of record sales as people desperately grope around for stocking-fillers usually leads to a vast number of releases from regular platinum-sellers, in the belief that the market at Christmas is more open to shrewd manipulation based on current trends than at any other time of year, as makers of charity records (and Cliff Richard) well know.

Early 1987 seemed to underline the lack of market definition, and at one point in February the top two places in the singles chart were filled by songs which were twenty-six and twenty-one years old – Ben E. King's 'Stand by Me' and Percy Sledge's 'When a Man Loves a Woman' – propelled to new triumphs by Levi's advertisements on TV and at the cinema. However, this apparent musical stagnancy signalled one of the great definable trends of the late 1980s and (on showing at the time of writing) the early 1990s – the increased power of both small and large screens as promulgators of regurgitation. And two other eminently successful singles from early in 1987 indicated important market forces emerging. Mel and Kim's 'Respectable' began the long stream of Stock, Aitken and Waterman successes which began to dry up only in 1990. 'Respectable' made play of another new and important trend, the new-found mass enthusiasm for house music, a minimalist disco sound emanating originally from the gay community of Chicago. The amazing rise to chart pre-eminence of Steve 'Silk' Hurley's 'Jack Your Body' in January and February showed that this stuff, apparently lacking all the usual accoutrements of a song – discernible melody, lyrical content, harmonic development – could shift units. 'Jack Your Body' was just a strong beat, a repetitive bass line and a few keyboard effects, with a very slight vocal input. All the musical elements were electronically generated. Music without singers or conventional instruments – this was an exciting, relatively new idea.

Well, yes and no. In fact, by mid-1982 'real' instruments on a pop record had become so rare that one of the thrilling novelties of the lush production sound achieved on ABC's album *The Lexicon of Love* was its use of a real string orchestra. For if Adam and the Ants gave a look to 1981, and if medley records caused distress, the real pop sound of that year, really of the early 1980s, was that of the newly reborn, regenerated and, above all, 'artistically' acceptable synthesizer.

It was, in a way, part and parcel of the move of dance music to the mainstream commercial centre, and when groups such as Human League, Soft Cell and Heaven 17 hit paydirt they did so with discs relying heavily on a definite, danceable beat. Soft Cell probably always intended that to be the case. Marc Almond's determination that his duo should have a sleazy, slightly tacky image fitted in well with a British mid-1970s idea of the disco. Almond was more open than anyone else about the disco as meat-market. But Human League and Heaven 17, or British Electric Foundation as they sometimes were and still are, were right out of the art-school mould, seeking to create a new music which perhaps owed something to classical minimalists such as Philip Glass, Steve Reich and John Adams. In fact, their new music owed more to Gary Numan than anyone else (although at the outset Numan seemed to take himself pretty seriously). I don't think it's unfair to suggest that for quite a few of those who actually bought them, singles like 'Are "Friends" Electric?' and 'Cars' were superior novelty records. Perhaps a more interesting influence was Brian Eno, whose use of the synthesizer, first with Roxy Music, and then as co-producer on a series of David Bowie albums, had shown a desire to use electronically generated music to break down some of the artificial boundaries around various styles and designations of music.

But before the art school synthesizer experimentalists got hold of it, the synthesizer had had three roles in pop music. Initially, it had been pure, unadorned novelty, intending to sound like something synthetic, palpably on unreal instrument and of limited expressive value. More ambitious, and more technically refined models sought to recreate all kinds of musical sound generated purely by electronic means – the computer equivalent, if you like, of the church organ, which also seeks to impersonate the sounds of 'real' musical instruments. Chicory Tip's 1972 hit 'Son of My Father' sold almost entirely on its science-fiction noise, synthesizer links. Then the synthesizer passed into bombastic rock, becoming an excuse for 'virtuoso' masturbatory epic compositions of little discernible merit even at that time. The prime exponent of this kind of synthesizer music was, of course, Rick Wakeman, who gave us, among others, *A Journey to the Centre of the Earth* and *The Six Wives of Henry VIII*.

Finally, the synthesizer was the staple of disco music. Some of the credit (if that's the appropriate word) for this must go to Giorgio Moroder, the man who invented Donna Summer, and had taken over where early pioneers of synthesizer-based dance music had left off. Stevie Wonder was part of this, too. The introduction to 'Superstition' remains, even twenty years later, one of the most memorable synthesizer figures, and it's a sad comment on the relative tastes of the British and the American record-buying publics in 1972 that where the latter were entranced in huge numbers by 'Superstition', the British preferred the challenging concepts lurking in 'Son of my Father'. Inevitably going back to the gay scene – where a high proportion of dance-music styles begin – Sylvester, with 'You Make Me Feel (Mighty Real)', managed to give one definition to the synthesized disco sound, as of course did Giorgio Moroder's achievement on Donna Summer's 'I Feel Love'.

So when the British art-school boys got going with their minimalist experiments in electronic sound, it was probably inevitable it was going to lead back to dance in the end, given that it was in dance music that the synthesizer had proved most usefully marketable. But it seemed, after 1983, that Human League, Heaven 17 and a host of imitators who rose and sank without trace had disappeared like just another fad. And the creator of the most successful synthesizer record of 1985 was not a British art-school neo-minimalist, but a DJ-producer who created an exciting sound using keyboards, voices and a collage of old news and documentary programmes, keeping a heavy finger on the digital delay button. Paul Hardcastle's '19' was perhaps more of a pointer forward than it seemed at the time. But then so was 'Jack Your Body'. And it's worth remembering that it was while Jackie Wilson's 'Reet Petite' was suggesting that the market was completely bankrupt that a WEA Artistes and Repertoire man called Bill Drummond and a guitarist called James Cauty got together to form The Justified Ancients of Mu Mu, a band opposed in every way to the 'traditional well-crafted song'.

I've perhaps been over-cynical and over-selective in this survey of what was selling to the public up to the beginning of 1987. No two people's remembered 'histories' of pop music will read quite the same, because the great genius of pop music, even when it's truly terrible by any imaginable yardstick, is to appeal to the gut instinct of the market at that precise moment. Although I've implied that it's all a matter of cynical manipulation, often it isn't. Very often when some new phenomenon scorches across the sky, it does so almost in spite of the apparent market rules of the time. Manipulation comes later with imitation. Once the technology existed, it was probably inevitable that someone would use sampling to achieve a successful breakthrough. It was just a matter of who, how and why.

4 · Scratching Where It Itches

One of the most important acts in the advance of sampling, indeed in the whole history of 1980s pop music, was The Justified Ancients of Mu Mu, who subsequently became better know as The KLF. The JAMs (as they're known for short) were the brainchild of a well-known figure on the Liverpool scene called Bill Drummond. Out for a walk on New Year's Day 1987 (walking off a hangover in some versions of the legend), he decided to turn his back on the history of pop music, on the electric guitar and – above all – on the 'well-crafted song'. To Drummond the natural means to this end seemed to be hip hop. He regarded it as the only area of pop culture which was moving forward, the only form in which anything new or exciting was happening. Hip hop was more than just a musical style, it offered a whole attitude, a style which for young consumers in the UK looked attractively alien. Successful new styles in the pop culture since rock 'n' roll have been in some measure rebellions against 'older' fashions, and hip hop, which had some claim to be a voice for an 'oppressed' minority, possessed a good measure of rebellious aggression. Its visual expression was the elaborate graffiti of the New York subway, the stylized territorial-marking system which was beginning to announce its presence in the larger urban centres in the UK. There are plenty of apologists – some very middle class and eminently respectable – for this graffiti as an 'original art form', and while some of the youths who've used it as a means of expression might cling to that argument in a court-room, it's scarcely the aspect which interests them. First and foremost, it's illegal. It's a way of expressing your disrespect for the authority that's treading you down. There were various illicit edges to the hip-hop culture; small wonder it appealed to Bill Drummond as he plotted legally dubious 'raids' on other people's recordings.

The most celebrated element of hip-hop culture is, of course, rap music, and rap had and has a life independent of that culture. Rap was to the black American urban youth more or less what punk was to its British white counterpart; and its crucial development took place at more or less the same historical point, in the mid-1970s. Black American sub-culture wasn't a 1970s novelty. Even during the days of slavery there had been some definitive black musical tradition. However, the decline of America's urban manufacturing industries in the late 1950s and 1960s created a new class of urban poor, a new black under-class who had originally been drawn to the large cities by the promise of work in the factories. But the new poor belonged to an age of mass communication, and an age where civil rights was an issue, the age of Martin Luther King. At the precise moment they seemed to fall into a new poverty trap, the black community was learning about pride, about rights, about the denial of rights, and thus about justifiable anger. It was unlikely that any future black sub-culture would be particularly quiet or restrained.

You could – at the risk of being glib and patronizing – chart the changing consciousness of black America in boldly stated and over-simplified musical terms. The slaves on the plantations had had Negro spirituals, religious songs which set their sights (as religous works tend to) on another world where all the apparently endless injustices of this vale of tears will be healed and rewarded. Something of this lingered in the gospel tra-dition, which produced many of the best soul singers. The spirituals were poached by white songwriters and performers

77

like Stephen Foster, and the ghastly white tradition of 'nigger-minstrel shows' sprang up, a tradition popular well into the twentieth century and responsible for evolving the career of Al Jolson. Meanwhile, the newly 'liberated' black community in the South, especially in New Orleans, developed a more secret, more hedonistic, illicit music called jazz, based around rhythms which subverted rhythm itself. In the second decade of the twentieth century, the white man got hold of jazz too, and eventually completely appropriated it. Then there was the blues, grievance music, in essence the spiritual without the religious optimism. The blues, you might say, is the music of the Great Depression, the late 1920s and early 1930s slump which hit town and country alike across racial barriers. A sense of energy returned to the black tradition with soul music, an energy stemming to some extent from gospel; at root, soul – although it had a wistful, ballad-orientated side – was good-time music. Like jazz, it went into the wider consumer market-place and was similarly 'stolen'. But then came rap. And the big difference between rap and all these other black musical traditions was its sheer assertiveness. Jazz, gospel and soul had had energy, but they hadn't been concerned with self-assertion in quite the same way. Above all, even when soul became enmeshed with a sense of protest, as was inevitable in the increasingly politically aware 1960s, it didn't have real anger. Rap, right from the start, was about anger. It was a vehicle for anger. It was the first purely black musical form designed for black people to assert and promote their own sense of worth in the here and now, and not some eternally postponed hereafter.

Inevitably, such a glib summary leaves out a great deal, and that great deal is at least part of the American tradition which went into rap. Jazz spawned artists like Cab Calloway and Louis Jordan, whose semi-comic songs were tied into the speech rhythms and patterns of the black community. Cabaret performers like Pigmeat Markham – a comedian rather than a musician – drew inspiration from a similar source; and when his appearance on the 1960s show *Rowan and Martin's Laugh-In* gave Markham a new lease of life leading to a minor cult hit 'Here Comes the Judge' (his long-standing catch-phrase), the combination of Markham's rhythmically organized comic patter and music on that single wasn't so very far removed from what we now know as rap. Younger comedians like Flip Wilson (with a US Top 30 album to his credit, whose title track, 'The Devil Made Me Buy this Dress', is one of the funniest monologues I've ever heard) picked up on the Markham tradition. Pride in these speech patterns and idiosyncracies was still something of a novelty in the 1960s – after all, Sam Cooke had been repeatedly upbraided during one of the recording sessions for 'A Change is Gonna Come' because of his natural tendency to pronouce 'ask' as 'axe'. That was only thirty years ago: anyone familiar with the special brand of Uzi-toting belligerence espoused by Public Enemy can imagine what might happen if a producer or a record-company representative tried to 'correct' their pronunciation to some 'ideal' received standard English.

These cabaret-style performers were showmen as well as musicians, and when the young James Brown came to put an act together, he decided that this element of show was very important. In this he wasn't so dissimilar from the people masterminding the Motown acts. Every Supremes, Temptations, Four Tops song had its own special set of movements the group would go through, but this was all choreographed and handed down from on high, so to speak.

Berry Gordy might have founded the first successful 'black' record label, but he didn't have any fancy civil-rights type notions about freedom of expression for his artists. There was a house style and that was that. And that house style placed soul-singing techniques within a fairly rigid pop production and sound framework, while ensuring that the lyrical content didn't get out of hand. You wouldn't find Motown acts making political statements about the position of black people during the upheaval of the 1960s and the rise of the Black Power movement. While James Brown was proclaiming 'Say It Loud, – I'm Black and I'm Proud', the Supremes were singing Rodgers and Hart and appearing at the Talk of the Town. When Motown did embrace social or even political issues, these were carefully ensured to be non-racial. The 'controversy' of 'Love Child', a song trailed as a daring story of illegitimacy, was so unintentionally hilarious and – dare one say it – camp as to make it ideal fodder for a high-energy gay club remake in the 1980s. Political songs like Edwin Starr's 'War' (a huge success in 1970) and the Temptations' 'Ball of Confusion', for all their impact at the time, sound to 1990s ears dangerously like novelty records ('War' has one of the great accidentally funny rhymes: 'heartbreaker' with 'undertaker'). These were political records designed to appeal to white liberal audiences, and now their concerns sound prehistoric. Yet the truly political black music of the 1960s, the songs which grew from protest and a concern to promote black consciousness, still pack an enormous punch. Apart from James Brown's 'Say It Loud' and Sam Cooke's 'A Change is Gonna Come', there's still something profoundly exhilarating about Aretha Franklin's 'Think', which, despite apparently having the lyric of a straightforward love song, centres on repetition of the word 'freedom'.

James Brown's individual, explosive, self-centred showman's delivery demanded a very different kind of musical framework from the pop style of Motown. He and his backing band of the time (due to ego clashes, the personnel of James Brown backing groups would change regularly) evolved a heavily rhythmic style, dense in its cross-rhythms, often very loud, but sparse when compared to the complex orchestrations of the traditional Motown sound. Drums, bass guitar and brass all featured heavily, sometimes at great individual length, which led to, among other things, the great rolling drum solo at the heart of

'Funky Drummer', a musical moment which was to prove the inspiration for a thousand samplers. For all its rhythmic and other subtleties and complexities, the sound surrounding James Brown was raw – just like the naked emotion of his vocal style. It was sensual, sexual. Brilliant producers though Holland–Dozier–Holland and Norman Whitfield were, it would be hard to imagine their production styles lending any credibility to any of their singers' claim to 'feel like being a sex machine'. James Brown's musical style made that claim natural.

The Brown style – musical and otherwise – was also arrogant, self-confident and self-promoting. James Brown became a fairly astute businessman, with his own chain of radio stations. Here was nobody's puppet – not even another black man's. Both musically and personally, Brown offered a role model to one section of the black community at a time of social upheaval. Ironically, he rejected the values of the civil-rights promoting Democratic Party, embracing instead the ideals of the Republicans, traditionally the businessman's friends, supporting Richard Nixon for the presidency and, eventually, in 1986 draping himself in the Stars and Stripes and proclaiming the virtues of 'Living in America'. America was so grateful that Brown was harassed into prison a couple of years later. R-E-S-P-E-C-T can still be hard to come by.

Brown's musical style, mirrored by the leaner, sharper black music to be found on the Stax label, was all part of what we loosely, and without much clue as to precise definition, label 'funk'. From 'Funky Drummer' to Rufus Thomas's 'Do the Funky Chicken', funk is much easier to recognize than to describe. A contemporary of Brown's who was, in his own way, equally influential was Sly Stone (as in Sly and the Family Stone). Not only was the very tough, quite 'heavy' (in a 1960s musical sense) sound ground-breaking in combining black music rhythms with the instruments of rock music, Sly produced a lot of quite political music in the early 1970s (especially on the album *There's a Riot Goin' On*). Given that his music was to prove a fertile source of samples, and, before that, of breaks and beats for rappers, it's either ironic or quite apposite, depending on your point of view, that Sly started out as a San Francisco DJ in 1965.

One of the key exponents of funk in the 1970s and 1980s was a man who as an individual was possessed of little talent as singer or musician or dancer. But George Clinton's talent for bringing people together, making things happen, and sheer showmanship was crucial to the development of black music and provided a vital musical background for the emergence of the hip-hop culture – and thus rapping, scratch mixing and all the other elements today's pop music takes so much for granted. Clinton created a series of personae (such as Doctor Funkenstein, Loopzilla) and outrageous shows, which blended funk with the androgyny of 1970s glamrock. Although the idea of 'creating a series of personae' may make Clinton sound like a precursor of Michael Jackson, nothing could be further from the truth. Clinton wanted – as Jackson never really has – to shock and outrage with only secondary regard to dominating the market. Two of the most important 'funk ensembles', Funkadelic and Parliament, were also Clinton's babies. Both 'One Nation Under a Groove', Funkadelic's surprisingly (but deservedly) large 1979 hit, and Parliament's 'P-Funk' provided a pattern for a type of radical black music which came out through the hip-hop culture.

The development of one black-music tradition into funk provided an important strand which went into the evolution of rap as we know it. Equally significant, though, was the non-American tradition and the political thrust which went with it. In the mid-1960s, a whole host of young black radicals had begun to view the civil rights movement of Martin Luther King as too slow, too peaceable, too respectful for their tastes, seeing it almost as another 'Uncle Tom'-style movement which allowed black people to be only what white people wanted them to be. These young lions – people like Eldridge Cleaver, Malcolm X, Elijah Mohammed – drew on an 'African' tradition, proclaiming Black Power and more or less stating that their aim was not equality but supremacy. Ironically, to finance their activities these groups still relied on the goodwill of liberal middle-class Whites. Tom Wolfe provided perhaps the most deadly and accurate analysis of the ideological cleft stick in which white liberals found themselves by the end of the 1960s in his famous description of one of Leonard Bernstein's parties for the Black Panthers, the essay which coined the term 'Radical Chic'. These movements – of which there were many splinters of varying radicalism, advocating varying levels of violence against the 'establishment' – looked back to a (possibly non-existent) Moorish past. Perhaps the most celebrated convert to the radical black viewpoint in the 1960s was Muhammad Ali, the heavyweight boxer who rejected the name Cassius Clay as a symbol of white oppression.

Such groups may have had some very valid and pertinent views on the social situation of the ethnic minorities in American society, but the proliferation of political groups espousing violence as a solution, added to the upsurge in levels of drug abuse in deprived urban areas, hardly made for calm and happy living in the bigger American cities. Black areas in New York's Bronx were riven by gang warfare in the early 1970s, but somehow out of this chaos a new culture emerged.

Somehow also a new tradition of parties sprang up, largely as an antidote to the upheaval and tension. The advent of portable but effective sound systems which made a good, loud noise allowed for a new breed of unofficial 'community DJ'. As with the graffiti, part of the fun of the parties lay in the illicit elements at the edges. To save money, and as a gesture against the oppressing authority, the party-goers would get the electricity to run the sound system by plugging into the nearest street lamp.

It's impossible to determine who 'invented' rapping – different names can be offered depending upon which tradition (or which record-company publicity hand-out) you come across. But there was one final, vital 'traditional' ingredient which made for the birth of rap. This was Jamaican 'toasting', talking to a rhythm in a particular patois, the rhythm of the speech and the rhythm of the beat working together. The Jamaican literary tradition has a special place for this kind of spontaneous creative act which crosses the barriers of poetry and music. Figures like Benjamin Zephaniah and Levi Tafari, who are considered bona fide poets by most of the British literary establishment, continue 'writing' these heavily rhythmic works, many of which are designed to elicit audience response and participation ('call and response' is one such poetic form, with the audience having a fixed rhythmic response, almost like a church congregation). The West Indian community in the US provided several of the DJs at these parties, and it was one of them, possibly Kool Herc, who began to 'toast' through an echo chamber (for that 'dub' effect which is so much a part of reggae music production) over the funk records that his audience preferred to his own selection of reggae in its simple and dub forms.

The records became the backdrop of the rhythmic patois, and the disc on the turntable would be there mostly to provide the basic rhythm – it would be there for its beat. It soon became clear that certain instrumental figures worked better than others as interludes when the DJ stopped talking, and it's said that Kool Herc was one of the first (some maintain *the* first) to buy records simply because fifteen-second instrumental bursts fit well into the breaks between his toasting. On a dual turntable sound system, the method was simple, if requiring dexterity. On one turntable the disc providing the rhythm would play, on the other the disc providing the instrumental break. The DJ wouldn't need all of both discs; usually he'd just require a single figure for the rhythm – the beat – and a single instrumental figure to fill in the gaps – the break. And so he'd just play the same part of the records over and over again, manipulating the discs manually, mixing in the instrumental break at the appropriate moments. And so was born the basic technique of the rap DJ, scratch mixing. The manipulation of a record produces its own rhythmic sound, the sound associated with scratching, an almost indescribable non-musical sound.

Rapping may have started this way with Jamaican DJs, but it quickly spread throughout the black community of the Bronx, through the communities of New York and thence to the west coast of the USA, to Los Angeles, and so to anywhere where there was a large black community with a sense of grievance. Here was a form of instant creativity, of instant statement, which didn't make such time-wasting demands as the acquisition of a formal musical skill like playing an instrument or singing. You didn't even have to be able to dance to rap; all you needed was to be able to talk in rhythm while the DJ provided the beats and breaks. It was also a form of expression which the white majority hadn't got hold of yet, a form of expression special to the black community. It was a suitable vehicle for pride and for anger, for asserting the self-worth of the community.

The first rap recording is traditionally held to be The Fatback Band's 'King Tim III' (although you could make out a sly retrospective case for Pigmeat Markham's 'Here Comes the Judge' if you felt so inclined). But it was 'Rapper's Delight' by The Sugarhill Gang which first suggested that there was a wider market for rap music. It also marked the first appearance of a 'dedicated' rap label – Sugarhill – which was to serve as a commercial vehicle for the most 'significant' rap record of the early 1980s: Grandmaster Flash's 'The Message'.

Back in 1979, anyone who knew nothing more of rap than 'Rapper's Delight' wouldn't have imagined that this was the voice of a radical political stance. 'Rapper's Delight' had one of the crucial elements of rap – it had buckets of self-assertive ego. However, to call it political in any sense other than, perhaps, reactionary sexually politics retrograde, would be to do both it and genuinely political rap records a grave disservice. 'Rapper's Delight' was packed with a lot of boasting about the sexual prowess of The Sugarhill Gang (one of whom laid claim to the sobriquet 'Super Sperm'), but the only way it ever got radical was in its ingenious *double entendres* and suggestiveness, making it the rap equivalent of a 'Carry On' film. Although from a completely different tradition, it didn't seem a million miles removed in attitude from a fairly recent (1977) black 'talking' record which had topped the UK charts, 'Float On' by The Floaters. In this *magnum opus* each of The Floaters in turn informed us of his astrological sign followed by his desired qualities in a woman (with a sung 'break' suggesting that any 'lady' fitting the bill should take his hand and accompany him to 'Love Land', which, if it emanated from a Floater's imagination, would probably have been a fate worse than death).

In fact, although this tradition of spoken monologues in both black soul and country music may have little direct connection with rap, it may suggest why the greater market may not have been so resistant to the sound of non-singing voices. There would, of course, have been a minority both in the UK and the US who would have been familiar with 'toasting' in its original reggae context, but this was a pretty small minority when it came to the actual record-buying market. However, there was a long tradition of talk in successful pop music, even if it was non-rhythmic talk, dating back to the tribute record 'Three Stars' (a 1959 single celebrating Buddy Holly, Ritchie Valens and the Big Bopper after their fatal plane crash) and encompassing figures like Elvis Presley, who recorded country talk songs such as 'Old Shep', the story of a ghost dog, and used the spoken word to great effect on his remake of All Jolson's 'Are You Lonesome Tonight?' Quite apart from the nauseating country tradition of talking songs like Red Sovine's 'Teddy Bear' (crippled boy melts truckers' hearts over CB radio), J. J. Barrie's 'No Charge' (mother spelling out to ungrateful child just what mother love really means, in a non-Oedipal sense, of course) and the daddy of them all, Wink Martindale's 'Deck of Cards' (soldier uses playing cards as Bible substitute), there was a somewhat less glutinous tradition of talking in soul music, which included such genuine classics as Diana Ross's 'Ain't No Mountain High Enough', as well as a whole range of introductions (Aretha Franklin's 'Angel', Gladys Knight's version of 'Help Me Make It through the Night', and the entire *oeuvre* of Barry White). Perhaps some of the soul tradition isn't entirely irrelevant in the development of rap. Isaac Hayes's long monologues on such albums as *Black Moses* were very involved with the raising of black consciousness and perhaps looked forward to such bona fide rap pieces as Gary Byrd's 'The Crown'. And Hayes's use of speech rhythm on his epoch-making 'Theme from *Shaft*' (the track which created the 1970s disco sound) wasn't a million miles from rap either. So speech (even on occasion rhythmic speech) and black music, indeed speech and pop music, weren't total strangers before The Sugarhill Gang opened up the market for rap.

A history of 'credible' rap would lead on from 'Rapper's Delight' to the significance of Afrika Bambaataa, who took the whole techniques of scratch mixing and set hip hop on the techno course by which it became familiar to the world at large, and the 1982 chart success of Grandmaster Flash and the Furious Five with their overtly political description of black urban deprivation, 'The Message'. But one of the great things about pop success and the pop consumer is the lack of interest in keeping things 'credible'. As far as your average listener was concerned, who didn't view music from the perspective of the Bronx or Compton, the next big rap record, the first major pop rap hit, had nothing to do with black culture. It was Blondie's

'Rapture', essentially a disco record, which culminated in Blondie's front person Debbie Harry pouring forth a wittily rhymed piece about driving in your car and being eaten by a man from Mars who eats all the cars, then eats up bars ('where the people meet') and finally 'eats guitars'. It was a very stylish vocal performance, capping one of Blondie's best singles (and one of their biggest hits in the US, if slightly disappointing in terms of its UK chart position), but it had about as much relevance to the 'real' rap tradition, to hip-hop culture as . . . well, as most of the 'rap' records which found their way into the UK charts over the next few years. The only relation it bore to much of the hip-hop culture was its insistence on naggingly repetitive rhymes. This facet of the rap vocal has remained constant through such antecedents as the rhymes of Cassius Clay/Muhammad Ali, to the seminal mid-1980s political rabble rousing of Schoolly D, and on to subsequent styles from the ranting of Public Enemy to the laid-back wit and hippy drawling of De La Soul and PM Dawn. But otherwise 'Rapture' was a brilliant pop record which exploited a trend and style before it was properly defined in the mainstream market's consciousness.

The next rap invasion in the UK charts came later in 1981 from two sources about as diametrically opposed as you could hope for, sharing only the common ground that neither had anything to do with the sub-culture to which rap genuinely belonged. 'Wordy Rappinghood' was a highly witty and articulate, extremely rhythmic single, and its performers, Tom Tom Club, being half of Talking Heads, had already showed a conscious awareness of 'funk' (members of George Clinton's Parliament had had some input to Talking Heads' 1980 album *Remain in Light*). Another Tom Tom Club single, 'Genius of Love', was to prove a very fruitful ground for samplers in search of breaks and beats and quite a few 'new' versions of 'Genius of Love' came out over the next few years. (In a similar way, Bobby Byrd's 'I'm Coming', provider of one of the seminal beats of the second half of the 1980s, spawned several tracks, culminating in an Eric B and Rakim single.) But although Tom Tom Club may have been respectful of the traditions, they were scarcely part of those traditions, and no one could claim that 'Wordy Rappinghood' was anything other than a very clever piece of arty elaboration. Like a lot of Talking Heads' music it was too clever by half. But it wasn't the only rap-related single in the UK charts in July 1981. Historians of rap and hip hop would want to forget this fact, but within two years of 'Rapper's Delight', rap was a fertile ground for novelty records. Hence The Evasions' 'Wikka Wrap', a more than usually feeble 'comedy' disc based around an impersonation of globe-trotting purple-prose-spouting TV journalist Alan Whicker, with a hook poached from a dance hit of the previous year (remixed with mild success in 1991/92), Tom Browne's 'Funkin' for Jamaica (N.Y.)'. The success of novelty records is often difficult to explain in retrospect; in this case a convincing explanation, if such exists, would probably be too surreal for words.

While the UK was lapping up such doubtful delights (it must grieve Americans that their restricted knowledge of Alan Whicker would prevent them from enjoying 'Wikka Wrap' to the full), the serious rap artists were getting on with some very important business. Afrika Bambaataa was – perhaps unwittingly – laying out a plan which would define much of the future of pop music (certainly of dance music). One thing that rap had done was to render musical instruments unnecessary. Providing you had a DJ (or two) manipulating the records with your breaks and beats, or you might if you could afford the luxury have your own drummer (or synthesized drum machine), all you needed to produce music was a microphone. Bambaataa had quit the New York gang life as the attraction of the new music style he'd heard from Kool Herc exercised a growing fascination over him. As an adolescent he'd imbibed a lot of the Black Panther message, and was very much at the radical edge of the black political view, although his childhood gang experiences had turned him against the more violent attitudes. He formed a small 'social group' (as the publicity literature likes to term it, although I suspect it looked like a gang even if it didn't behave like one) called The Zulus, studied the techniques of Kool Herc and then started acting as DJ himself.

One thing which immediately distinguished Bambaataa from much of his sub-cultural competition was his eclectically catholic taste in music. In this, as in much else, he set the trend for the era of the sampler. For Bambaataa, colliding corny TV themes with James Brown tracks was part of the excitement. He also listened, as few Americans of any cultural origin did at that time, to electronic European acts like Kraftwerk, Gary Numan and the Japanese Yellow Magic Orchestra, acts who were far removed from the sweating, growling sensuality of funk. And it was his interest in this kind of music, his incorporation of it into his public performance, that led Bambaataa to form the ambition of creating 'a black group that had a record with just electronic instruments', indeed, taking this to a logical conclusion, having 'no band except a synthesizer'. Having recorded tracks which proved to have a cross-over dance appeal like 'Zulu Nation Throwdown' (Bambaataa originally objected to the post-production addition of strings to this track, rather foreshadowing the distaste Eric B and Rakim would exhibit for the Coldcut remix of 'Paid in Full') and 'Planet Rock', he went on to work with producer Arthur Baker (responsible for Freeez's 'I.O.U.' and New Order's 'Confusion', and one of the most distinctive producers of electronic-based dance music in the mid-1980s), produced tracks like 'Looking for the Perfect Beat' (the home of the title of 'Beat Dis') and became one of the most revered figures in hip hop. He proved his eclecticism by working with figures as unlikely as John Lydon (previously

Johnny Rotten), although he never quite achieved the major market appeal many predicted for him. Undoubtedly he was ahead of his time in his early 1980s eclecticism. Grandmaster Flash, more or less an exact contemporary on the hip-hop scene, achieved success by keeping things a lot simpler, a lot less involved and perhaps a little less radical lyrically. While white American audiences may have been ready in the early 1980s to dance to 'Zulu Nation Throwdown', this didn't mean that they wanted to buy it, with its heavily black-orientated message, for home consumption. Grandmaster Flash's 'The Message' described an urban, rat-infested deprivation which was much easier to relate to.

'The Message' was the first serious rap record to cross over into the mainstream in the UK, reaching the Top 10 within a month of official release. Like 'Rapper's Delight', it was a product of the Sugarhill label, but its anger and frustration was a long way from the effusions of Super Sperm and his colleagues. Its success was unusual not only because it was rap but because it was released almost exclusively in the twelve-inch format, then a somewhat rare event as the twelve-inch was (slightly) more expensive. 'The Message' cut across most of its chart competition of the time (Autumn 1982) simply because it sounded like the authentic voice of the ghetto – especially to those who (like myself) hadn't been within a million miles of anything which could properly be styled a ghetto. Not only were the lyrics completely arresting, the *engagé* style of delivery was entirely new, and the musical sound was unlike anything which the UK market had ever experienced before. Not a musical instrument in sight, just the rapper(s) and the DJ manipulating his discs on his 'Wheels of Steel', ensuring that every break between stanzas of the rap was filled by the same memorable hook, a synthesizer keyboard figure. For the first time, the mainstream public heard the rhythmic swishing noise a disc makes when being moved by hand on the turntable. It all had a certain novelty appeal, but you could scarcely accuse a record as basically serious (and compelling) as 'The Message' of being a novelty record. Sadly the actual appearance of Grandmaster Flash and his Furious Five proved to be something of a let down. They turned out to be much more of a glitzy old-fashioned style act than 'The Message' had promised (closer in presentation to The Detroit Spinners than anyone dared imagine) and tracks like 'Adventures of Grandmaster Flash' proved to be more like The Sugarhill Gang's narcissistic ranting than the social concern of the initial UK success. Still, the Grandmaster managed to turn the chart trick twice more in the UK, but not before various other unlikely figures had brought the word 'rap' into complete chart disrepute.

It may be that the British response to 'The Message' was partly provoked by a new political sense which had been awakened to some extent by a series of inner-city riots in 1980 and 1981. These had occurred in areas often identified for shorthand purposes as 'black' areas, although the ethnic mix was usually more diverse than this might suggest. Particular headline-grabbing flashpoints had been Toxteth in Liverpool and Brixton in London. A feeling was abroad, especially among those of liberal opinions, that the gap between the affluent and the poor was opening up to a width unseen in the UK since the worst days of the 1930s depression. This sensation would later grow stronger after the Thatcher Government's landslide post-Falklands election victory in 1983 and the confrontational nature of the year-long miners' strike of 1984–5. It may be that the growth of a UK rap industry later in the 1980s had something to do with the growth of a 'new under-class' who took their attitudes and style from their more defined American counterparts. But even if this were the case, it was hardly suggested by the first genuine scratch mix hit by a UK artist, as the artist in question was one of the great cynical entrepreneurs in the popular-music business.

Malcolm McLaren's career as the mastermind (and financial beneficiary) behind The Sex Pistols has been well charted. By 1982, no one imagined that the man who'd given the world *The Great Rock 'n' Roll Swindle* was entirely lacking in monetary motivation or completely devoted to art for art's sake in any project he undertook. After all, McLaren had gloried in the 'swindle' element of the career of The Pistols. Just after 'The Message' had put socially concerned rap music, complete with DJ-operated scratch mixing, on the popular agenda, McLaren returned to the market-place with a whole new set of products – new, exciting musical styles filched from all over the world, especially from the streets of New York. In chart terms his greatest success from this campaign was his 1983 Top 3 hit 'Double Dutch', based around popular girls' skipping rhymes. But in late 1982 it was McLaren – and neither Grandmaster Flash, nor yet Afrika Bambaataa, who made some of his best recordings in that year – who made the mainstream record-buying public aware of the whole concept of 'scratching'. The single with which he did this was 'Buffalo Gals', the choice of song here being itself part of the joke. Colliding an old American square dance with modern New York DJ styles was an act of perverse eclecticism which would have out-Bambaataa'd Bambaataa. Just to show how old-fashioned and highly unsuitable (and completely without social message) the original was, he recorded a perfectly straight version, complete with country fiddle and cries of 'yee-haw', for the single's B-side. McLaren's sense of 'fun' took him further. Rather than using beats and breaks as backdrop and punctuation for some coherent whole, McLaren set out to make the dislocation of scratching the whole point of his exercise. Unrelated non-musical sounds were mixed in, the noise of the record itself being manipulated on the turntable was highlighted and the snatches of the original 'Buffalo Gals' were so incoherently and unpredictably interjected that the effect was almost an anti-song. It was, in its way, a brilliant sort of post-modernist joke. The beat was so terminally dislocated that it was almost impossible to dance to (undermining one of the central concepts of the rap/scratch mix track), unless you were an intolerable show-off who'd managed to memorize every little jump on every mix. Like the 1987 work of The Justified Ancients of Mu Mu, 'Buffalo Gals' was essentially collage, but collage which set its face against preaching any message which might 'redeem' its dislocation.

Perhaps by leaping on rap and scratching so cynically, with such admiration for the style and such disdain for the content, McLaren was simply divining what would be the prevailing mood of the later 1980s, the era of the 'Big Bang', deregulated markets and go-getting hungry entrepreneurs following the Gordon Gekko creed of 'Greed is Good' (articulated by the anti-hero of Oliver Stone's 1987 movie *Wall Street*). And perhaps by their (relatively) enthusiastic response to the McLaren treatment of the genre, the UK public indicated that their interest in it at this stage of its development was as much for the sake of its novelty as for its content and potential. And certainly two of the next three hit singles using or alluding to the idea of 'rap' were straightforward novelty records of a pretty unpleasant kind.

The exception was Gary Byrd's 'The Crown', a paean of praise to the contribution of the black man to the development of world culture and history. In some ways, although Byrd was a DJ, 'The Crown' owed as much to mainstream soul and the monologue tradition as to the scratch mixing and cutting of Bambaataa and Grandmaster Flash. Gary Byrd had provided part of the spoken commentary on Stevie Wonder's 'Black Man' (a track on the 1976 double album *Songs in the Key of Life* which also celebrated the contribution of the different ethnic groups to American history) and Wonder returned the compliment by singing a section of 'The Crown' which bemoaned the lack of formal education about the achievements of the black communities provided by the official United States curriculum. Admirably slick though it was, 'The Crown' had the sound of a spoken soul song.

Balancing the success of 'The Crown' (which reached the Top 10 in July 1983) were Kenny Everett's 'Snot Rap' (March 1983) and the immortal 'Rat Rapping' (chart debut for Roland Rat in November 1983). While the Everett single, supposedly a monologue by one of the hilarious personae he adopted on his TV programme, merely used the word 'rap' in its title to denote that there wasn't much in the way of singing going on, 'Rat Rapping' actually homed in on the scratching technique (partly to work in a joke about rats and fleas) and incorporated the sound of 'scratching', that sound of the record's physical manipulation which was becoming recognizable to the public ear. As the Roland Rat character was essentially arrogant, this made for a good parody of the assertive element of rap as well. Did this mean that the moment rap was established in the British market, the moment 'The Message' had got across, the industry had assimilated the form, eaten it and then regurgitated it as novelty?

In fact, the next part of hip-hop culture to make an impact was break dancing, the physically energetic style which involved spinning around on the floor and made extreme demands on the performers. Two singles by Break Machine, promoted by a highly visual dance presentation, pushed the concept of break dancing to the fore, and it became one of 1984's crazes. And there were signs, albeit sparse to begin with, of a cross-over and acceptance of the scratch and cut-up techniques in the mainstream. Duran Duran's chart topper 'The Reflex' used scratching as part of its attention-grabbing in the hook of the chorus, as well as employing a visual equivalent on the video for the single. Grandmaster Flash and Melle Mel's (nominally) anti-cocaine rap, the ambiguously titled 'White Lines (Don't Don't Do It)', a sparse, neurotic single which could have been at least half-infatuated with the habit it purported to decry, proved to be one of 1984's top-selling singles (in a year when singles sales were generally high). The Grandmaster was, in fact, keeping the rap flag flying at this time. Not only was there a third Top 10 hit in early 1985 ('Step Off'), but the eclectic combination of talents which made up Chaka Khan's successful 'I Feel for You' included a Grandmaster Melle Mel introductory rap, complete with initial scratching. (This rap was subsequently reprised more or less in its entirety and perhaps to slightly more baffling effect on 'Step Off'.)

Rap began to grab the headlines and attention in both the UK and the USA once more in 1987, when The Beastie Boys were boosted, by a carefully orchestrated campaign of 'outrageous' behaviour, to the status of teen rebels. This white middle-class trio had carefully studied and copied the dress styles and language of the hip-hop culture, to great short-term success (their album *Licensed to Ill* enjoyed a lengthy spell at the top of the American album charts), although ultimately their self-assertive noises seemed as ludicrous as those three years later of Vanilla Ice. '(You Gotta) Fight for Your Right (to Party)' might have carried a message of great hedonism, but if the only right you need to fight for is your right to party, then a bad attitude somehow seems less appropriate. With hindsight, '(You Gotta) Fight for Your Right (to Party)' seems like a rap, mildly bad-mannered, version of The Beach Boys' 'Fun, Fun, Fun'. Certainly, set against the serious, confrontational pronouncements of Public Enemy later that same year, it's hard to take The Beastie Boys very seriously (unless, of course, you're one of the people whose Volkswagen suffered serious damage as a result of the craze they inspired for stealing car insignia).

It was in 1987 that both Public Enemy – serious advocates of Black Power with an aggression rarely seen since the days of Huey P. Newton, Malcolm X and others – and Eric B and Rakim came to public attention. That year rap became critically respectable and began to show its UK sales potential: 'Paid in

Full' and L. L. Cool J.'s 'I Need Love' were both hits in the second half of the year. Public Enemy's *Yo! Bum Rush the Show* was selected as *NME*'s album of the year (and Public Enemy showed a remarkable resilience as critical favourites when their subsequent album *It Takes a Nation of Millions to Hold Us Back* won the same accolade the following year – to retain the *NME*'s critical favour and have a Top 10 album is a pretty fair achievement), and several other style-conscious magazines gave the album *Paid in Full* a high rating. Nothing like the same kudos had been accorded to Run-DMC when they had briefly threatened a 1986 rap breakthrough with their reworking of heavy metal group Aerosmith's 'Walk this Way'. But suddenly rap was extremely trendy, especially with the advent from other directions of The JAMs and M/A/R/R/S.

In spotting hip hop as the area of the future at the end of 1986, Bill Drummond showed a certain amount of prescience – it wasn't quite the area for adulation it was about to become. There was a sizeable cult following at that time, and various individual hits like 'Bang Zoom (Let's Go Go)' by The Real Roxanne ensured some profile for hip-hop scratch and cutting techniques. But it was probably the eclectic groove-raiding of Afrika Bambaataa (who had appeared live in the UK in the summer of 1986) which appealed most to Drummond – the concept of a group without members, music without instruments.

Rap has become a commercial success over the past four years or so, to the extent that a chart without a sprinkling of rap or rap-associated records in it would now be as remarkable as the presence of Grandmaster Flash and the Furious Five was ten years ago. Many of the more critically adored acts have found a sales barrier beyond which they cannot break. It's unusual, for example, for a Public Enemy single to rise past Number 18 even in a poor sales week, but then the Public Enemy message is designed to alienate as much as anything else; and personally I find that if you've heard one Public Enemy single, then you've heard the lot. The same could be said of the deliberately controversial acts like NWA and 2 Live Crew, whose sexism and racism has sent liberal white critics into spasms of doubt about what line to take. Hard-core rap remains a minority taste, and the rap that does cross over in the UK tends to be based around easily recognizable samples of tried and tested hits. Thus De La Soul's biggest singles to date have revolved around samples from such wonderfully eclectic sources as Steely Dan, Daryl Hall and John Oates, as well as a rewrite of a Curiosity Killed the Cat hook line. PM Dawn's biggest single world-wide, 'Set Adrift on Memory Bliss', leaned heavily on the proven hit-making power of Spandau Ballet's 'True'. All of (MC) Hammer's samples have been easily recognizable and dominant in their particular track.

And there's one (sad) sense in that however much imaginative rap music there is around (De La Soul's debut in 1989, A Tribe Called Quest's in 1990, PM Dawn's in 1991), rap music in the UK still suffers from what you might call the Roland Rat effect. To date only two rap records have topped the UK charts, only one of which didn't depend pathetically upon a previous hit. That unique achievement belongs to Partners in Kryme's 'Turtle Power', a fascinating narrative of the plot of the first Teenage Mutant Ninja Turtles film. The other chart-topping rapper is Vanilla Ice, whose 'Ice Ice Baby' owed its success almost entirely to the use of Queen and David Bowie's 'Under Pressure' as a break. And Vanilla Ice's posturings as a rapper were one of the more ludicrous sights and sounds of recent years. Whatever his claims about being 'black inside', the few facts that seem to have been established about his background suggest that his experience of poverty, deprivation and being part of an oppressed culture (as he would have us believe that he is) are about on a par with those of Roland Rat.

Fans of hard-core acts like NWA and 2 Live Crew would find

the inclusion of their darlings with the likes of Hammer, Vanilla Ice, Partners in Kryme and possibly even De La Soul and PM Dawn insulting. None the less, one of the healthy things about the rap scene is the diversity of influences and attitudes contained within it. The UK tour by Anthrax and Public Enemy suggested that certain preconceived barriers between musical genres may be coming down (although Run-DMC's collaboration five years ago with Aerosmith didn't achieve this). I welcome the success of the more sophisticated rap acts like PM Dawn, but history suggests that the shelf life of successful rap acts is short and getting shorter. Just like the shelf life of successful mainstream pop acts in fact. However, one thing is clear: as long as there are microphones and record collections, rap will remain a musical option, especially for people with no other outlet. Hammer is reported recently to have said that 'rap is easy' and requires no talent. Surely the fact that it never required conventional talent was part of its appeal, part of the reason for its success. But the talent to spin the wheels of steel, to cut the records into one another, to pick out the breaks and beats, to 'play the records' as though they themselves were a musical instrument, that's a real talent too, without which a lot of the current pop scene couldn't have happened. Even if it *can* all be done on computers nowadays.

5 · Kick out The JAMs

Everything about The Justified Ancients of Mu Mu has been shaped into the form of legend by the protagonists themselves. Almost every move they have made, under whatever pseudonym, has been accompanied by a carefully calculated burst of publicity. Only one event in their career, the catastrophic copyright action brought by the Swedish group Abba, wasn't a direct result of their own orchestration; and even that they managed to turn to some kind of publicity advantage – but it cost them their first album.

We've already encountered the first element of their legend – Bill Drummond's creatively inpiring New Year walk in 1987. Drummond had been working in the rock business for some time and was probably best known as Echo and the Bunnymen's manager, producer and publisher (stories about this part of his career abound). He had also handled another Liverpool band, Julian Cope's The Teardrop Explodes. When the charms of management waned, Drummond resuscitated his career on the other side of the music business fence, as it were. In 1978 he had co-founded an early independent label, Zoo Records; post-Bunnymen he joined the corporate rat-race as an Artistes and Repertoire consultant for WEA. It was in this capacity that Drummond became friendly with a post-punk guitarist called Jimmy Cauty and he invited Cauty to join him in the Justified Ancients project. Cauty claims that he understood instinctively what Drummond was up to and that he found the idea as irresistibly right as Drummond did. The anti-song, anti-instrument band was an idea whose time had come (as I've tried to show, it wasn't all that new an idea anyway).

The Justified Ancients of Mu Mu inevitably needed their own record label. Not only was the idea of collage based around scratch and sample, with an essentially dance-beat base, an incredibly difficult one to sell to a major label; not only were the anonymous personae which the members of The JAMs intended to assume more or less directly contrary to the whole personality-based star framework which the major record labels have always felt happier working within; not only was the idea behind The JAMs to a large extent the intention to wave two fingers at the conventional music establishment; aside from these considerations was the certainty that both Drummond and Cauty knew that they were going to be flouting copyright to an unprecedented and flagrant degree. This wasn't going to be copyright infringement of the 'does "My Sweet Lord" sound like "He's So Fine"?' type; this was straightforward purloining of other people's recorded materials. And so the KLF label was formed, the letters KLF purportedly standing for Kopyright Liberation Front. In fact, from very early on in the concept's history (it seems somehow limiting to refer to The JAMs, or The KLF, or even The Timelords, as a band), The KLF served as a useful – mildly confusing – alternative name. Given his history as an early leading light in the punk 'indie' movement, Drummond can honestly – perhaps even uniquely – claim to have been at the birth of two great booms which helped to change the expression on the face of British pop music.

One thing that's always been notable about The JAMs/KLF image and publicity is its forthright cynicism. There's a strong sense about much in their public pronouncements and in the initial impact of their product that Drummond and Cauty are taking everyone for a ride for their own amusement and – they hope – profit. The Timelords' *The Manual (How to Have a*

Number One the Easy Way) at first reads like a huge, cynical prank. Many of the early JAMs records contrive a sound of near chaos. In so far as they ever talk publicly about their work as JAMs/KLF, Drummond and Cauty wouldn't, one suspects, be caught dead prattling on about their 'art'. Pop musicians who regarded their work as somehow 'serious', the Stings and Bonos of the business, were something they were undoubtedly reacting against. And yet the very first JAMs release was, for all its cynicism about much contemporary pop music and public attitudes, a deeply serious social and political statement. Devotees of Robert Anton Wilson's 1970s science-fiction trilogy *Illuminatus* perhaps wouldn't have been so surprised that out of apparent chaos and haphazardness came a serious end product, for the whole JAMs/KLF product had borrowed the *Illuminatus* symbol of the single eye embedded in the upper part of a pyramid and adapted it, for use as their own symbol, replacing the eye with a portable stereo ghetto blaster. The *Illuminatus* trilogy posited a world run by a secret society where all the apparent abstract anarchy and chaos loose in the world was part of a larger and sinister scheme.

Another aspect of the publicity and legend which Drummond and Cauty forged which is worth noting is the actual elusiveness of the duo themselves. Every new product they have launched has always required some elaborate masquerade which promotes something – or someone – else to the foreground of the action. Their relations with even the sympathetic press have been guarded in the extreme, usually involving some elaborately staged 'event'. This has made it difficult to describe them as 'based' anywhere in quite the same way that Echo and the Bunnymen and The Teardrop Explodes, for example, were 'Liverpool bands'. The JAMs tracks on which they performed their own rap vocals over-stressed, to a misleading extent, a shared Scottish origin, but these same early releases depended very much on the London music scene for immediate propagation and elevation to cult status. (The 'Madchester' craze lay a couple of years in the future then.) A lot of the early support vocals specially recorded came from London too – the lovers' rockers on 'All You Need is Love' and the gospel choir on 'Downtown'. And, of course, 'Downtown' is essentially a London song (which may explain why it never quite had the sales and chart impact it deserves).

It was in March 1987 that the first KLF product was released, if 'released' is quite the right word. In fact only 500 copies of 'All You Need is Love' were pressed, which proved to be a canny move for reasons both planned and unforeseen. The exclusiveness of the release helped to build up interest and create a mystique about the product. Since this gambit, quite a few hit singles have started life as illegal or exclusive club releases subsequently legitimized by major record companies (DNA's reworking of Suzanne Vega's 'Tom's Diner' in 1990) or finally surfacing in 'legitimate' form with a ready-made audience salivating for the chance to buy (The Source's retread of Candi Staton's gospel song 'You Got the Love' and Bassheads' 'Is There Anybody Out There?' in 1991). One shouldn't forget, though, that this is a tactic which in its time worked for Jaap Eggermont's original 'Stars on 45' medley.

Pressing only 500 copies was also quite a shrewd move financially – it saved money at the time and upped the under-the-counter price of a copy into the region of £30. So that when, within a month of the initial release, three major record companies took out injunctions and obtained a court order that the single be not merely withdrawn but physically destroyed, all copies were conveniently out of the way to re-emerge as collectors' items in an unspecified future. This was a trick which Drummond and Cauty worked to greater effect with five copies of their debut album. And the fact that their first ever release attracted, *in parvo*, the subsequent, more graphically destructive, fate of their album, does give rise to the thought that this 'unforeseen' setback to The JAMs might have been on both occasions part and parcel of the plan and the publicity. Certainly with both the original version of 'All You Need is Love' and later with *1987: What the Fuck is Going On?*, it became easier to create market mystique around a product which legally couldn't exist and to which the public had no right of access. It helped Drummond and Cauty to continue to get favourable coverage from the music press, too. Human nature being what it is, most music journalists prefer to champion tastes and acts which the general public haven't yet acquired.

But whatever the usual vagaries of taste of the music press and whatever their general motivation, 'All You Need is Love' was something rather special, something which managed – and still manages – to hit the *Zeitgeist* nail fairly and squarely on the head. And it made an assumption rare in a pop record – it assumed co-operative intelligence on the part of the listener. It also tried hard to shock, on several levels at once. The record's very title was a sort of challenge, appropriating The Beatles' anthem for the Summer of Love (1967) and very quickly exploding it. A derisive rendition of the opening of 'La Marseillaise', a blast of the Fab Four singing 'Love, love, love' as the record is slowed down, and that's it for the old idea of love and peace, as the cry of 'Kick out the jams, motherfuckers' (courtesy of the MC5) makes clear. Shock tactics from the word go; also one component sample which was to last into the KLF chart-topping days of 1990 and 1991. That cry of 'Kick out the jams', with or without the motherfuckers, resurfaced on 'What Time is Love?' the track which eventually on its third go round turned The KLF into large-scale rave-scene heroes.

Exploding nice 1960s myths about love in such a brusque manner served a twofold purpose. There was the musical message: who stood more for the supremacy of the well-crafted song in pop music, even twenty years on, than The Beatles? What was more representative of pop music as art than The

Beatles' outpourings of 1967? The JAMs' 'All You Need is Love' tore all that up with a vengeance. But more important than this musical satire was the social comment, the collage depiction of 'Love' in the late 1980s, love and sex in the wake of AIDS. The first words to be heard on 'All You Need is Love' after 'Kick our the jams, motherfuckers' were 'sexual intercourse' and 'no known cure', evidently lifted from some documentary source. Tabloid sex-goddess Samantha Fox provided part of the soundtrack, with her Stock, Aitken and Waterman disco anthem 'Touch Me'. Sam Fox had been created as a masturbation object by the very newspapers which were taking a high moral line on the subject of AIDS and promiscuity; but it didn't seem to strike the editors and proprietors of such papers that thundering on about morality on pages 4 to 20 and in the editorial column and printing a picture calculated to titillate on page 3 (or 'page 7 fellas' come to that) might contain at least an element of self-contradiction. Nor did it seem to lessen Sam Fox's credibility as an icon of all that was virtuous in the tabloid universe that her cries of 'Touch me, I want to feel your body' were aimed at the very social group the same tabloids were blaming for the spread of the HIV virus, namely sexually active gay men – to judge from the style of the production and the venues where the disc was most popular.

The JAMs threw Samantha Fox into the sampler along with a quick snatch of children singing 'Ring-a-Ring o'Roses', a playground song usually thought to describe the symptoms of bubonic plague, the disease which had cut through Europe with devastating and monotonous regularity between the thirteenth and seventeenth centuries. Also present were a female lovers' rock (soft reggae) duo singing a repeated rhyme in which an HIV-infected mother bewails the damage done to her child against a background of repeated cries of 'Shag' provided by the mastermind JAMs. And yes, the basic essential of rap was thrown in: a highly exaggerated Scottish accent, owing as much

105

to the kind of impersonation you'd expect from Russ Abbott as to regional origin, proclaimed the merits of The JAMs as artists (who else would have had the nerve to use as their first words – the first they spoke themselves, that is – 'We're back again'?), weaving in thematic observations about AIDS around this.

Despite Drummond's professed opposition to 'the well-crafted song' at the moment when 'All You Need is Love' was made, inevitably the samples and elements of the collage were arranged in a form reminiscent of typical song structure: intro, verse (the rap plus Sam Fox's panting plus any other extraneous effects such as the playground rhyme), chorus (the lovers' rock). And like all good pop songs, the record moved towards constant repetition of the 'chorus', throwing in background cries of 'Ancients of Mu Mu' and 'Justified' – another thread throughout all KLF work right up to 1991's collaboration with Tammy Wynette, 'Justified and Ancient' (itself a reworking of a track from the forcibly destroyed *1987* album). In some versions of 'All You Need is Love', especially the version cleaned up for radio (the second half of 'motherfuckers' getting obscured as it later did on radio mixes of 'What Time is Love?'), there was a final flourish, too, a sort of coda, with a snatch of 'The Lonely Goatherd'. Whether this was supposed, in view of the disc's subject matter, to pack any sexual punch isn't so clear. You can read any number of things into it: a sniggering and schoolboyish glance at 'solitary practices' or even bestiality; an ironic reflection on the conventional boy-meets-girl, boy-marries-girl story of the lyric, and the way in which that simple concept has been blown out of the water by the HIV virus; a sneering reference to the sexless world of *The Sound of Music*; or maybe it's just a joke, thrown in as a bit of culture shock to jar the listener and to provoke people like me into making elaborate and pointless pseudo-cultural observations.

Drummond is on record as regarding the adulation immediately offered to The JAMs by the music press as something of a joke. He loves, when recounting the story, to dwell on the haphazard nature of the whole enterprise, the lack of concern for 'quality' in any conventional sense, and doubtless he'd hate me pointing out that all KLF product is meticulously crafted. Where there are jarring discrepancies and awful clashes of style, beat, rhythm, these always work, much as the clashes and grinding gear-change juxtapositions in 'The Waste Land' work – to use a pretentiously grandiose but ultimately apt allusion – and work better for being stark and raw rather than, as Eliot if uninfluenced by Pound would have had them, nicely prepared and elegantly worked in with pseudo-eighteenth-century 'pleasing numbers'.

And so with The JAMs, when Dave Brubeck's classic recording of 'Take Five' is thrown into the melting pot of 'Don't Take Five (Take What You Want)' – one of the tracks from 1987 to survive the litigious attentions of Abba and reappear more or less intact on The JAMs' greatest hits compilation *Shag Times* – there's no clever attempt to prepare the listener for the complexities of the five-in-a-bar rhythm which gives the Brubeck track the main point of its title, nor is there any hinting at the distinctive 'cool' jazz sound for which the track is noted. One of the characters in Roddy Doyle's novel *The Commitments* suggests (in the forcible manner of a typical Doyle character) that jazz is the absolute opposite of soul, because it's essentially intellectual, whereas soul is earthy and 'of the people'. Given that the hip-hop tradition which The JAMs were using as their basis was directly descended from soul music and had its roots in expressing the feelings 'of the people', the intrusion of Brubeck is more incongruous in its way than the conflation of Wagner with Jimi Hendrix in 'Candyman' (a track on The JAMs' second album *Who Killed The JAMs?*). But there's no excuse, no subtlety about the Brubeck sample; it's so bald you'd scarcely call it a 'sample' in quite the same sense in which people talk about 'samples' of 'Funky Drummer'. It's just a blatant quote, sticking out like a sore thumb amid a laid-back rap about shopping (here used as a kind of metaphor for sampling), and doubtless Drummond, when mythologizing the lack of concern for 'quality', the desire for speed and economy of production, would pretend that this is because it was the easiest way of doing it. But in fact, although the juxtaposition of the Brubeck with the rest of the track is initially jarring, repeated listenings reveal it to be quite carefully integrated from a rhythmic viewpoint (the use of scratch sounds achieves an unobtrusive continuity), the change back from five in a bar to the more straightforward simple four being especially well done. This could be good luck, but I somehow doubt it.

As criticism, even of pop or rock music, this may seem amazingly subjective; but then one of the obvious effects of such post-modern music (and one of its probable intentions) was to subvert and topple the old 'objective' standards of judgement. It comes back to the 'two fingers' element of the whole JAMs project; the fact that in their initial and probably most potent combination Drummond and Cauty were issuing a series of distorted reflections of the world around them. Hence the chosen album title *1987*. Hence also the fact that the second album, *Who Killed The JAMs?* although released early in 1988 was very much a sequel to *1987*, its final track including the chimes of Big Ben at midnight on New Year's Eve along with the voice of the then star of BBC 1's *EastEnders*, Leslie Grantham, urging us to 'Kick out the old'. The chimes had been sampled from a special forty-five-minute turn-of-the-year edition of the soap. Perhaps this offered the underlying view that The JAMs were in danger of turning into a soap. Or again perhaps not. The point about this chaotic collage – chaotic in the sense that no apparently consistent frame of reference is maintained – is precisely that the listener is left without an objective correlative, to use T. S. Eliot's term. As I've already said, the first work from The KLF stable assumed a co-operatively intelligent listener.

Not all consumers of popular music look towards the genre to provide them with intellectual stimulation, which may explain why real popular success, the kind that the 1988 KLF publication *The Manual* insists is the only real reason for getting involved in pop music, didn't happen for The Justified Ancients of Mu Mu in this first incarnation. Of course, the album *1987*, with its sampled *Top of the Pops* chart rundown and scream of 'Fuck that, we want The JAMs', seemed to imply otherwise, but consistency of outlook is the last thing you should look for from an organization whose artistic *raison d'être* is to mix, scratch and unsettle, even shock. Still, even though popular success had to wait, on the basis of one single release, a series of injunctions, plus a few sneak previews of an album which was clearly going to present immense legal problems, with a few outrageous comments (that flair for publicity and self-mythologizing), The JAMs/KLF became the darlings of the media. At this point they were masquerading under the aliases of King Boy D and Rockman Rock (partly as a way of avoiding any awkward legal documents which might come flying in their direction), aliases maintained throughout the two JAMs albums. The first album *1987: What the Fuck is Going On?* (expletives were at the outset a very useful and cheap way of shocking) was heavily trailed in the music press in late June of its title year, and the timing was impeccable. On 11 June, Margaret Thatcher had won her third term as Prime Minister (with another three-figure majority) and those who weren't too enthralled at this prospect were feeling especially depressed. Conventional democratic opposition politics didn't seem to work any more, and there were fearful mutterings about what lay ahead. The phrase 'poll tax' began to be heard, and there seemed relatively little chance of the new homeless under-class, becoming increasingly evident in the major cities, being offered any relief. There was also some fear, as it turned out mainly unjustified, that a third-term Thatcher Government might essay some socially repressive legislation in the arena of personal morality, the only attempt at which to date has been the spectacularly useless Section 28 of the Local Government Act, a legislative clause forbidding local authorities from 'promoting homosexuality' and phrased so vaguely as to be impossible to apply in any practical manner.

Thatcher's victory constituted, for her opponents, another depressing blow in a not very encouraging year. The Zeebrugge ferry disaster in March that year seemed to many to be not merely a tragic accident but one precipitated by the profit-margin motivated attitudes of a company (Townsend Thoresen) merely in keeping with its age. If ever a year characterized a decade perfectly, 1987 was it – the twelve months of unscrupulous dealing following the 'Big Bang' which deregulated the rules governing stock-market dealing, a year in which property prices boomed and exacerbated the divisions betwen the haves (particularly the new ostentatious breed of haves) and the have-nots. Not a few people cheered when the world stock markets crashed in October 1987, feeling that, unlike 1929, the money markets were so far removed from any real-life events that a catastrophe to brokers couldn't make things any worse for the rest of the country. I can't see any evidence that this view was very far from the truth. For people who didn't like the way things were, there seemed to be little way of effecting real change and little way of offering a rational critique of situations. Style triumphed over substance every time. Even hightly publicized charitable efforts now needed to be telegenic (you could devote an evening's TV to cute little kiddies in need, but the elderly, being by most aesthetic lights of the time less lovely to look at, weren't really suitable for such treatment), or else topical (in which case the *Sun* would gather Stock, Aitken and Waterman, Sam Fox and anyone who had had a Top 40 hit within the previous two months into a recording studio to come up with something in the name of 'charity').

The fragmentary, pirated critiques The JAMs offered worked so well because they were new and because of the cynicism partly (apparently) motivating them. They were, you might say, corporate raiders of the groove, except that their heavy adopted Scots accents came over as the voice of the minority. 'Don't Take Five (Take What You Want)' is partly about the legitimacy of sampling absolutely anything you feel like using, partly another absurd, surreal rant about The JAMs themselves; it's got references to nuclear arms proliferation (still a live issue in 1987), Middle East destabilization, and that old bugbear tabloid sex (Mandy Smith gets in there somewhere).

'Don't Take Five' was nowhere near the toughest or most subversive track on *1987*. Indeed by any standards it was pretty easy going. 'The Queen and I', colliding Abba, The Sex Pistols and the National Anthem is now, except for a few lucky individuals, lost for ever; and it was this track – by common consent the album's classic – which caused its own destruction. Somehow, the forces attacking the original 'All You Need is Love' had been prepared to compromise, and a revamped version had been possible. Abba weren't even interested in taking a test case on sampling to court. Although I doubt that Drummond's subsequent defence that The JAMs were only doing to Abba what the Swedes themselves had done to the English language and American pop music would have come over very well or convincingly in a court-room. Indeed I wonder now whether The JAMs really cared about saving the album – after all, they'd done it and that was that. Their supposed mission to Sweden to intercede with Abba–master-minds Benny and Bjorn seemed more calculated to offend. Plans to present a fake gold album (inscribed 'for sales in excess of 0') to a prostitute dressed as one of the Abba females and to play 'The Queen and I' at 3.30 a.m. outside the HQ of Polar Music

(Abba's publishing company) hardly seem likely to win you friends. It made good copy for an article in the *New Musical Express*; it didn't save the album. What remains (legally) is 'All You Need is Love', 'Don't Take Five' and the spirit of 'Hey Hey We're Not The Monkeys', which The KLF incarnation of the project has managed to milk almost to death in 1991 under the new title 'Justified and Ancient'.

While the Abba problems were building and the music press were trumpeting The JAMs' praises, Drummond and Cauty had changed tack temporarily and came up with a 100 per cent genuine club dance record, still the result of nifty collage whose philosophical method offered a blueprint for their first 'proper' hit twelve months later. 'Whitney Joins The JAMs' actually first appeared in August 1987 attributed to Kopyright Liberation Front. It was a simpler, more professional, altogether slicker work than much of The JAMs' previous offerings. (A *Melody Maker* article in July, discussing *1987*, referred to it as 'an admirably ugly record', meaning it constituted a fine response to the slick style world, both pop and political, around it.) Ostensibly it told no political tale, made no comment on the world. To a background mainly dominated by the theme from the incomprehensible cult American 1960s/early 1970s thriller series *Mission Impossible* (famous for its beginning with the self-exploding tape detailing the assignment while the theme ran in the background) and the orchestral stabs and guitar riff from Isaac Hayes's 'Theme from *Shaft*', that famous distorting guitar noise which changed the sound of 1970s soul music, the story is told of how The JAMs want to get Whitney Houston to join them. 'Mission impossible, we were told, she'll never join The JAMs.' Taunting fragments from the introduction of Houston's 1987 multi-national chart-topper 'I Wanna Dance with Somebody (Who Loves Me)' keep on surfacing as one or other of The KLF men utters a few grovelling cries of 'Please'. With a touch of Mantronix thrown in, these elements (surprisingly few when you consider the feverish juxtapositions of 'All You Need is Love') meld together over a repetitive dancebeat somewhere in the vicinity of 120 beats per minute until the Whitney Houston intro is allowed to reach the point at which Whitney breathes 'Ooh yeah' alluringly. This, of course, becomes part of the 'narrative' and the first line of Whitney's chorus ('I wanna dance with somebody') gets into the song, while there is general rejoicing that, as the voiceover tells us, 'Whitney Houston's joined The JAMs'.

This was something more selective, more considered than the previous KLF work, and for all its commercial expertise (it's a much stronger single than 'All You Need is Love', but given that it leans heavily on two big hits – Houston and Hayes – in a much more obvious way than the previous single did, that's not surprising) and its danceability, some of the earlier work's urgency is lost. All the impudence is still there, though, not least in the basic joke of apparently justifying the theft inherent in the Whitney Houston sample (at the time of the single's release, anyway) by weaving this elaborate aural fantasy of a conversation asking her permission. And while there's no political comment to be found here, I can detect a half-admiring, half-scathing attitude to the star this fantasy is being spun around. 'I Wanna Dance with Somebody' was a very good, very efficient pop record but it highlighted everything which was wrong about Whitney Houston's career. Possessed of what was clearly a very strong, potentially ravishing voice which wouldn't have disgraced one of the great soul singers of the 1960s (not quite in the Aretha Franklin mould, but potentially the equal of her cousin Dionne Warwick), she was allowing herself to become more and more part of a synthetic process in which her voice was allowed less freedom than Phil Spector had given your average Crystal or Ronette. Despite an apparent artistic freedom many of the female singers of previous decades would have killed for, Whitney Houston was giving off clear signs that she wanted to remain locked within a very narrow, safe range, not stretching herself. The possibility that she'd ever take a chance and do something like join The JAMs looked implausible in mid-1987 when she was at the height of her career, and, despite rumours that she might be planning something along these very lines when her star seemed to have waned somewhat, I still regard the eventuality as unlikely – a good deal more unlikely than the KLF collaboration with Tammy Wynette.

In fact, 'Whitney Joins The JAMs' was in a double-edged way contriving to be both ironic and complimentary, exactly the sort of good professional pop with few (if any) rough edges for which Whitney Houston was well known. At the time, though, as now perhaps, the image of the KLF aegis wouldn't have suited anyone with a desire to play safe. While the advent of the rave scene and many figures with similar – if derivative – ideas, along with that old mellower Time, have rendered Drummond and Cauty less extreme, while they've become part of the mainstream, even to the extent of cracking the US market, they still try where possible to cultivate an image of difference. And in my view they're still market leaders in creative cynicism, as their remarkable 1991 success shows if you read it right.

Their end of 1991 single release, the reworking of 'Justified and Ancient', a track from their Top 10 album *The White Room* (and, as I've said, itself a reworking of 'Hey Hey We're Not The Monkees' from *1987*), could be said to constitute a Christmas single. The novelty value of Tammy Wynette's involvement – real and honest involvement, not merely some fantasia spun around a sample – suggests that the Christmas market may have been somewhere in their mind, the ultimate pop-statistic reward of the elusive Christmas Number 1 (an honour never achieved in the UK by a female soloist until 1992). They're too aware of the market to have any other real intention in releasing a single at the end of November. But they had a more authentically 'verifiable' stab at cracking the Christmas market at the end of 1987 with what in my view has been their most acccomplished piece to date (a clumsy way of saying it's my favourite KLF product). 'Downtown' combined all that was best about the 1987 JAMs: the pointed collision of material, the sheer danceability and the social critique. To date 'Downtown' remains about the only decent pop record to address the subject of homelessness. Plenty of rap acts have attacked poverty and squalor and racism to good effect, and coincidentally one of the few other convincing pop portrayals of street life, The Pogues and Kirsty McColl's 'Fairytale of New York', was also specifically targeted (with a great deal more success) at the 1987 UK Christmas market. But for sheer anger, irony, attack and a good beat, all adding up to a pungent message, 'Downtown' is hard to better. A quite remarkable achievement from a genre whose forays into this kind of social comment usually produce such patronizing guff as Ralph McTell's 'Streets of London' (not to be excused for belonging to a different age) and Phil Collins's 'Another Day in Paradise'.

There's an added irony to the effectiveness of 'Downtown', in that Drummond and Cauty were getting rather sick of collage and cut-up and the whole hip-hop business by this time. The market had, by this juncture of the year, caught on to the sample collage single. 'Pump up the Volume' reached Number 1 at the end of September, immediately spawning the Coldcut remix of Eric B and Rakim's 'Paid in Full'. When he started his master plan, Drummond had regarded hip hop, scratch mixing, rap and black dance music as the only area where anything at all was happening in the pop music business. In an interview with *Melody Maker* published in December 1987, the official JAMs/ KLF view was somewhat different: 'Hip-hop's gone now. It's just another form of mass-produced black music. Do these package tours, boys. Wear these plastic tommy guns, boys. They're just like the white rock stars. It's just careerism.' Any mission to 'liberate the groove' was denied. They also insisted that 'Downtown' was intended to be completely sample free. In fact, they portrayed the inclusion of the sample as an act of regression. In at least two interviews to promote the single, allusion was made to the text of the Book of Proverbs: 'As a dog returneth to his vomit so a fool returneth to his folly.'

Perhaps. Perhaps not. With that title it's hard to believe the story completely. To produce its effects 'Downtown' collides the London Gospel Community Choir, recorded specially, singing a gospel Christmas carol which revolves around the angels singing 'Glory, hallelujah, Jesus Christ is born', a church organ, some sleigh bells, police sirens and a rap describing London life in late 1987. Spliced into this are various brief moments from Petula Clark's 1964 single 'Downtown', a song which was, of course, a celebration of the attractions of London's night life. The samples mainly concentrate on key words such as the title (obviously), 'rhythm' (as in 'of the gentle bossa nova') and the phrase 'neon lights are pretty'. In the same *Melody Maker* interview in which they announced that hip hop had 'gone', Drummond and Cauty further insisted that the inclusion of the Petula Clark samples had been down to the 1 in 960 chance that the original single 'Downtown' had been both in the same key and had the same number of beats per minute as the untitled track being made out of the other components listed above. As the first word (or first two words) of the song's rap is 'Downtown', you do wonder about this account of things. But then the lyric could have come after the discovery of the amazing coincidence.

Surrounding the rap, then, are nostalgic naïve back references to a view of London at night as a happy panacea for all your problems and happy, enthusiastic references upwards to glory and celebration. Inside the rap, remarkably disciplined and non-self-referential by JAMs/KLF standards, both rich and poor in London's West End are viewed with pity. 'Got the cash/Gonna buy trash/But you ken it's all a lie.' The down and outs aren't sanitized; they're 'Dying in the dead of night/With your Special Brew'. The affected Scotticism lets the side down slightly, but it's as good a summary as any of the late 1980s *nouveaux riches*, all feeling, since the October stock-market crash, an unfamiliar breeze. As the choir's cry of 'Glory' is subjected to some digital interference, the rap asks 'What glory? In a wine-bar world? In a tenement block?' There's an intensity about both the delivery of the rap and the performance of the choir, as well as the dense mix, which gives a sinister urgency to the whole, particularly when the rap ends with the enigmatic question 'In Leicester Square/Did you do it clean?' leaving the field to the 'Hallelujahs' and 'Glories' and 'Jesus Christ is born todays' of the choir. Only after the rap is over do Drummond and Cauty allow Petula a relatively lengthy free spin, carefully selecting the part of the song with the now more or less tasteless words 'Downtown/ You'll find a place for sure'. By this point even the Gospel Choir sounds pessimistic. If, as Petula Clark wanted us to believe, 'Downtown everything's waiting for you', then this account of 'Downtown' can't leave you in much doubt that in 1987 that's a threat and not a promise. No wonder it wasn't a massive Christmas hit, and it's so aggressive, so committed and – above all – so continually applicable, that no wonder The KLF manifestation of The JAMs haven't tried to resurrect it. Although as The JAMs were recently resuscitated for the more adventurous but, compared to the glory days, decidedly limp 'It's Grim up North', perhaps there's still a chance one of these fine Christmases. Ironically, a remix of Petula Clark's 'Downtown', treated with no irony whatsoever reached the UK Top 10 a year later, as more and more young people flocked down to the West End of London to find 'everything waiting' for them.

I've devoted a lot of space to a few releases which could easily be dismissed as pretentious, middle class, cultish and (in a way) elitist. The 'pop music is simply entertainment' lobby were never going to get much joy out of The Justified Ancients of Mu Mu. But I'd contend that these tracks do work on an entertainment level and represent a level of creative energy which led a lot of people (myself included) to believe that sampling, far from being a question of navel contemplation, auto-digestion and self-reference, was something which could inject pop music with a dynamism and maturity hitherto unknown. It seemed to promise a growing-up, a taking stock, a step forward; it used its past not merely as a nostalgic frame of reference, but as an instrument for social critique, indeed as an 'instrument' in the purely musical sense. And this multi-faceted, many-voiced, protean project also seemed to offer a new blueprint for that old warhorse 'the pop group'. It all suggested that in future groups would be entirely – and admittedly – creatures of the studio, that the studio was where it all started and finished. This was the logical conclusion of The Beatles' decision to abandon live performance. Further, by refusing to admit to a definite, real identity (admittedly partly for legal reasons), Drummond and Cauty were taking the whole star-machinery of the music business and subverting it. This has been a consistent element of their post-1987 careers.

What The JAMs had started, others seemed initially to promise to carry on and fulfil, and it was possible to feel a sense of excitement again. After all, excitement is crucial to successful pop music. And although The JAMs didn't immediately reap what they sowed, it seemed at the time that they had helped clear a path for this great new thing to happen. As it turned out, things were somewhat different, and the immediate progress of their career suggested that the initial optimism was probably unjustified. And, when we come on to their existence as The KLF in 1990 and 1991, it becomes clear that, however good the product, the original premise, the original revolutionary zeal had evaporated, leaving only a sense of humour, production expertise and a cynicism you'd either love or hate.

Inevitably, once the year 1987 was gone, the music press's loyalty began to wane slightly and the notices for *Who Killed The JAMs?* were less adulatory. The second album was more dance orientated, more along the lines of 'Whitney Joins The JAMs' than any of the spiky chaotic creations of the early days. Clashing 'Ride of the Valkyries' with Hendrix had its own amusement value, but it didn't have quite the same impact, partly because the album's verbal concerns were mainly self-regarding: surreal Jack Londonesque tales like 'The Porpoise Song'; ironic chat-up lines like 'Candyman'; even party records – 'Burn the Bastards', for all its aggression, is a hard dance track putting the repeated line 'JAMs have a party' to Sly Stone's 'Dance to the Music'. Wagner apart, the range of tracks plundered is narrower. It's all much more dance-music based, although anyone trying to spot every sampled reference would still give up in despair before the second of the eight tracks was over. But there was nothing as off the wall as 'The Lonely Goatherd' or Scott Walker singing Jacques Brel.

'Burn the Bastards', with its New Year chimes, was very much a suicide note for The Justified Ancients. Throwing a mutilation of the title track of the year's best-selling album (Michael Jackson's *Bad*) it urinated in the face of the music scene. The JAMs were vacating. As for the bastards who were to be burnt, it was probably anybody and everybody. '1987: What the Fuck Have We Done?' was the question posed without any hint of the answer. It's the angriest track on the album, the nearest thing to a 'Downtown' or an 'All You Need is Love' packed with incidental detail designed to wave a couple of fingers in the direction of rival samplers. (James Brown's already over-used cry of 'Can I take it to the bridge?' is echoed as the New Year approaches with a shout of 'Take me to the bells'.)

So The JAMs were officially dead. But Drummond and

Cauty had their revenge planned and it took them to the top of the charts. 'Doctorin' the Tardis' was a title lampooning Cold-cut, who had hit the Top 10 in March with an imaginative, slightly too-knowing collage entitled (as a rather feeble joke) 'Doctorin' the House'. S-Express's April Number 1 proclaimed a revival of 1970s music, promoted with a video full of 1970s clothes and colours (for over four years now people have been desperately promoting the cause of 'the decade that taste forgot'). Everyone was doing what The JAMs had done, and doing it with some success, although as we shall see, legal problems meant that no one was making much money directly out of records. Novelty records were getting back in on the act too. Morris Minor and The Majors' awful 'Stutter Rap (No Sleep 'Til Bedtime)', a parody of The Beastie Boys, coming like all parodies about six months too late and, like most, promulgating the concept of comedy without humour, had been a Top 10 hit at the start of the year. Harry Enfield's 'Loadsamoney (Doin' up the House)' – was there to be no end to these endlessly inventive 'house' jokes? – had reached the Top 10 in May. Enfield's novelty record is something of a tragedy in its own way, and an illustrative little nugget for the historian of popular culture. Originally the character Loadsamoney, a yobbish plas-terer who'd made a packet conning his clients, was meant as a satire on the new breed of rich people generally thought to come out of Essex. Although Enfield had made his character a plasterer he clearly – as a comedian of moderately left-wing sensibilities – intended him to represent the worst tendencies in the young, tastelessly conspicuous, wealthy men of all classes. Unfortunately he created a hero with whom these people could identify rather than a target for satire. Enfield lost control of his monster. All over Britain people went around saying 'bosh, bosh, bosh – loadsamoney' in aggressive pseudo-London accents. A novelty single was inevitable.

'Bosh, bosh, bosh – loadsamoney' are the first words spoken

on 'Doctorin' the Tardis', where they are intoned by someone pretending (by electronic means – usually the best way) to be a dalek. These four words aptly sum up the purpose of the disc. But it's quite a little pop-culture weather vane in its way. Apart from the Enfield reference and the Coldcut snub, there's a harsh riposte to the 1970s revivalists, as for the main core of the disc three pieces of music are used. One, inevitably, is the theme from *Doctor Who*. But, although the disc's ostensible *raison d'être*, that's merely sandwiched between the opening bars of The Sweet's 'Blockbuster' and the main refrain (indeed sole content) of Gary Glitter's 'Rock and Roll Part 2' with the lyric 'Rock 'n' Roll, hey, Rock 'n' Roll' superseded by 'Doctor Who, Doctor Who, Doctor Who, the Tardis'. Two classically awful records of the 1970s, two records heralding the arrival of teeny glam rock, two records which typify why the 1970s were well worth escaping (however admirable a camp joke the whole Gary Glitter persona may be); and Drummond and Cauty conflated them with a TV theme, but left the ambience of the two 1970s records very much stamped over the whole proceeding. It was done with panache, even with a great sense of camp. The dalek noises around the fringes were mere icing on the cake. Some dalek lines (such as 'We are the superior beings') were authentic quotations from the TV series; others (the impersonation of the DJ shout of 'You what, you what, you what' put smack in the centre of the record-buying public's attention by Steve Walsh's version of 'I Found Lovin' in late 1987) were patently not authentic dalek speak.

The BBC declined to put 'Doctorin' the Tardis' on any of the three Radio One playlists. It reached Number 1 in three weeks. Drummond and Cauty had used the appropriate and one-off name The Timelords for this release, although the presentation had KLF stamped all over it, right down to the pretence that the group was actually fronted by an old Ford (Ford Timelord) who supposedly did all the group's interviews. KLF's *Manual (How to Have a Number One the Easy Way*) is (rightly) scathing about this particular piece of promotional tactics.

The Manual, a cynical work which is both funny and yet – if you ask anyone in the record industry – pretty accurate, reads more or less like a goodbye note. It describes in some detail the work which had gone into 'Doctorin' the Tardis', a rare example of something done for cynical reasons succeeding in its aim, purporting to offer this as advice to the aspiring hitmaker. At least one group, The Bingo Boys, followed *The Manual* with some success, reincarnating themselves as Edelweiss (of 'Bring Me Edelweiss' fame; ironically, the basis for this profit from The JAMs' advice was an Abba song, 'S.O.S.'). But the end of *The Manual* reads like a valediction, an acknowledgement that The Timelords was a one-off, that that kind of success wasn't really what the KLF concept was about. 'To quote the most heart-shuddering moment in teenage pop, the closing line in "Past, Present and Future" performed by the Shangri-Las . . . "It will never never happen again." If we do have Empiricals that line is it. We would never be allowed to get away with it a second time.'

But, of course, they did. As the book's final sentence said, 'The White Room is calling'. But even those master manipulators probably didn't quite realize the significance of those words back in 1988. Although with The KLF one can never be entirely sure.

6 · Hitting the High-tech Groove (Not Entirely Legally)

It might be useful to try to define a sampler. As I don't possess – and have never shown any aptitude for – scientific jargon, such a definition will inevitably strike anyone deeply involved in electronics and acquainted with the wonders of technology as rough and ready. This 'technical' chapter is very much written from the point of view of a layman, a medieval peasant who has wandered into the modern world and is liable to assume that radios, TVs and sound systems are actually inhabited by little men.

The sampler was made possible by digital sound. 'Digital' because rather than being recorded on magnetic tape, it's converted into numerical signals and then fed into a computer. Anyone who owns a compact-disc player has a digital playback system – the numerical signals stored in the CD are converted back into sound. The great advantages to the consumer of this breakthrough in sound reproduction were, first, that the quality of the sound could be improved to a previously unimaginable level, eliminating the surface noise which was part and parcel of the process involving magnetic tape; second, that a lot of sound could be stored in a relatively small space. The usual upper limit of the CD is eighty minutes of sound; and, of course, the CD is smaller than the standard seven-inch single.

But it was the impact of digital technology in the studio which made the new approach to music possible. The computerization of sound made it possible as never before to record lots of different real sounds and then edit and play them back simultaneously in remarkably little time. A sound recorded on to magnetic tape is, more or less, fixed. You can edit it, of course, by a fairly laborious process, you can speed it up and slow it down, perhaps even turn it round, but those are about the limits of your flexibility, and the time this takes can seem endless. Some of the original samplers were slow by comparison with today's models, but even these were a vast improvement.

The key revolutionary aspect of the sampler, and what has given it the hold it now has, was that it allowed you to do with 'real' sound all the things which had hitherto only been possible with synthesized sound. Musical instruments involving electronic and computerized components had been around for some fifteen to twenty years before the first dedicated sampler made its appearance in 1981. But where these had involved 'real' sound, that sound had been stored on magnetic tape – as with the Chamberlin and the Mellotron, of which more later – with all the drawbacks of inflexibility that would inevitably entail. Where the sound had the potential for flexibility, it was entirely synthetic, imitative, but artificial. Because of its greater flexibility, it was this synthesized sound – produced by a 'synthesizer' – which seized the interest of musicians in the late 1960s and 1970s.

To try for the definition: a sampler is a digital recording device which allows the operator to store, manipulate and play back real sounds which have been fed into it. In fact, it's a thoroughly ingenious box of tricks whose possibilities seem so near endless that, to someone with my technical grasp, it almost has a life of its own. A good part of this chapter is devoted to my experiences with a real 'live' sampler, and I hope that these experiences will provide more elucidation than the attempt at a definition.

First, though, a little history. There's a case to be made that the first 'sampled' record was 'The Singing Dogs (Medley)' by

The Singing Dogs. This unbearable novelty Christmas hit of 1955 – even more unbearable than most novelty Christmas hits – consisted of a series of dog barks at various pitches carefully and expertly edited to produce a sequence that sounded like a medley of Christmas tunes (starting with 'Jingle Bells'). It wasn't a sampled record in any digital sense; it was simply a masterpiece of editing and engineering. The same technique – much more clumsy and blatant, though with an end result equally intolerable – could be seen on Chris Hill's two 'Renta Santa' hits in the 1970s ('Renta Santa' in 1975 and the thrilling sequel 'Bionic Santa' in 1976). Here Hill interwove a tedious narrative about Santa Claus with short, hilariously apposite bites from recent hit singles. There was no attempt to place these extracts in any consistent unifying rhythmic or tonal context; the whole exercise was purely one of editing. At least The Singing Dogs aimed for some kind of tonal or melodic unity, painful though it was. But neither of these 'sampled' records involved putting the 'sampled' sound through any distorting or adaptive electronic process.

In high-tech pop, first came synthesizers. Attempts to synthesize sound reach quite a long way back into musical history. What else are most organ stops, lovingly labelled 'flute' or 'oboe' or 'viol da gamba', but attempts to recreate an instrumental sound through another medium? The synthesizer tried to do the same, but in the context of late twentieth-century electronics rather than wind and pipes. As I've already tried to illustrate, synthesizers created sound from scratch, allowing the player to control everything from a keyboard. The synthesizer sound became quite a fixture in early 1970s pop music, finding particular favour with would-be flamboyant keyboard wizards like Rick Wakeman of Yes, who produced synthesizer-keyboard extravaganzas such as *Journey to the Centre of the Earth* and *The Six Wives of Henry VIII*. The most famous synthesizer was probably the Moog, which was also favoured by avant-garde(ish) 'serious' musicians like Walter (now Wendy) Carlos, who released seemingly endless albums of synthesized Bach.

At around the same time as the early synthesizers (the late 1950s) came an instrument called the Chamberlin, almost immediately – by amazing coincidence – followed by a British near-twin called the Mellotron. These instruments followed on from developments in the use of magnetic tape (developments mainly pioneered in the 1940s by Pierre Schaeffer, who is credited with inventing many of the terms of tape technology). The Chamberlin/Mellotron was a small keyboard, rather piano-like in that each key produced a visible physical reaction. However, rather than strings and hammers, the Mellotron keys were each attached to an individual piece of tape which the action of the key would roll past a head designed to make the tape 'play'. On each tape was what sounded like a recording of that note played on stringed (or other) instruments. The Mellotron was designed to allow you to have your own portable, 'sampled' (to jump the technological gun again) string orchestra on tour with you. Rock groups addicted to lush, strange string sounds – such as Genesis in the early 1970s and The Moody Blues – made great, even excessive, use of the Mellotron, although very often its users (especially Genesis) tended to produce a sound bearing no resemblance to anything on earth.

At the end of the 1970s, out of Australia came the first machine you could a 'sampler' – the Fairlight Computer Musical Instrument. The Fairlight, being a computer, was of course digital, thus allowing its user to feed in 'real' sound and then manipulate and replay it. This in itself was a remarkable advance, although it was at the time seen as only a side effect of the Fairlight. But equally important was the element of the machine's operating software known as 'Page R'. This was the mother and father of all 'sequencer' software, and it's the sequencer which allows the sounds which have been recorded, manipulated, edited and so on to be reproduced simultaneously without any further stringing together by the operator. The original 'Page R' allowed only eight separate parts to be so strung together, but even so it was a necessary breakthrough, especially as a compositional tool.

Many pop musicians took with enthusiasm and alacrity to the Fairlight but seemed only to use it as though it were some kind of elaborate synthesizer which made a new and special noise of its own. Peter Gabriel inevitably employed one, but it hardly inspired him to some new and thrilling musical departure. The Fairlight arrived just at the right time to preside over the burials of a few pop careers, to provide the keynote sound for some expensive flop albums. Notable casualties included Heaven 17, whose third album, *How We Are*, was Fairlight ridden, and The Human League, who followed up the enormously successful multi-platinum *Dare* with *Hysteria*, an album soon found reduced in price in record shops throughout the land. More successful from an artistic viewpoint (despite a 'serious' critical slaughtering at the time) was Scritti Politti's *Cupid and Psyche '85*, another album reliant for much of its impact on 'Fairlight programming' as the credit always ran, but even this album seemed to bear out the fact that most of the musicians who got hold of the Fairlight were fascinated by it but unaware of its potential.

It was actually some Trevor Horn protégés in the ZTT stable who put the Fairlight's sampling potential in the centre of the musical stage. The Art of Noise, as the culturally loaded reference of their name suggests, were interested in more than 'mere music' in the terms in which most pop musicians understood the word (or most practising classical musicians, come to that). Their brief was the music in all sounds, and they used the Fairlight to this end on their album *Who's Afraid of the Art of Noise?* from which came the unlikely Top 10 single 'Close (to the Edit)'. Extraneous and unmusical noises looped and sampled through their Fairlight included a car door slamming and an engine starter, along with various 'sampled' orchestral stabs (in many ways the start of the fashion). This was The Art of Noise as pure Art. In a slightly later incarnation they were to become little more than a novelty backing band for unlikely luminaries such as Duane Eddy, Tom Jones and the supposedly computer-generated 'TV personality' Max Headroom (actually actor Matt Frewer in a latex head mask with cunning computer tricks played on his image). Anne Dudley, one of the original and most artful Art of Noise members, could subsequently be seen taking quite a number of credits for musical involvement in Pet Shop Boys projects. It's no coincidence, given this, that PSB Chris Lowe (by all accounts an orthodox keyboard wizard) became one of the most successful pop musicians to incorporate the Fairlight CMI and use it both as musical instrument and as sampler. Of course, the Fairlight as now used by The Pet Shop Boys is something of an advance on the original instrument – at the last count we were up to Fairlight Series III.

The Fairlight CMI offered sampling as one of a range of possibilities. The first specifically dedicated sampler machine in the modern sense appeared around 1981, surprisingly not in Japan or in Australia, but in the United States – the Emu Emulator, invented by the Emu company's founding father Dave Rossum. An article in a recent hi-fi magazine suggests that Rossum had little idea just how significant a tool he'd come up with. When asked in the early 1980s if he regarded sampling as the 'future of the sound industry', apparently he laughed at the implausibility of the idea.

At its most basic level, used least inventively, a sampler is just another piece of hardware in the producer's armoury. It stands in the stack along with lots of other pieces of hardware, impotent without an audio cable, an amplifier/mixer and a pair of speakers. I describe it as 'just another piece of hardware' when used 'least inventively', but perhaps it's fairer to say that now that the use of the sampler is a commonplace, it's just another tool to be mastered rather than a venerated object providing creative inspiration. Which is perhaps more healthy in the long run. The same hi-fi article which waxes lyrically about the 'dedicated' sampler's inventor's view of his baby, suggests that the machine's future may lie more in its functions in post-production and as a piece of recording equipment than as an instrument capable of generating sound. This suggests, in fact, that the inventor is a little behind the times, as it's probably already equally important for such functions. For a non-hi-fi buff such as myself who isn't obsessed with the 'toy' element in technology this doesn't matter too much. The fact is that the sampler isn't going to disappear suddenly.

And even as 'just another piece of hardware', it's a pretty remarkable object which saves time and money on a vast scale. Once upon a time if you wanted a decent rhythm track, you had to play it, or hire session men to play it for you, and go on recording it, track by track, until it was right, until everything fitted together. Usually it would be necessary to try and get at least one full performance of every element of a song that you wanted to record down on tape. With a sampler and a sequencer, two bars of a basic beat is more than a luxury; it's a positive extravagance.

How do you put a track together using a sampler? There are probably as many different answers to that as there are record producers. The description which follows is very far from definitive; indeed, it's purely personal, as non-technical as the procedure will allow (non-technicality made all the more necessary by my own almost wilful scientific ignorance), and can be seen on at least one level as simply an essay entitled 'My Day in a Studio'. The studio in question was the creative workshop of Rex Brough, known in the music business by various pseudonyms including The Red King (co-producer on Definition of Sound's first album) and the King half of King John. It was, of course, Rex who did all the hard technical labour.

As I've said repeatedly in one form or another, the great

advantage of the sampler is that when you want to make a track from scratch, you don't need to take any musical instruments or indeed to be possessed of any ability to play musical instruments. The only ability you do need is that of spotting what small elements of other people's works might fit well together; which rhythm tracks, bass lines, melodic figures, snatches of lyric, spoken words – or, to put it simply in the jargon, which beats and breaks – could fit together. I imagine that any recording artist (be s/he producer, singer, rapper, whatever) who lives by the sampler will always have a blank cassette loaded when listening to the radio, and will probably be an inveterate channel hopper (something there wasn't much point in being a couple of decades ago before the advent of commercial radio). After all, you can get a lot of beats and breaks from the radio, and quite a bit of the stuff which Rex and I fed into the machine in the course of our sessions had started life in various (now unidentifiable) radio broadcasts. But apparently many artists, especially producers, feel that the sound quality of material transmitted on the radio just isn't good enough. I've always thought that samples which highlight the quality flaws in the original source are quite fun (the scratched copy of 'Walk on the Wild Side' which provides the punctuation to A Tribe Called Quest's 'Can I Kick It' springs to mind as an excellent example), and for all his furious professionalism, my collaborator on this project tended to agree with me. Anyway, whatever source you get your raw material from, the cassette of breaks and beats should feed the sampler.

The equipment which was used in the process I'm going to describe was: an Akai S1100 digital sampler (there was an Akai S900, an earlier less-swish model in there somewhere, too, acting as a separate storehouse for spoken word samples); a mixing desk; Yamaha DX100 electronic keyboard; and an Apple Macintosh computer. The sequencer software package we used was Passport Mastertracks. Also helping things along was an Opcode Studio 3 Synchronizer and Midi Interface. I don't mention these names for reasons of commercial sponsorship, or because they were at the time of writing the last word in up-to-the-minute state of the art (which they weren't). In some ways we were operating relatively primitively. An eight-megabyte board attached to the sampler would have given us much more memory (samples are stored exactly the same way as computer files, requiring room in the memory). We didn't make use of the multi-track machine, which most professional recordings would. On the other hand it could have been more primitive; we could probably have managed with just one sampler (plus computer package) and the mixing desk.

The material I wanted to turn into a dance masterpiece included a bass-line and rhythm culled from the twelve-inch mix of a British pseudo-soul hit of 1987, as well as the drum rhythm from the B-side of that same disc. This second element turned out later to be too inflexible (a polite way of saying just too boring) and Rex elbowed it in favour of one of the most popular beat samples in the business (Bobby Byrd). I also had on my cassette of breaks and beats and other things a weedy but catchy synthesizer figure from a mid-1980s gay-club favourite ('Endless Road' by The Time Bandits, a group of whose origins and subsequent whereabouts little is now known or remembered) and some chords from another high-energy floor filler of that time, 'Ti Sento', by the Italian group Matia Bazar. These latter choices were fairly unimaginative – early 1970s funk would have been much more useful. But the four truly distinctive elements I had to hand were: a Wagnerian tenor singing the four-note '*Blutbruderschaft*' motif from the second act of *Götterdämmerung*; a three-note horn blast from the same source; a line of football commentary taken from a video of the TV coverage of the 1991 Spurs v. Porto match; and, best of all, a cartoon cat with the creepiest voice you ever heard enouncing the line 'But the third bowl of porridge was just right'. This last item was worth all the rest put together.

Putting a track together differs from eating in many respects, but in this case the most significant was that porridge had to wait until the end of the day. You start – well, we did – with the rhythm. And so the first rhythmic phrase I'd recorded was fed from the cassette into the sampler (in exactly the same way you'd record on to a cassette in the first place). There's always too much of what you record; as I've said, two bars of most beats or breaks is an extravagance. But this is where the sampler performs the first of its magic tricks, as an editing machine. In this case the bass figure was allowed to run twice before being chopped into two discrete phrases running alternately (so that the second could be made subtly different from the first in a way that it wasn't in its original form).

To help in editing, to make it virtually perfect and rhythmically exact (vital with 1990s techno-dance music), the sampler has its own small visual display, which portrays the sound as a graph. This display means that you can locate the precise beginning of each measure much more easily than by manipulating a reel of tape. You can see exactly what you're editing and be sure of precisely what you're doing. Recorded sound is reduced to basic, visible, separable units, and can be worked on almost the way you'd make a drawing or painting more accurate or more graphic. Even figures played on the Yamaha keyboard can be reproduced visually through another display produced through the sequencer, so that you can augment or diminish your chords and rewrite your music as if you were dealing with something written on manuscript paper, rather than something you may have plucked out of your head. This graphic aspect means, conversely, that you need never write anything down, or make the effort to remember anything you've played.

Once the figure is edited precisely it is retriggered on the sequencer. The result of this is that a loop-like effect of endless repetition of the figure is achieved. I say 'endless', but in fact the sequencer is programmed to take the figure through 120 measures initially.

As you're editing, apart from sheer precision with the start and finish of beats, you also have the option of varying the tempo of the figure you're working on. For convenience, we opted for the standard 120 beats per minute (the usual 'four on the floor' tempo), but this is in no way necessary. Varying the tempo raises or lowers the pitch.

There is another visual display involved which I've already mentioned – that produced on the computer VDU by the sequencer. Generally this display lists each track line by line, identifying each track – each element or figure that's been fed into the sampler – by name (a name which the producer/performer can assign according to his or her whim). After the sample has been fixed and is played through, the display follows the tracks through all 120 measures, showing by means of a series of blocks whether or not each track is active in that measure – a black or filled block indicates that there is, a white or empty block that it isn't. This display is particularly helpful when editing the track (in the sense of song or number) as a whole, allowing you to work in unlooped variations in the various figures that have been sampled. After all, it's the unpredictable elements that tend to make even the most mundane of dance tracks memorable. But the elements which make up the rhythm track also need to have some kind of predictability about them to make dancing possible. Dance records with shifting rhythms have a limited appeal. The commonest and most effective way of putting variety into a rhythm track is to eliminate part of it momentarily, to take out the steady pulse of the beat for a measure or two so that only incidental percussion keeps the rhythm going in that time.

In the package that we were using, certain pre-sampled

percussive sounds were available, saving us from the need to feed them into the sampler from outside. Many samplers come with a library of such sounds, or offer the capacity to retain such regular percussion features as bongos and tambourines on the machine's permanent hard-disk memory. There are, of course, separate digital drum machines, pioneered by Roger Linn (a standing joke on many Stock, Aitken and Waterman releases is that the drummer credit will go to 'A. Linn'). Such an instrument did not, however, feature in this day's work. When, after three beat samples had been fed in and doctored according to the method above, Rex felt that something lighter but sharper was needed to underline the beat, the percussion was added and edited like the other samples.

The keyboard turned out to possess power beyond my wildest dreams. Some of the time we used it simply as a synthesizer keyboard, and through it fed several 120-measure performances on to their own separate tracks. These tracks encompassed four completely separate styles, with varying instrumental sounds: rhythmically repeated minor triads, very common in much house music; frenetically repeated single notes, which form ideal complements to the triads; descending scales and similar figures; and finally the melodic line from the opening of Mozart's Piano Concerto No. 24 in C Minor, K. 491, which is, after all, well out of copyright. The discrete keyboard performances were all separately edited. It turned out that the bottom notes of some of the triads had acquired, more or less by accident, a hollow tone, rather like the sound you get on a piano when one or two of the strings on a note have gone. This accidental sound was so pleasing that the bottom lines of the triads were separated out on to their own track, to give a separate sound timbre which could be used on its own. The triads and repeated notes had been recorded using a piano simulator (although the result didn't sound much like a piano to me, not even a fortepiano as beloved by the advocates of period instruments); the rest with a distinctly synthesized sound, to capture the 'techno' feel so popular in 1991 and 1992.

However, the keyboard had much more going for it than its role as a synthesizer. It also had its part to play in doctoring what had been fed into the sampler. At the simplest level, a note on the keyboard was designated to trigger the sample, particularly useful when editing the rhythm tracks. But this quality really came into its own when the two Wagnerian samples were thrown into the grand scheme. The sound of the hefty Wagnerian tenor crying *Blutbruderschaft* ('Blood-brotherhood', an important concept in the final episode of The Ring Cycle, and a telling leitmotif in this opera), after it had been edited down to those simple four notes, was fed into the keyboard with the result that when you played the keyboard in certain designated areas, you got that note as though sung by the tenor in question backed by the Orchestra of the Met., with each group of four notes producing in turn each of the vowel noises of *Blutbruderschaft* in the correct sequence. Obviously there was some electronic distortion on this, and added to the rhythm track only the most devoted of Wagnerians would probably be able to spot what was really going through the system here. In addition to which my enthusiasm at the keyboard led me to try and play the whole 'Ride of the Valkyries' figure with these resources, which probably wasn't such a good idea on a dance track – the 9/8 rhythm of all Wagner's Valkyrie motifs sits pretty ill with the 'four on the floor' we were using. When I calmed down and just fed three- or four-note descending sequences (akin to the original sample) into the mix, these proved much more fruitful, and gave Rex something to edit down into occasional stabs of tenor noise, allowing once or twice the unpredictable surprise of the full motif or three-quarters of it. This was an area where a good professional was of much more use than an enthusiastic amateur.

After the tenor had been subjected to this treatment, the same thing was done with the three-note horn blast. This time I was more cautious at the keyboard, and in the end the horn blasts were used only singly or in groups of two and only towards the end of the track to provide some further unpredictable element of variety. As these blasts were edited down, Rex mixed in quite a good deal of echo, which worked rather well, having almost a feedback-like feel and acting as a counter to the insistent rhythm. Later quite a lot of these echoing atmospherics got mixed into other elements of the whole, creating at one point a sound rather like the noise made by the materialization of the Tardis in *Doctor Who*. As Rex commented at the time, 'echo always helps'.

Of course, to anyone used to dealing with this technology every day, the ability to manipulate whatever sound you've put into the sampler through the keyboard will seem as mundane as the miracle of pressing a switch and making an electric light come on. And that's as it should be. If you're in awe of the machines, then they take over and your creative ability is stunted and tailored according to the power of the hardware. Putting operatic tenors through the process described above is no big deal to some people, most notably in this instance, Chris Lowe and Neil Tennant, who claim to have incorporated the voice of Luciano Pavarotti into the 'Ah – Ah – A-a-ah' figures which were so crucial to the success of their fourth Number 1 'Heart'. (Tennant and Lowe have accordingly rather wittily claimed they laid all the groundwork for Pavarotti's later success.) But that such complex computer-generated noises should be so easily reproduced, once you can get through the initial editing process – something made easier by the visual graphic displays inherent in this kind of technological recording process – does bring home how much, to a computer-literate generation, this technology simplifies the concept of music making. However much the punk ethos despised musicianship (and looking at the Rick Wakemans and other 'musicians' of the rock world in the first part of the 1970s this despising is not only understandable but also necessary and healthy), it wasn't possible to get very far if you couldn't manage a few rudimentary chords on your guitar, bass, keyboard, whatever, even if you then decided to mar the sound with feedback. But even though you use keyboards which look something like the traditional piano/organ keyboard, in all this process you don't have to possess any knowledge of how to play it for real. It's just a way of controlling other people's music making which you've fed in there. Again, real musical knowledge is an advantage but not necessary, providing you're not profoundly deaf. But if you edit properly, it's a question not of whether you passed Associated Board exams, but of whether you pressed the right buttons at the right time, with the right element of imagination. Music-making made supremely easy, if not supremely cheap. Although in the later 1980s, the desire of the whole Western world to plunge into credit agreements and the co-operation of most retailers in this process meant that getting your hands on the equipment wasn't as difficult or even as initially costly as were the standard guitar, bass and drums necessary to start your own 'beat' group in the 1960s or punk group in the 1970s.

Back in the studio, Rex decided to add some more 'pure' music to the proceedings, and plugged his guitar into the set up. The guitar figures he produced at strategic points as the whole track played back weren't put in the sampler. Having twiddled around at the guitar to his heart's content, he then ruthlessly edited what he'd played using the sequencer's graphic masterplan on the Apple Mac's monitor. Again, the point of the guitar was variety, surprise, so to keep it going all the way through would have been otiose and marred the impact. Just a few Ennio Morricone-inspired twiddles somewhere in the centre seemed to meet the case.

At last it was time for the porridge. I'd been told – but I'd never have guessed – that it was possible to feed straight from the soundtrack of a video into a sampler, simply by plugging the video and TV into the general system. (It's vital in a studio to have enough sockets to plug in everything you need.) Once the phrase 'But the third bowl of porridge was just right' had been captured inside the machine it could be edited and then messed around with like everything else. Although with a spoken phrase like this which was to recur at certain but by no means necessarily regular intervals, we used from a separate unit offering certain studio effects the tool of digital delay – the device which creates a stuttering effect with selected syllables or notes.

This was the first day's work. There were other vocal effects to be fed in at a later date, but the last piece of work for the day was to create a series of different sixteen-bar phrases, using the monitor as a guide once more.

The result of that day's work wasn't by any means a master-piece blockbusting smash hit, but neither was it markedly inferior to a lot of dance music to be heard in clubs and at raves. (It may have been about four to eight beats per minute too slow to be a first-rank rave single.) And even though the producer's concentration had been heavily called upon (at one point he temporarily lost one line of the rhythm, but this didn't prove too difficult to retrieve), the whole process had been a great deal of fun, especially for me – but then I don't have to spend all day, every day with those machines. I imagine when your livelihood depends upon it, when record companies are breathing down your neck to produce on time (or when you're trying to produce something which might interest them enough to want to breathe down your neck in the first place), then the fun goes out of it.

So, providing you can afford the equipment and are computer literate, you can make your own music. In this way the sampler has changed the face of the pop and rock industry quite significantly. This is why there are so many dance records around now, why the dance culture has taken such a hold – it's easy to do. There's also the drug question, unfortunately; the way in which this kind of creativity has grown up around a frenetic amphetamine industry, the way that clubs – and in particular parties or raves – have become little more than retail outlets for sellers of ecstasy and similar easily transported, concealed and consumed drugs. But these considerations don't belong in this chapter.

Another factor introduced by the sampler is that anyone with room to spare can create a home recording studio. One of the prohibitively expensive parts of trying to make a demo in the old days was the hire of the studio. If you've got the sampler (and related hardware) and the mixing desk, you've got a studio you don't have to hire. The prices of the equipment may look steep when put down in black and white: the mixing desk we were using would cost something slightly more than £4,000 to £5,000 (at the last count) and an S1100 Akai Midi digital sampler comes for about £2,500 (£3,000 to £4,000, with the extra memory board). You can get perfectly adequate samplers for under £1,000, though, even before you need turn to the second-hand market. Yet the cost of getting together even such moderately expensive equipment as we were using is no larger than the hire of a 'proper' studio for three days. And the end result will, unless the technology defeats you, sound slick and professional (if you want it to) and not as though it's been recorded in the garage (unless you want it to). Although the way I've described our 'session' makes it sound very much like a professional and an enthusiastic amateur in a bedroom, what we actually produced sounded nothing like that.

And if you're lucky enough, the end result will be so successful that you'll be able to afford all the studio time you want, with all the top session men, all the best 'real musicians'. Or alternatively, you can just buy a more expensive sampler – perhaps the £8,000-plus Emulator III, the latest, most expensive descendant of the first ever 'dedicated sampler' or, if you want to be really flash, the New England Digital Synclavier, which is a musical production system incorporating the most advanced commercially available sampler in the world, and which is as much a descendant of the Fairlight CMI as anything else. The Synclavier apparently allows for polyphonic sampling, resynthesis, hard-disk recording (and it probably makes the tea as well). And with a sampler, who needs the hassle of 'real' musicians? No wonder the KLF manual advised aspirant hit makers to throw away their instruments.

7 · Pump up the Volume

'This has got to be the greatest record of the year.' Those were the opening words on the best-known edit of 'Pump up the Volume'. Usually that kind of claim can be fatal, and it may not, for all listeners, have been immediately borne out by a single which heard off guard in the wrong circumstances could sound like a slightly disjointed tribute to the minimalism of such jackmasters as Steve 'Silk' Hurley or Farley Funk. One of the great things about 'Pump up the Volume' was its insidious subtlety, the way it could impinge upon the consciousness of people with no professed interest in dance music; the fact that it employed, very unflashily, such a multiplicity of voices, of breaks and beats that, given enough exposure (and here 'enough' could be a fairly small amount for the spell to work), one of them was almost certainly bound to hit a nerve.

Whether or not it was 'the greatest record of the year', there's little doubt that 'Pump up the Volume' was one of the most significant, as well as one of the most distinctively different chart-toppers of 1987 (or of quite a few other years). It wasn't merely a showcase for the possibilities of all the technology I discussed in the preceding chapter; it showed that all that sophisticated machinery could put together something which could shift units. But in a broader context it marked a watershed in the history of pop music. 'Pump up the Volume' could be said fairly to be the hit record which marked pop music's advance into modernism, which acknowledged that the old-fashioned staple of its diet, the song, had just about run its course. It announced the arrival of irony in the mainstream; not verbal irony of which there'd been a certain amount (Elvis Costello, The Pet Shop Boys), but an ironic view of recorded sound itself. And what was happening here to pop music had happened before in other art forms. The music business may have subsequently proved to be difficult ground for a revolution to take permanent root, but after 'Pump up the Volume' things could never be the same again. It's worth considering how it worked.

Taking apart 'Pump up the Volume' sample by sample, if possible, would yield the titles of a lot of dance records which became known to a wider public largely through being employed by M/A/R/R/S. Some of the genius of this single consisted in identifying the potential of this 'alliance' of small parts of cult dance records which hadn't quite broken into the ordinary market-place. By Autumn 1987, Public Enemy could do no wrong as far as the music press was concerned, but their record sales became more visible – most importantly, in this context, in terms of chart placings – from 1988 onwards. In the 1987 context of 'Pump up the Volume', the aggressive choric cry of 'We're gonna git you' had a good deal of novelty value. In fact, most rap records still had mainstream novelty value at this point, especially those of such excellence as Criminal Element Orchestra's 'Put the Needle to the Record', the sampling of whose title line made an important contribution to the wit of 'Pump up the Volume'. Novelty wasn't notably lacking either in the quasi-mystical sound of the Israeli chanteuse (raised to an even more mystical pitch by the simple expedient of speeding her up), who came floating in after 'the drumbeat goes like this' when the needle has actually been put on the record. Subsequent exposure (at a more natural pitch) on the Coldcut reworking of 'Pump up the Volume' which served as the basis for that production team's remix of Eric B and Rakim's 'Paid in

Full' exposed the Israeli contribution as Ofra Haza's 'Im Nin Alu' (which was, in the natural and cynical way of things in pop music, released in its own right with a very 1988 beat underpinning it to become one of the less likely Top 20 hits in history).

It's impossible to over-estimate the immediate impact and influence of 'Pump up the Volume'. The Coldcut team had theoretically been doing this kind of thing in their own right, in an Art of Noise kind of way. Their 1987 endlessly refashioned and restyled 'Beats and Pieces' was a collage constructed not so much from musical samples as from noises – bicycle bells, doorbells, with a stray snatch, and scratch, of Vivaldi providing a rare and brief musical interlude. But when they came to the Eric B and Rakim track in the immediate backwash of M/A/R/R/S, the influence was so great that the remix of the rap track which they produced was, effectively, simply the highlights of 'Pump up the Volume' with a few of their own amusing non-musical effects thrown in (the endlessly copied 'This is a journey into sound' introduction, and the infinitely wittier interpolation of Humphrey Bogart direct from one of his soundtracks 'replying' to one of the exhortations to 'pump up the volume'). Their (sampled) bass line and beat aside, Eric B and Rakim came over as somewhat superfluous to proceedings amidst all this essentially English (perhaps even, in 1987, essentially London) wit, when their cynical rap about commercialization and motivation was allowed to poke its head above the elaborate Coldcut sound-collage parapet. The two rappers were quoted as hating the remix because of its use of 'disco' music which they apparently felt to be somehow either feminine or effeminate. The absurdity of the macho posturing of even the most talented rap artists usually condemns itself when represented in cold print, and this assertion seems to me no exception. But Eric B and Rakim's displeasure didn't have any effect on the mainstream record-buying public. Despite their feeling emasculated by the Coldcut treatment, 'Paid in Full' put

Eric B and Rakim in the UK Top 20 and (allied with some rather fawning adulation in the music press) gave them a following.

And for all the music press's influence, it was basically the decision of the Coldcut team to souse 'Paid in Full' in 'Pump up the Volume' which did the trick. There wasn't even any attempt to disguise what had been done. A lot of the 'techno' sound effects of the M/A/R/R/S single were trimmed back, small details like the interjection of 'Pump that thing' were played up, quite a lot extra was added. But if there'd been no 'Pump up the Volume' there'd have been no 'Paid in Full' remix. No 'Paid in Full' remix like this one, anyway. Just as without 'Pump up the Volume', there couldn't have been any 'Beat Dis' by Bomb the Bass, even if the title had been purloined from Afrika Bambaataa's 'Looking for the Perfect Beat', because most of that disc was pure 'Pump up the Volume'.

Schoenberg once said that if he hadn't been Schoenberg then someone else would have been. This highbrow intrusion is quite resonant in its comparison. The ascetic atonalism of the twelve-tone musical system with which Schoenberg (for good or ill) is linked in the minds of most people with any interest at all in music didn't really come naturally to him, as anyone familiar with his earlier works will know. Lavish pieces like *Verklärte Nacht*, *Gurre-lieder*, *Pelleas und Melisande* are all written in a lush, huge orchestral style akin to that of Mahler and Richard Strauss, clearly influenced by the mature works of Wagner (in particular *Tristan und Isolde*), and Schoenberg could probably have gone on writing quite happily like that for ever. Well, not 'happily', that was the problem. He felt there was something wrong with music, that it needed to be purged, that a new start needed to be made. The conventional tonality which had stood everyone in such good stead right up to the end of the nineteenth century (in the cases of composers like Brahms and Tchaikovsky) was sliding, from a purist's point of view, into decadent and indeterminate chromaticism – rich, syrup-like and sticky. Schoenberg was terribly good at writing in that style, but he was also a man of strong opinions with an almost puritanical devotion to his art. He therefore saw it as his duty to 'purify' music, rescue it from decadence, effectively by starting again. To start again he abandoned the whole framework of tonality (the minor and major scales) which had governed Western music from the sixteenth century. He even returned to a simpler concept than the system of modes which had prevailed in all known music through the Middle Ages. Music, in the Schoen-bergian system, consisted of twelve basic notes, a sequence of twelve semi-tones. Everything was constructed from these twelve notes. Schoenberg started 'modern music' as we know it by going back to these twelve discrete notes, seeing each as of equal and distinct value, abandoning the idea of diatonic tonal relations between selected notes, and putting forward the idea that composition should consist of 'rows' using the twelve notes in the way implied by this system. Putting it crudely (but by no means inaccurately) Schoenberg solved the 'problem' in music as he saw it by the simple expedient of taking music to bits.

I hark back to the birth of modernism in music at precisely this moment in my discourse not to try and claim some bogus credibility for the M/A/R/R/S project, but simply because I do see resonances of Schoenberg's 'reluctant revolution' (as a series of South Bank concerts in 1990 rather limply labelled it) in Dave Dorrell's 1987 project. The advent of minimalist house music in the UK charts early that year couldn't prevent the British music scene looking as though it was largely dominated by the dead and the practically retired. The commercial music scene of 1987 became – *pace* The Pet Shop Boys and Stock, Aitken and Waterman – a world where a fairly forgettable biopic pushed a fairly average retread of 'La Bamba', an old rock 'n' roll song in Spanish, to the top of the charts in both the UK and the US. The nature of pop music is such that it would scarcely show its 'decadence' in the form of an obsession with chromaticism. The sure sign of decay in the pop-music market-place is an endless stream of violently successful reissues and cover versions. 'Pump up the Volume' cut through all that.

Yes, but that doesn't make it art, some might say. And had 'Pump up the Volume' emanated from some small dance label, from the heart of the hip-hop scene or from musicians known primarily for their past involvement with dance music, then it would be hard to call it anything other than a lucky cross-over. But it emerged from a liaison between groups (a bit of a down-market term, really) signed to the very art-conscious 4AD label. 4AD were perhaps best known at this juncture for The Cocteau Twins, an ensemble given to swirling musical sounds without rhythm, overladen by poetic recitations and 'dreamy' (a polite term for unintelligible) lyrics. 4AD was about 'Art' with a capital A, almost painfully so if your viewpoint was that pop music was meant to be fun and possessed of a good beat even when it had pretensions. 4AD had previously little to do with fun. And the two groups – ensembles, perhaps – who combined uneasily to create M/A/R/R/S were very much of the 'Art' lobby. Up to that point both A. R. Kane and Colourbox had shown every sign of being more interested in pop music as some kind of higher, indefinite, arcane (pun fully intended; after all, where did the name come from in the first place?) form for enlightened listeners. Colourbox had shown an interest in scratch-mix collage techniques, even a certain sense of humour in putting such tracks together, but there was an anti-commercial sense of high art even where there was humour (underlined once again by the 4AD connection). As anyone who ever bothered to turn over 'Pump up the Volume' and play what was technically its double A-side companion 'Anitina (The First Time I See She Dance)' would know. The M/A/R/R/S project wasn't just intended as a piece of fun. And there was no JAMs/KLF-style impulse to annoy or outrage. While the intention to make a very good dance record was there, so was the 'artistic' intention, the desire to find a new way forward for pop music.

You can't take pop music apart and produce a twelve-tone system though. Well, you can, but it wouldn't shift many units, and scarcely anyone would notice it. And there isn't much point in staging an artistic revolution if no one notices. When Picasso, faced with a similar visual problem to Schoenberg's musical poser, started on *Les Demoiselles d'Avignon* and 'solved' the post-impressionist dilemma by reducing visual subjects to their constituent geometric form, his aim wasn't that no one in the world should notice his drastically novel approach to painting. However much the twelve-tone system contributed to the removal of contemporary serious music from the popular domain, and even though he was scarcely the most populist of individuals, Schoenberg intended the 'new music' of himself and his leading pupils (the Second Viennese School) to be noticed, to create the kind of controversy that it did. These two 'revolutions' of course took place more or less simultaneously, being part of the process of deliberate disintegration I discussed in such sweeping terms in the first chapter. And like the key literary modernist text discussed there, Henry James's 'In the Cage', both 'revolutions' sought to change the context of the basic tools of the trade, having broken the elaborate construct of centuries of 'progress' in each art back to its constituents: the twelve notes of Western music, the basic geometric form of the cube, the word as object taken out of its original context.

It's the question of context which has particular resonance when applying this apparently grandiose analogy to 'Pump up the Volume' and its artistic ambitions. These ambitions were much loftier than those of Bill Drummond and Jimmy Cauty. 'Loftier' because less steeped in cynicism, and also in an old artistic sense because much more removed from the grimy, everyday world with which all JAMs/KLF enterprises were besmirched. Given the background of the participants and the label on which it was launched, 'Pump up the Volume', for all you could dance to it, for all that it got to Number 1 on its fifth week of release, had much more of the arty ivory tower about it than any of The JAMs' less commercially successful releases. Drummond and Cauty had 'formed a hip-hop group' and gone on a series of highly organized, (ill-)disciplined raids on famous recordings to make a statement about their times. 'Pump up the Volume' was the result of careful consideration of recorded sound, acknowledging that this, rather than any musical system, is the basis of pop music, and an attempt to see what happened if you broke that down to its constituent elements and – like Picasso or Schoenberg or T. S. Eliot – started to rebuild the same basics in a recognizable but different manner. It differed from all the rap usage of breaks and beats in that it was nothing to do with the necessity of MCs fronting a DJ or two playing with their wheels of steel. Rap methods had evolved from live performance; 'Pump up the Volume' was a pure studio record. The uneasiness of the collaboration (which, if rumour is to be believed, is understatement on a grand scale) ensured that there was no chance of discovering whether it could be realized live. Just as it ensured there was no question of a follow-up, which is probably just as well. It was the follow-ups which exposed just how much of the wit and invention of the debuts of Bomb the Bass and S-Express (as well as the earlier Coldcut productions) had been novelty and sheer serendipity. In any case, how do you follow perfection?

So what did this perfection consist of? Well, to begin with there were several different edits. The original twelve-inch edit was probably the most minimalist, using far fewer of the samples, especially those vocal breaks which gave the radio edit much of its hook, helping to push the single up the charts so rapidly. The original minimalist version, being much more pared down, was particularly useful to club DJs who could thus start compiling their own versions of 'Pump up the Volume' as the mood took them. I remember hearing an excellent mix in a club when the vocal line of Whitney Houston's 'So Emotional' was played over the top of the 'Pump up the Volume' bass and recurrent piano figure. It brought out all the qualities of Houston's voice with a freedom and strength the production of her records doesn't usually confer. I offer this personal recollection partly in evidence towards the contention that much of the best in pop music is about the fleeting moment, the ephemeral lucky accident.

One thing that's remarkable about 'Pump up the Volume' is the blank simplicity of the drum beat. None of the tricksy, subtle rhythms of James Brown's 'Funky Drummer', which everyone else has subsequently sampled to death; just a straightforward drum hitting each beat regularly. Initial rhythmic interest is supplied by other percussive effects, introduced separately – first, a hollow electronic drum-sound pitched on two notes an octave apart, then a tambourine pattern. That's the order they appear on the 'pure' twelve-inch version. The more familiar radio edit starts from the electronic pitched tone, with voices and drum rolls preceding the basic beat; here the tambourine doesn't arrive until the familiar nagging bass line heralded by the single resonant piano note (made electronically resonant, no doubt). The sound of a record being scratched – something you don't need an actual record to make if you've got a sampler – precedes the injunction to 'pump up the volume', which kicks off the piano, bass and sometimes the tambourine, according to edit.

The most striking thing when one returns to 'Pump up the Volume' is how little of it involves actual music. The basic elements I've just described are usually present throughout in one form or another (except when a sample from Stock, Aitken and Waterman's 'Roadblock' intrudes – the sample which nearly became a 'courtblock'). Most of the samples used are of rap vocal lines which have a sort of 'anthemic shout' about them –

Public Enemy threatening vengeance, Criminal Element Orchestra demanding the needle on the record. Apart from the Israeli singing, which is so dependent on the kind of quarter tones not employed in conventional Western music as to seem unearthly and not especially musical, the rest tends to be so processed and electronically treated as to be reduced to the status of sound effect. Particularly popular at various pitches are sounds 'phased' so as to seem to approach the listener, pass by and then disappear out of earshot. There's also a pulsating radio signal, used to greater effect in Bomb the Bass's 'Beat Dis', and possibly derived from the ironically named DTI's plug for illicit mobile broadcasting stations: 'Keep this frequency clear'. Vocally the samples tend to do little except draw attention to the dance and hip-hop roots of this experiment (the voice does keep enjoining the listener to 'dance, dance'), but smuggled in there at one moment, after a struggle in which the second half of the phrase is meaninglessly and repeatedly matched with an oriental vowel noise, is Henry Ford's observation that 'History is bunk'. Which could, of course, serve as the motto for the whole enterprise. By not falling back on melodic pop the way The JAMs did, M/A/R/R/S managed a much more subversive attack on the 'well-crafted song', even if it didn't have the social critique ambitions of the tracks on *1987*. And there was probably less 'music' involved than in Coldcut's arty 'Beats and Pieces', with its ostentatious doorbells; but by not wearing its pretensions on its sleeve, and more importantly by making sure that the rhythm track was so insistent and driving, 'Pump up the Volume' reached a market others could only dream of. And all this from the same label as The Cocteau Twins.

Although M/A/R/R/S and The Justified Ancients of Mu Mu were creating their music by the same technological means, their aims at this juncture were, I think, markedly different. Which isn't to say that Drummond and Cauty didn't want people to dance to their music, or that they didn't want it to sell. Of course they did, and they were nakedly honest about this later (especially in *The Manual*). But the impact of a JAMs release relied on the listener actively recognizing and identifying the constituent samples that had gone into the work. If you don't know that the beginning of 'Whitney Joins The JAMs' is actually the *Mission Impossible* theme, then you're going to miss the joke. Just as if you don't understand the resonances of The Beatles' 'All You Need is Love' as the great hippy summer of 1967 anthem, then the point of their first single might be a bit lost on you. When they sampled Scott Walker singing Jacques Brel's 'Next' on the *1987* album, that was meant to be a reference understood by those who knew the song (as well as a tribute to one of the true individuals of pop-music history).

With 'Pump up the Volume' on the other hand, it wouldn't matter at all if you'd never heard of the records which provided the constituent elements. Most people (myself included) still haven't, and only the most wilfully eclectic of record collectors would say that all the principal sources there were part of the shared experience of mainstream pop history. 'Put the Needle to the Record' is a good dance track, but it hardly resonates for most people in the same way as even the *Mission Impossible* theme (let alone any Beatles single).

Both The JAMs and M/A/R/R/S knew what they were about in these instances. The latter never had to decide whether to carry on like that; Drummond and Cauty proved, on their second album and with most KLF releases, that they were perversely capable of playing it both ways. Because there's an implicit schizophrenia in basing your material on what other people have already recorded. Are samples supposed to be recognizable? Or are they used because they're useful? Is a recognizable sample ironic or a homage? The same question applies to an unrecognizable sample too. After all, what the public (and in particular the legal department of the record company holding the copyright on the sampled recording) may not detect, the producer or artist is very well aware of and has consciously lifted (except in cases where, in ignorance, the sample turns out to be of something which had been itself sampled – the Lolleatta Hollaway effect). In the course of our recording described in Chapter 6, Rex Brough confided to me that he often samples from records which especially irritate or annoy him, working out a subtle revenge on things he dislikes by subjecting them to his technological domination and doing them to death; and he did, in fact, choose one of the samples which went into our track on this basis.

The over-sampled beat from James Brown's 'Funky Drummer' seems an obvious example of something which has been used for all possible reasons. It's a good and infectious dance beat; musicians working in dance music, especially black music, are conscious of the debt they owe James Brown as the 'Godfather of Soul', possibly even the 'inventor' of 'funk as we know it'. When Public Enemy used 'Funky Drummer' quite openly on 'Don't Believe the Hype', they obviously had both attitudes in mind. (After all, James Brown did record 'Say it Loud, – I'm Black and I'm Proud' when Stevie Wonder was still doing cabaret numbers.) George Michael's motives for borrowing it – rather late in the day – are somewhat more abstruse; perhaps, one dares to suggest, to prove that he was still 'in touch' with the music scene around him (*Listen Without Prejudice Vol. 1*, the album on which the sample can be found, was clear proof that he was nothing of the sort). Pop Will Eat Itself's motivation – examined in greater detail in Chapter 8 – manages to combine admiration and irony (no mean feat, and perhaps the exemplary attitude for approaching pop music).

But the vast majority of tracks which have sampled 'Funky Drummer' (probably) had little intention of any kind when doing so, save that of providing a good beat. No homage, no irony, possibly even a vague hope of 'Funky Drummer' not even being detected (if the speed was changed enough or the sample edited to an unusual enough pattern). In these cases, as with 'Pump up the Volume', it scarcely matters a damn whether or not the listener recognizes it. The listener might, if detecting something obscure or particularly well hidden, be allowed a certain smug sense of pride, and thus increase whatever initial pleasure the track provided, but that pleasure never depended – and was never meant to depend – upon recognizing the constituent samples. And sadly, in a majority of these cases, what is being produced isn't something markedly different, something you are meant to see as marking a break with the past like 'Pump up the Volume', but just routine dance music. For Dorrell and Co. history might be bunk, but – as I've already said – they didn't have to produce a follow-up.

And I should say that the implicit suggestion that sampled records which demand the listener to recognize the samples used tend to be somehow wittier and more inventive than those which don't is merely wishful thinking on my part. What more immediate or obvious contradictions of this contention could there be than anything by Jive Bunny and the Mastermixers? Or – more contentiously, I'd assert – the output of MC Hammer in the days before he dropped the MC. Most Hammer samples are instantly recognizable and have little real purpose or wit behind their employment. There is an argument to be constructed about the use of the repeated figure from Prince's 'When Doves Cry' on 'Pray', but I suspect that it's an over-ingenious and specious line of debate. For the record, it goes like this: Prince is among the great black artists in pop history, a never-failing source of invention, who has shown when he feels like it that he can create the goods which shift the units. 'When Doves Cry' is his most successful single to date (the top single in the US in 1984, and still his biggest hit to date in the UK in sales, though not in chart-placing, terms). Hammer's use of it is both homage and boast. He seeks to do what Rembrandt did in his self-portrait which consciously echoed Titian's *Man with the Blue Sleeve*, once thought to be possibly a portrait of the poet Ariosto. He seeks to place himself on a par with someone he admires from the past (though if this argument were correct, I suspect Hammer would have been rash to consign Prince to history quite so rapidly). A further dimension is added in that Hammer has employed a sample by Prince, who always dedicates his albums to God and is known for a strong (if rather idiosyncratic) religious belief, on a track called 'Pray', which exhorts its listeners to adopt religious faith as a means of survival in modern society.

It's a splendidly pretentious argument, but most of Hammer's sampling is too vacuous to justify it. In fact, to call it sampling is to dignify it with a subtlety it really doesn't possess. Much of the time his 'sampling' is more like his bastardization of The Chi-Lites' classic 'Have You Seen Her', which purports to be Hammer providing a rap commentary and new lyrics while stumbling across the song on the radio. It is difficult to know whether this or 'Here Comes the Hammer', a 'tribute' to James Brown relying solely on 'Super Bad' and including some superimposed shots of James Brown dancing with Hammer (or a Hammer impersonator) in the promotional video, is the less imaginative and inventive. But then Hammer was never really about the music. He was a brilliant marketing ploy, rap made palatable for the mass market and dressed in style (the baggy trousers were, and were intended to be, every bit as memorable as the music). Hammer was a black man rapping non-threateningly for Whites, about as far as you could hope to get from Public Enemy or Ice-T. In fact, there was a superb and surely completely unintentional irony – or suitability – about the choice of Hammer to provide a rap theme for the big box-office film of late 1991, *The Addams Family*. Charles Addams's original 1940s and 1950s *New Yorker* magazine cartoons depicting Gomez, Morticia *et al.* were meant as a sardonic comment on the American nuclear family and the notions of happiness through that unit which were being stereotypically peddled through advertising, TV and movie images in an attempt to return to conservative values after the upheaval of the Second World War. The 1960s TV series with John Astin and Yvonne de Carlo managed to retain something of that macabre, subversive quality. However, the 1991 movie, for all its special effects and splatter, ended up as a paean to family life and solidarity, an essentially cosy and warm piece. Who better to provide a theme song for an Addams Family castrated of cynicism and subversion than the man who'd made rap music so cuddly that Partners in Kryme's 'Turtle Power' sounded hard core in comparison? Perhaps it should be acknowledged in passing that the result, 'Addams' Groove', is possibly the only rap track to date in 12/8 time.

All of which is something of a digression from the point that it's pretty difficult (if you're old enough to remember and have a memory) not to be aware of what Hammer is sampling. But that consciousness doesn't mean that you're meant to be conscious. And my parenthetical point about age isn't so parenthetical when considering this issue. A sizeable portion of the market for pop music is young enough to find no resonances at all of even a 1984 single like Prince's 'When Doves Cry'. Plundering the back catalogue for breaks and beats need have little or nothing to do with homage, just as recording a cover version may have little to do with the desire to extend the boundaries of interpretation of a song. Even when the effect of collage and sampling is as deliberately old-fashioned and nostalgia-inducing as Jive Bunny's 'Swing the Mood', where the old rock 'n' roll songs were presented in a more or less straightforward medley, a good percentage of those actually buying the record would be coming to these songs for the first time. Just as, before sampling had made its impact, songs like 'Stand by Me' and 'When a Man Loves a Woman' wouldn't necessarily have been too familiar. For all the cleverness involved in 'Pump up the Volume' and

The JAMs releases (as well as several sample-orientated singles which followed), sampling offered an even more inexhaustible way for those with less imagination but a yen for stardom to raid the archives. Nothing to do with homage; nothing to do with irony.

Of course, the 'pure music' lobby, those who still clung to the idea that pop records were somehow about live musical events, found the idea of music produced by cutting other people's records up and simply collaging through a machine deeply disturbing. This sense of resentment, particularly evinced by some rock musicians who'd made their names in the 1960s, hasn't gone away. Roger Daltrey's remarks about 'drum machines' at the 1991 BRITS awards jamboree when presenting The Cure with the award for Best British Group showed an in-built resistance on the part of the older establishment to music which didn't come from a good old-fashioned group with 'real musical instruments'. This attitude seemed to have spread back to the younger generation of music critics by the end of 1991, with groups like R.E.M., Nirvana and Ride – peopled by 'real musicians' – being obsessively championed. But with these critics there was less of a sense of moral outrage at the supremacy of technologically created music.

Is there in fact a 'moral' issue here? Is the creativity of a M/A/R/R/S or KLF somehow less genuine than music created from scratch? Can there really be creativity in quotation? This question leads back to those other 'crises of faith' in 'higher' art. Both literature and music leaned heavily on quotation and reference back to a previous tradition when they were trans-forming themselves into something modern and modernist. You could call *The Waste Land* just a collage of other people's lines (especially after Pound had edited out most of Eliot's linking, rather prolix, pastiche verse), and it's not too far fetched to see it as a work of literary sampling. Similarly the literary echoes consciously summed up in Joyce's *Ulysses*, its use of sound collage, were all discrete sounds fed through the digital sampler of Joyce's literary imagination to produce part of a (supposedly) coherent narrative.

Even before the twelve-tone system had been evolved, classical music had employed quotation, reference and sometimes downright plagiarism, very much in the same equivocal spirit as many pop musicians and producers now use sampling. Sometimes – back in the days when there was a constant demand for novel settings of the mass which might be immediately accessible to the populace – it was simply the question of poaching a good tune from the popular domain and using it as a basis. The old medieval tune, '*L'Homme Armé*', popular in Europe for a couple of centuries, inspired literally hundreds of masses between the fifteenth and seventeenth centuries. Mozart, Haydn and Beethoven would all borrow tunes if they felt they could use them, especially if they were looking for a theme to be varied. All three of these composers were also heavily given to self-reference. Most wittily of the three, Mozart had Don Giovanni sit down to dinner to be entertained by a tune from *The Marriage of Figaro* (a double-edged comment on the way that music can be taken out of context). Beethoven's later work is full of cross-reference, with many of the themes of the demanding late string quartets echoing – or even simply quoting – themes found elsewhere (especially in the more or less contemporary *Missa Solemnis* and Choral Symphony). But it was the composers of the late nineteenth and early twentieth centuries who turned reference, both internal and external, into a feverish near disease. Bruckner admired Wagner so greatly that he transformed part of his Seventh Symphony into a tribute packed with direct quotation. Echoes of Wagnerian motifs can be found too in the more modernist operas of Richard Strauss, especially his *Salome*. Despite Debussy's repudiation of all things German in the shadow of the First World War, he also offered direct Wagnerian reference (to *Tristan und Isolde*) in his opera

Will Pop Eat Itself?

Pelléas et Mélisande (quite naturally, as both involve doomed lovers who seem almost anxious to embrace their fate). The work of Gustav Mahler is so packed with self-reference, themes linking one work with another, that there's almost a sense in which you could call parts of his Ninth Symphony (the last he completed) a 'megamix'.

More relevant, though, in this context, are probably two works of the latter half of the twentieth century – Luciano Berio's *Sinfonia* (1968) and Shostakovich's Fifteenth Symphony (1972). The latter, its composer's last major work, is more sparingly straightforward in its referential frame. The first movement quotes – openly and directly – the famous theme from the overture to Rossini's *William Tell* (famous as the signature tune for the 1950s TV series *The Lone Ranger*). The finale is built around a Wagnerian leitmotif used throughout The Ring Cycle to denote 'Fate', but in several senses of the word – fate as inevitability, but also the courage to face one's fate, even the serenity that comes from accepting it and going to it gladly. A man who managed to survive (just) an active creative career under Stalin, sticking coded messages to the future in pieces which were none the less found politically correct and acceptable, would probably have had more chance than most to embrace the idea of fate both as inevitability and as something to be faced with equanimity, so there's no mystery about the way in which this simple but telling cadence permeates what seems on the whole a good-natured piece. The use of the Rossini is slightly more abstract and must be seen as an ironic comment on heroism, especially nationalist heroism. The theme occurs in a movement which can seem superficial, and that's not, I suspect, an accident. As with pop sampling, context is all.

Berio's *Sinfonia* is much more a work in the spirit of 'Pump up the Volume', employing verbal and non-musical sound quotations. Readings from Levi-Strauss's *Le cru et le cuit* (the title of which provided Fine Young Cannibals with something to call their ridiculously successful second album) and Samuel Beckett's *The Unnamable* (nicknamed by some 'The Unreadable') vie with quotations from Debussy's *La Mer* and works by Schoenberg, as well as a Mahler scherzo which started life as a song. The effect throughout the piece is one of intense mosaic and it's obviously at least in part an attempt to solve the question of how one actually goes about writing 'classical' music at that (or indeed this) juncture of 'high' cultural history. But it's also intended as an elaborate consideration of issues of identity, a play between land and water, and a tribute to Martin Luther King.

Like much late twentieth-century 'classical' music, Berio's *Sinfonia* makes heavy demands on its listeners, and requires a certain familiarity with many of the atonal idioms it employs. It's not accessible in the manner of, say, 'Pump up the Volume', although that too has its idiomatic demands which render it as unlistenable to some ears, as many would find the Berio. But whether you consider *Sinfonia* to be a pretentious load of old junk or a work of towering genius (and both views are held), the fact remains that its being compiled at least in part from quotations doesn't prohibit its being imaginative. The fact also remains that in the late 1960s a 'classical' composer had recourse to stylistic devices – even if not involving technology – which would strike certain people in pop music as desirable, even necessary twenty years later. I suppose the principle is something like a broken down motor bike or car – to get it going again you might have to take it to bits first. Or you might just kick-start it into life by shock tactics.

I remember when 'Pump up the Volume' appeared, and was followed by a rash of records – the list headed, as mentioned earlier, by Coldcut's 'Paid in Full' remix – which assumed a working knowledge of the M/A/R/R/S single itself. There was the possibility of a golden age of invention and creativity, even alongside the baleful presences of Tiffany and Debbie Gibson, and despite the rise of *Neighbours* as a major popular cultural event. At last a new departure, at last a new dawn, at last something to get excited about. But then in pop music real success is a poisoned chalice because it demands a sequel. And dawns and departures can't, by their very nature, last for ever.

8 · Dirty Cash

Ripe and ripe, then rot and rot. Taken broadly, that's the natural cycle, and it has its own mirror in the course of human affairs. The honeymoon gives way to routine, which often ruins the illusion.

Pop music is an illusion business and honeymoon periods are notoriously short, as the near-momentary careers of various manufactured teen-market stars of the late 1980s all too clearly prove. But what happened to the form of music which 'Pump up the Volume' launched as a marketable, profitable commodity shows how a similar process of ripening then rotting takes hold as much of styles as of personalities. Ironically, it was partly through the insatiable desire of all sections of the industry – record companies, TV, radio and the music press – for specific and identifiable personalities that the seeds of an inevitable decline were sown. What started out as an ambitious experiment degenerated into something at best predictable and formulaic, at worst monstrous and fearsome.

After 'Pump up the Volume' everything was miraculously changed. Apart from the collage record, the only other great and remotely durable phenomenon to explode on the UK pop market as big business around the end of 1987 and the beginning of 1988 was Kylie Minogue. The phrase 'remotely durable' eliminates Bros, who emerged to grab their fifteen seconds of fame at around the same time as Kylie – January/February 1988 – but who were already on their way out before the autumn weather turned the leaves to flame, as 'September Song' might put it. A short honeymoon, but almost eternal by the standards of Vanilla Ice and Chesney Hawkes.

'Miraculously changed' is inevitably a bit of an exaggeration. It was (approximately) in February 1988 that the first great barrage of successful collage sample records began to emulate the success of M/A/R/R/S. In the immediately wake of 'Pump up the Volume', the Coldcut remix of 'Paid in Full', essentially derivative of but as influential as the M/A/R/R/S single, reached the Top 20. The aftermath of the Christmas market and the inevitable decrease in singles sales at the start of the year allowed, as it had done twelve months before, straightforward house music to make its sales mark felt with numbers like the Beatmasters' 'Rok da House', Jack 'n' Chill's 'The Jack that House Built' and Krush's 'House Arrest'. None of these was an especially huge or epoch-shattering release. The 'news' as far as records which were actually selling went, revolved around the sudden vogue for female solo singers, preferably pseudo-pre-pubescent ones. The unlikely troika of Belinda Carlisle, Tiffany and (inevitably) Kylie created a chart-trainspotter's record by becoming the first trio of female soloists to achieve consecutive Number 1s in the UK; a trick turned again towards the year's end by Whitney Houston, Enya and Robin Beck, a yet more diverse trinity.

The sample-dominated records which exploded on to the market in the last fortnight of February were 'Beat Dis' by Bomb the Bass and 'Doctorin' the House' by Coldcut (featuring Yazz on vocals). Even more than the remix of 'Paid in Full', these singles were clearly post-'Pump up the Volume', hence the time gap between it and them. When 'Beat Dis' entered the charts at Number 5 on the first week of release it was regarded as a phenomenon. In 1988 it was still unusual for an act with no chart history whatsoever to debut in the Top 10, and previously such a high first-time entry had been achieved only by Neil's

'Hole in My Shoe' (1984), a novelty cover version performed by a character well known from the popular cult TV series *The Young Ones*. Bomb the Bass had no such advantage. 'Beat Dis' made its impact mainly on the strength of the record and the market's awakened, keen appetite for this collage sound.

The internal antagonisms among the participants in the M/A/R/R/S project had made it difficult and more importantly pointless for the music press and the pop-gossip journalists of the conventional press to try to seize upon any personality within that group and build him up into a fully fledged pop personality. In any case, the whole 4AD ambience of the experiment had been a bit too arty for all that, even if there had been any purpose to or possible candidates for this doubtful treatment. Bomb the Bass and 'Beat Dis', though, had a photogenic 'personality' with a 'story'. And so nineteen-year-old Tim Simenon found himself being touted as the first heart-throb of sampling. Very quickly, the legend was built, the legend that Simenon had made 'Beat Dis' on cheap DJ and recording equipment in his bedroom, single-handedly, from elements in his record collection. Simenon became the first of the high-profile DJ samplers, the first to be turned into a star and not just a faceless figure manipulating discs and twiddling knobs somewhere behind pouting female singers, dancers or rappers. Of course, the legend was a bit of an exaggeration, although Simenon seemed happy enough to play along with it and indeed gives the impression of having come to believe it himself in the fullness of time. In fact, Pascal Gabriel, whose name was to crop up a lot in the development of this style of record, was heavily involved in the making of 'Beat Dis', and his commitment to Bomb the Bass as a group (although it was rapidly subject to promotion as a name under which Simenon could operate as a sole Svengali to various vocalists) was sufficient to mean that he owned 75 per cent of the rights to the second Bomb the Bass single 'Don't Make Me Wait' (which was a rewrite of 'Let the Music Play', a 1984 almost high-energy dance hit for American singer Shannon). Many of the more distinctive elements of 'Beat Dis' can be attributed to Gabriel's influence – the slightly camp touch of the Thunderbirds' '5–4–3–2–1' countdown was the kind of consciously kitsch effect he was fond of at that time.

Whatever the truth of the matter, there were attractions for all concerned (except maybe Pascal Gabriel) in going along with the bedroom story. There was the star-making aspect, giving the mainstream press a better handle on the collage-sample phenomenon than the idea of several producers, engineers and a DJ putting the product together by committee. It also gave a suggestion of careless spontaneity and suggested the possibility that anyone could do this kind of thing with the right technology. It was the best plug for do-it-yourself records since skiffle music propounded the idea that you could create an entire musical ambience with a cheap guitar and a washboard. Also, the average record company, even independent companies like Rhythm King and Mute (who were jointly responsible for the release of 'Beat Dis'), preferred having a face, a specific personality, to front the product. And when all's said and done, it's a better story, the ultimate rock myth – youngster makes record under own steam and manages to break through against all odds with it. Practically every Elvis Presley and Cliff Richard film from the early 1960s offered a variant on that narrative. Everyone loves overnight success, and no one likes to have the illusion ruined by something as inconvenient as the facts.

'Beat Dis' is possessed of a contrived (well, to my ears, anyway) air of roughness which helped to keep the illusion alive. It's a great dance record, but it already suggested the best way to mainstream success through sampling. Compared to all The JAMs products of 1987, and Coldcut's experiments of around the same time, and even to the highly organized 'Pump up the Volume', it's a blend of homogeneous elements. The bits that were designed to hook were the Thunderbirds' countdown, the continued quote of DTI's 'Keep this frequency clear' and the pseudo-electronic bleep which followed close on that. The majority of records lurking round it in the charts were conventional songs with lyrics – until the great techno-domination of late 1991, that would usually be the case – so 'Beat Dis' gave the impression of being another blow against 'the well-crafted song'. But just as you can describe most JAMs tracks in terms of 'verse-substitute' and chorus, so it is with 'Beat Dis'. Indeed, Pascal Gabriel has always, in producing records, thought first and foremost in terms of the 'song', believing that you can still make a 'well-crafted song' out of sampled components.

And of course 'Beat Dis' continued in the direction of 'Pump up the Volume' in one very crucial sense – the effect of the collage was, at best, to make a statement about music rather than about any subject outside music. Where most JAMs songs up to 'Downtown' had been about something more than production technique and showing what fun you can have with a sampler, and where 'Pump up the Volume' had attempted to assimilate new and unconventional musical sounds, 'Beat Dis' was simply a highly commercial, fairly successful, eminently danceable smash-and-grab raid on various sounds and breaks from records which took Simenon's and Gabriel's fancy. It had a good deal of wit about it, and the whole technique was sufficiently new for the product to sound like something new, a further step in this exciting progress to a future and a new pop music which understood and assimilated and made something out of its past.

Appealing to the public in only slightly smaller quantities at exactly the same time was Coldcut's 'Doctorin' the House', which seemed even cleverer and wittier. Drawing on the same range of materials they'd already shown themselves to be capable of dragging into a collage in their remix of 'Paid in Full' or their less well-known 'Beats and Pieces' (a 1987 collage single which more or less avoided conventional musical instrument samples, going instead for a neo-Art of Noise mixture of doorbell chimes and percussive effects, with just a snatch of Vivaldi added for good measure), Matt Black and Jonathan More, the two DJ-producers who made up the Coldcut team, had produced a heady, above all funny brew which threw film dialogue, a musical excerpt from the soundtrack of *The Jungle Book* and the specially recorded vocals of their protégée Yazz at a house bass line. The disjunctures seemed terrific at the time; but a few years on it sounds uneasily like a very special, very clever kind of novelty record. The JAMs' early discs still amuse, entertain and above all mean something. 'Pump up the Volume' will always be, if nothing else (and it's a lot else as a work of pop-culture art), a great dance record. 'Doctorin' the House' isn't really about anything except its own cleverness. This is, of course, terribly post-modern. Post-structural criticism had promised that the only valid subject of texts would be the texts themselves (although it's debatable that the great high priests of this critical school intended everything in the world to be treated as a text which contained the seeds of its own destruction). But there's something, in retrospect, awfully over-knowing, disturbingly arch, about what Coldcut were up to in 'Doctorin' the House'. This is perhaps an unfair criticism, because it presents the producers with a catch-22: if it's a joke, then it's just another novelty record – Benny Hill's 'Ernie' with a sampler, or an update of 'Renta Santa'; if it's 'art' or even, to use a less emotive and contentious term, 'experiment' then it fails to be 'about' anything and fails to 'get anywhere'. To be appallingly subjective for a moment, I know that in 1988 I regarded 'Doctorin' the House' as a highly entertaining, deeply subversive single that might be leading somewhere. At the end of 1991 the only part of it which seemed to foretell the future was its ending – the crazed science-fiction B-movie cry of 'They're coming! The Plastic Men are coming!' followed by the chorus of 'Plastic Man'. With the dehumanized robotic rave music which arrived three years later, the 'Plastic Men' could easily be said to have arrived.

The next big sampling sensation also struck the world – especially the record-buying world – as innovative and new. S-Express's 'Theme from S-Express' reached Number 1 in three weeks in April 1988. An irresistibly infectious blend of 1970s dance tracks with various voice effects thrown in, it described itself as 'a trip'. Aside from the obvious drug reference here, a conscious throwback to the psychedelic days (the acid house craze and the re-emergence of hallucinogens as a necessary adjunct to club culture still, at this point, lay a few months in the future), the concept of sound as 'a trip' had already been used extensively in collage since Coldcut had purloined the phrase 'This is a journey into sound' from an early stereo-sound demonstration disc. 'Enjoy this trip', the S-Express single instructed the listener after a Spanish '*Uno, dos, tres, cuatro*' countdown, which I remember first hearing on Debbie Harry's minor 1987 club hit 'Feel the Spin', and which from this point on resurfaced over and over again, reaching its lowest point on one of the worst records of 1990, Andrew Lloyd Webber's covertly produced 'update' of 'Itsy-bitsy Teeny-weeny Yellow Polka-dot Bikini' by Bombalurina.

The S-Express record was a classic artefact of its time. As the instruction to 'enjoy the trip' suggested, it was a celebration of hedonism, another burst from the affluent end of the 1980s. The disc came as part of a style package, with a promotional video very consciously using early 1970s colours and styles and implicitly pushing early 1970s attitudes to sex. 'I got the hots for you' was the disc's constant refrain, something of a far cry from the insistence upon abstinence and safe sex which was now common coin (even though such topics didn't really find their way into the average pop song). The disc was issued through the same Rhythm King/Mute channels as the Bomb the Bass hit, and once again a 'personality' emerged as front man for the production sound. In fact, the S–Express disc in its twelve-inch format actually carried pictures of the main protagonists on its sleeve, but as the female participants seemed to be there to impart a bit of glamour and generally look sultry and exotic, the publicity machine this time seized upon Mark Moore, one of the co-producers, and designated him the man who was 'responsible' for S–Express. By a mildly ironic coincidence Moore's co-producer was Pascal Gabriel, who thus found his role on a hit single underestimated and downgraded for the second time in under three months. Gabriel's taste for camp kitsch was much more up-front on the S–Express project, which was from the start intended as a visual product with a specifically flamboyant image.

As with the Bomb the Bass single, the disparate elements thrown into the melting pot were very much homogenized on the 'Theme from S–Express'. The whole pseudo-1970s sound (the 1970s as it might have sounded if refracted through 1980s technology) was very carefully achieved and the outcome was extremely commercial. Again, an effect of verse and chorus was achieved even without lyrics and singly conceived original melody, and to this day Pascal Gabriel thinks firmly of 'Theme from S–Express' as a good old-fashioned 'song'. The 1970s revival idea, although it has never quite taken off properly (it keeps stuttering and starting, as the similar success of the 1970s psychedelia-based 'Groove is in the Heart' in 1990 shows), was quite fortuitously timed. Coincidentally with the S–Express single, a remixed revival of The Jackson Five's first hit from 1970, 'I Want You Back', was in the Top 10. This revival, though, owed as much to the use of the distinctive piano-based introduction of The Jackson Five single in Eric B and Rakim's 'I Know You Got Soul' as to any yearning for the previous decade. In fact, in raiding the doubtful treasury of 1970s disco, the S–Express team were following in the footsteps (inevitably, perhaps) of The JAMs, most of whose second album had drawn on 1970s dance-music sources.

You could equally argue from the records whose success was coeval with S-Express's debut that the Moore/Gabriel combination had got their record released just in the nick of time. Yes, it was innovative and great fun, a good dance record, much less self-conscious than Coldcut's hit, but it entered the charts at the same time as the first wave of sampling-based novelty records. The medley-record craze of 1981 had provoked a parody centred on a medley of badly sung pub cabaret songs in typical inept pub cabaret style wittily entitled 'Star Turn on 45 (Pints)' and credited to Star Turn. This highly amusing idea was resuscitated, as Star Turn on 45 (Pints) reached Number 12 in the charts in May 1988 with 'Pump up the Bitter (Brutal Mix)' – the parenthesis being a side glance at a particular style of pared-down and hard-core house music. The same chart housing both this supreme example of the humourless parody (although a remarkably speedy reaction by the standards of most parodists) also gave a home to Harry Enfield's 'Loadsamoney', already discussed beyond its merits, and that hazard of the music market in May, the obligatory football record. The offering in 1988 was something of a departure. Instead of the usual choral rant which had been the staple of the football record since the 1970 England World Cup Squad had topped the charts with 'Back Home', the Liverpool team, noticing that one of their key players happened to be black, assumed that a rap employing all the currently trendy modes of record production might be a good idea. Hence the release of 'Anfield Rap (Red Machine in Full Effect)' which reached the Top 3 (a rare success for a club side, surpassing the previous peak of Number 5 achieved by Chelsea's 'Blue is the Colour' in 1972 and Tottenham's awful enough to qualify as surreal 'Ossie's Dream' in 1981). The Liverpool record proved, if nothing else, that the notion that all black men could rap properly was deeply wrong (my mind was not changed on this point by the *double-entendre* laden contribution the same player, John Barnes, made to the England/New Order collaboration to commemorate the 1990 World Cup).

Yes, in the blink of an eye, the same thing had happened to sample records as had happened to rap. Ripe had quickly turned to rot; scratch and mix parodies had come to pass. On top of which LA Mix's Top 10 hit, 'Check this Out', released in May and popular for the next month or two, sounded like a parody even though that wasn't the idea. It was the first real 'bandwagon' sample hit, overtly retreading what everyone else had done so far, and not making any significant attempt to innovate or create its own style. Its use of samples, almost all of which had appeared elsewhere on one of the sample collage hits of the previous nine months, was predictable – almost knowingly and deliberately so – and gave the air as much of a medley record as of an avant-garde raider of the groove. And it was at this juncture that Bill Drummond and Jimmy Cauty offered their derisive and highly successful deconstruction of the whole process and sent 'Doctorin' the Tardis' to Number 1. After all, if the whole purpose of the technology is just to play around and show how good your mastery of the technology is, 'Doctor Who, hey, Doctor Who' is as valid and intelligent a lyric as 'Doctorin' the house, we're doctorin' the house'. It certainly packs about as much meaning syntactically and grammatically.

In 1987 Drummond and Cauty had had the doubtful advantage of never having to follow up a hit and being, in any case, pioneers in their field with no emulators to worry about. M/A/R/R/S might never have issued a follow-up to 'Pump up the Volume' for all the wrong reasons, but, given the difficulty of providing a sequel to anything received with enormous acclaim, their internal difficulties might be deemed to be a blessing in disguise. Because all the successful, innovative British production teams – Bomb the Bass, Coldcut and S-Express – now had to find some way of following up their successes. With hindsight, disappointment was inevitable. At the time, when these acts seemed like potential trailblazers, anything might have been possible.

Although these three teams had operated through independent labels, the necessity to find follow-ups to their initial successes shows how much these 'outsiders' had already been consumed by their industry. The pressure to provide a front man for Bomb the Bass and S-Express was part and parcel of this consumption, of course. A phrase from a 1970s Joni Mitchell song springs to mind here: 'stoking the star-maker machinery behind the popular song'. Coldcut had chosen to push Yazz to the front of 'Doctorin' the House', and their few future (and minor) hits using their 'brand' name always advertised the name of whichever vocalist was being 'featured'. As a result, Coldcut very quickly receded (from a publicity viewpoint) to behind their controls, leaving 'stardom' to their 'creations' (of whom Yazz and Lisa Stansfield were probably the most notable). And perhaps the very arty, tricksy nature of 'Doctorin' the House' hadn't left the majority of record buyers – who usually don't care over much about 'directions' in popular music – quite so eager for more.

That, of course, is another catch-22 about the tricky art of the follow-up. The public want something similar, but not identical, and judging by history in this matter, they are easily disappointed. So how far can you depart from your formula if you want to follow up a success? And to what extent can you risk being accused of producing something that's just 'the same old song'? The compromise entailed in achieving the right balance for continued and long-lasting success is a difficult one which few have judged correctly, and as pop music gets older the shelf-life of its successes, on the whole, gets shorter.

S-Express maintained their 1970s image for their next release, 'Superfly Guy'. The original *Superfly* had been a movie soundtrack by Curtis Mayfield, one of the most respected and revered of the old soul men, whose work with his group The Impressions in the 1960s (especially 'People Get Ready') was seen as both musically and lyrically vital in the development of a black soul–music culture. While the soundtrack to *Superfly* unquestionably had its merits, there had been a certain irony that Mayfield, of all people, had undertaken to write for what was one – a key one, indeed – of a string of tokenist movies about black detectives, of which *Shaft* had been the initiator. Loosely known by the collective title of 'blaxploitation' movies, these had been subsequently agreed by commentators to be anything but liberal portrayals of black people as heroes, but rather – in the villains depicted – semi-subtle ways of enforcing racist stereotypes and – in the heroes' deeply unsympathetic attitudes to women – perpetuating a myth about black men and sexual relationships.

This aspect of *Superfly* probably passed by the S-Express team completely. For them it was just a useful 1970s peg on which to hang another highly accomplished dance track; but where 'Theme From S-Express' had, for all its homogeneity, still contrived some spiky juxtapositions (cries of 'Drop that ghetto blaster' and various other pieces of speech thrown into the blender), 'Superfly Guy', whatever sources it plundered, came across as a more or less straightforward dance track. The thing which prevents my describing it as a song isn't the disparity of its elements but its absence of much in the way of lyrics aside from 'Superfly guy/Let me take you higher'. A perfectly good pop single, but nothing unusual, nothing a major record label wouldn't have been able to handle, 'Superfly Guy' defined S-Express as a highly professional production team who knew how to make quite catchy dance records. 'Quite' here in the sense of 'fairly', and less catchy with each successive release. The follow-up 'Hey Music Lover' was, it's true, slightly more adventurous, its electric piano and rap ingredient making it more multi-textured than its immediate predecessor, but then it was lifted from a more imaginative source (with all due respect to Curtis Mayfield), an old Sly and the Family Stone track. It was also coincidentally S-Express's last major hit to date. Linking everything in to an identifiable 1970s image hadn't helped to extend the team's shelf life, either, just as it subsequently did nothing to make Deee-lite permanent residents in the public's heart. In fact, the image, the 'personality', became something with which to get rapidly disenchanted.

Apart from the fact that Tim Simenon's chart career has proved more durable, there's a good deal that's similar about the subsequent career of Bomb the Bass, except that there was one inevitable cliché to which Simenon succumbed, the easiest cliché in the pop and rock music business. The third Bomb the Bass single, released in November 1988, was a straightforward song, featuring vocalist Maureen. It was indeed a good old-fashioned cover version of an older song, in this case 'I Say a Little Prayer' (the Bacharach and David song which had been definitively recorded by Aretha Franklin in 1968). Cover versions are a part of pop life, as old as the business, and it's generally fair enough that each 'generation' (given that a pop generation lasts somewhere between five and seven years) should wish to recreate old songs of any merit in its own style. But there was little about the sparsely produced, slowed-down arrangement of 'Say a Little Prayer' to suggest that Tim Simenon would make a particularly sensitive arranger of other people's songs (nor was there anything especially compelling about Maureen's vocal delivery). The style and tempo of this performance had been more or less lifted from (or to put it politely 'inspired by') a cover version of 'Anyone Who Had a Heart', another 1960s Bacharach and David classic, by Smith and Mightys. To have had to resort to a straightforward cover version within twelve months of a thrilling debut rather showed that Bomb the Bass (or Tim Simenon, at any rate) weren't the beacons of progress and development 'Beat Dis' might have led one to hope. However clever the production techniques behind the old song, this all reeked of the state of the art in 1986 and early 1987.

This might seem harshly unfair on poor old Tim Simenon, who has managed to continue having large-ish hits through to 1991, despite the hole blown in the marketing of a new single early that year by a temporary change of *nom de guerre* by the BBC's ludicrous over-sensitivity to the word 'bomb' for the duration of the Gulf War. The man has a living to make, after all. But then that's the problem, of course. To make a living in the pop business you have to maintain a steady output and originality becomes difficult under those circumstances. Unless you've arrived on the scene with some master-plan (such as that denied vociferously by The JAMs and the KLF) of how to move forward both your chosen form and your career simultaneously.

What all the first sample collage records had in common was exuberance and, part and parcel of that, a sense of irony. Not necessarily the irony that smirks behind the hand and undercuts, but that which is alive to meanings and nuance acquired by temporal and spatial juxtaposition. However, the more routine the inclusion of samples became, the more a sample was chosen simply because everyone else used it and it was a conveniently useful kind of sound (James Brown's 'Funky Drummer' springs to mind), and the less there was any real sense of the layers of meaning this might have for various generations of listeners. A lot of record buyers, we know, wouldn't recognize a lot of samples and probably wouldn't care about that fact. But there's a world of difference between using a sample to make a point and using a sample to save yourself the work or the musical effort. Likewise there's a good deal of difference between using a sampler and breaks from your favourite records to create a track because it's the only means at your disposal, because you really don't have any alternative resources and can't afford any, and doing it because you want to jump on the bandwagon and exploit the latest fad.

James Brown samples form an interesting paradigm here. Lawyers for Polydor Records believe that James Brown's back catalogue is probably the most heavily sampled of any artist's. There's a good chance of this, as rappers were scratching and mixing James Brown tracks before the sampling technology was available and, since the technology of sampling as we know it was developed, 'Funky Drummer', with its distinctive rolling beat, has graced more tracks than can probably be traced and identified. Indeed Polydor Records has claimed that James Brown is so sampled that two of its legal executives spend the whole of their time simply tracing and dealing with instances where James Brown discs have been plundered. In each case, the man himself has to be contacted and the indications are that he's quite flattered. One might say that that much is inevitable. None of this new attention has harmed his career at all, and he doesn't let anyone quote from his records for free. James Brown has, in fact, built a whole new career on the back of being extensively sampled. I can't imagine that Polydor Records would complain, either. The James Brown back catalogue has become extremely remarketable in the wake of his sampling superstardom.

In fact, quotation in a sample lies second only to quotation in a TV advert as an excuse to reactivate an old record. We've already seen that the use of the beginning of 'I Want You Back' on Eric B and Rakim's 'I Know You Got Soul' led to a (remixed, sadly) reissue of The Jackson Five's record. Coldcut and M/A/R/R/S both sampled 'Im Nin Alu' by Ofra Haza, with the result that the original itself (with a suitable dance mix) found an unlikely brief berth in the Top 20. More recently, the success of PM Dawn's 'Set Adrift on Memory Bliss', so heavily dependent on Spandau Ballet's 'True', prompted not just a re-release of that single but a whole greatest-hits collection. If properly alerted so they (and the artists involved) can have their copyright pound of flesh, a strategically placed sample from some old hit can work wonders for an act's entire back catalogue.

Apart from 'Funky Drummer', the most frequently quoted James Brown number must be 'Sex Machine', or, to give it its full title, 'Get up I Feel Like Being a Sex Machine (Part 1)'. As with 'Funky Drummer', most usage made of samples from this track has been predictable and routine. 'Get up, get on up' makes a useful rallying cry, but samples have mainly concentrated on the 'discussion' James Brown has with his musicians before the track starts ('I want to get into it, you know, moving it, doing it') and on his mid-song cries of 'Can I take it to the bridge?' and 'Can I count it off?' Imaginative use of James Brown samples is, and always has been, rare. At the worst end of the spectrum, a James Brown reference seems to be included in the hope it will confer some kind of 'soul' respectability. Arguably the most pointless sample of 'Funky Drummer' yet is that by George Michael on 'Waiting for the Day'. The rolling rhythm adds little or nothing to the meandering, unmemorable melody, but in the deliberately 'low profile' publicity for the *Listen Without Prejudice* album on which the track first appeared (the reticent George didn't want to give interviews, but was prepared to allow London Weekend Television to make him the subject of a *South Bank Show*) it was something to talk about which was, sadly, more interesting than most of the tracks on the disc. Obviously George Michael – who has had the distinction of duetting with Aretha Franklin – liked the idea of being able to put himself in the same breath as James Brown. But there was a faintly patronizing air in the discussion of this sample, a suggestion even that this technological device had somehow been graced by its use by such a talented superstar.

Whereas all George had done was to slow the beat down somewhat.

There are, in my view, two records which sample James Brown with real wit and style. One was an independently released single which squashed Brown together with Donny Osmond, some demented trumpet playing and an American demagogue ranting against rock 'n' roll. Unfortunately Coco, Steel and Lovebomb's 'Love Puppy', made in 1987, remained unknown to the Great British Public. The nagging delays to which Donny's agonized cries of 'Someone help me' and 'This is not a – puppy love' were subjected infused a kind of eerie, androgynous sexuality into a record always seen as the acme of asexual teen pap. To put Donny Osmond alongside James Brown with extracts from 'Sex Machine' and then have an American demagogue effectively denouncing both as part of the broad church that is rock 'n' roll ('that rotten, lewd, lascivious junk called rock 'n' roll', as the sample describes it) showed a ready wit which deserved to meet with more public response than it did.

The other great James Brown sample came on Pop Will Eat Itself's 1989 album *This is the Day . . . This is the Hour . . . This is this!*, an album which was treated with reverence by sections of the music press. By the time this disc was made, 'Funky Drummer' samples were already old hat, and James Brown's tortuous career had taken another strange turn in that he had been arrested, charged, tried and gaoled for, among other things, shooting at the police. Using only a drumbeat, a low piano note, a grumbling bass and a few record scratch noises, PWEI related the story of James's arrest, four-letter language and all, thumping 'Funky Drummer' through the middle of proceedings. A verse–chorus structure is provided by Brownian interjections of 'I want to get up and do my thing' and other obvious moments from 'Sex Machine' to be met by a frenetic guitar and a shout of 'Not now, James, we're busy' from the assembled ranks of PWEI. That shout gives the track its title.

The thing about 'Not Now James' that makes it so distinctive is, predictably, its energy and imagination. In fact, the whole PWEI album suggests that sampling did still have something to offer, even if the dance acts had turned it into just another technical trick. But then PWEI weren't a dance act; they were, before they started feeding disparate elements of pop into their sampler, a greasy rock band. By the late 1980s that was the least respectable thing to be in the music business; maybe that's why they felt they could still take risks. No one respected rockers then and no one could make anyone in PWEI look like a teen heart-throb. They didn't have any major hit singles to follow up. And they retained a keen sense of irony as well as a desire as keen as The JAMs had had in 1987 to push everything as far as it would go. PWEI probably wouldn't offer you a particularly lucid definition of post-modernism, but they have a much more arresting sense of what collage can achieve than most of the dance acts. And they also know that there's no point in watching pop eat itself unless the end result is to find a new dish to put on the menu.

But then PWEI were, for those who'd regarded the advent of sampling and collage as something exciting, a beacon of sanity by the end of 1989. They still sounded dangerous and different, and had quite a lot to say. They also didn't make any significant impact on the market, which meant they didn't have the great problem of mainstream follow-ups to mainstream hits, and the inevitable deterioration into tame routine. In market terms they hadn't quite ripened, so they couldn't start to rot. But after the initial excitement and novelty (in the best possible sense) Bomb the Bass, S-Express and Coldcut had turned out to be honourable disappointments. That was how their style of music seemed to have turned out. But that thought still didn't prepare anyone for the true horror of the Monster Bunny from Hell.

9 · Mix-omatosis

By the time the monstrous Jive Bunny phenomenon gripped the UK, signs of rot in the popular-music business were fairly widespread in more senses than the purely intellectual. It wasn't just that artists, managers and promoters seemed to have run out of any ideas which could run and run; more important was the simple fact that people didn't want to buy the product in anything like the same bulk which had once been the norm.

The decline of the pop single in all its formats was so acute in the late 1980s that in 1989 the British Phonographic Industry changed the rules for the award of silver, gold and platinum discs. The certified sales level for a silver single went down from 250,000 to 200,000, a gold dropped 100,000 to 400,000, and – most tellingly – the platinum level was slashed from 1 million to 600,000, a whole (new) gold disc fewer. Since 1984's six million-plus-selling singles, only one release – Jennifer Rush's 'The Power of Love' in 1985 – had gone platinum. In fact since Jennifer Rush and to the end of 1991 only one single had passed the million-sales mark – Bryan Adams's mystifyingly successful '(Everything I Do) I Do It for You', a record whose main interest in future years will surely be as a statistic rather than a piece of music.

Three years without the award of a platinum disc, even in years of relative slump, was something remarkable and, for the industry itself, alarming. Even multiple releases of individual singles in different formats (different mixes, different sleeves, collect the set and be a completist – this was a tactic particularly favoured by Iron Maiden and had helped them to make some artificially high chart debuts) were doing nothing of significance to arrest the decline of the single and, despite the fact that a lot of the marketing in the record industry has always revolved and continues to revolve around the singles chart, unless something dramatic happens in the near future, the gentle death of the single looks more or less certain. But to ensure that the platinum award for the single didn't become extinct, and to ensure equally that an industry always keen on making conspicuous awards to itself, like all branches of the entertainment world, thus validated its existence by such 'proofs' of popular success, it was necessary to make this drastic rule change so that platinum records could flow again. It was a sign of the comparatively meagre sales of singles over the years since 1985 that the 600,000 target for platinum was still a pretty stiff one, and between 1989 and 1991 only seven platinum singles were awarded (two to the same disc, the vacuous Bryan Adams phenomenon, and two to reissues).

The first of these downgraded platinum awards came nine months into 1989. It was made to a dance record which was a collage of old discs, mainly cover versions of very well-known hits of the rock 'n' roll era, making much use of digital delay, topped and tailed by an Irish showband impersonating The Glenn Miller Band playing 'In the Mood' (or, so inept was the impersonation, more probably Joe Loss, the British bandleader who appropriated 'In the Mood' in the 1940s as a signature tune). Throughout this collage, an irritating drum sound ensured that the regularity of the beat was never in doubt. The whole thing had been put together, incredibly cheaply, by two Sheffield club DJs, and had initially been something they'd done for the amusement of their own audiences. The original, unreleased, unreleasable version made use of extracts from the well-known versions of the songs featured – *echt* Glenn Miller, Elvis

Presley, Everly Brothers and so on. Copyright costs for such discs would have been so prohibitive that it was much cheaper – though still by no means free – to use cover versions, or, as in the case of the Glenn Miller tune, get someone else to do a recording and use that instead. The whole thing was cheap and, to my ears, sounded it. Several of the segues didn't work (that leading into 'Wake up Little Susie' springs to mind) and there was no sense of daring collision and juxtaposition in this, merely lack of resource. There was an equally inexpensive-looking video to promote the disc, a compilation of various bits of old film, featuring either people dancing in the rock 'n' roll era, footage of some of the stars involved or hilarious shots of planes and cars crashing (whether human lives had been lost in these moments so lovingly thrown together wasn't mentioned), many of which were subjected to the digital treatment so that they ran backwards and forwards, 'stuttering' where the music appeared to do so. To provide a sense of continuity, a crudely drawn cartoon rabbit, coloured so as to stand out from the black-and-white footage, wandered across the screen throughout the proceedings. This rabbit had a name – it was Jive Bunny.

The temporary but phenomenal ascendancy of Jive Bunny (and the Mastermixers) proved something of a flashpoint for those who cared about pop music, and a surprising number of column inches were devoted to deploring the advent of the Bunny. Some – like an article in *NME* at the end of 1989 – strained every sinew to be fair, partly I suspect out of a perverse desire to be different. But love or hate the Jive Bunny singles, it can't be denied that they permeated the public consciousness more than most other pop records of the decade, more so than many acts which out-sold them. Because of their calculated nostalgia, the Jive Bunny singles also crossed an age gap, making some mark with people who'd lost contact with pop music and pop singles. It's hard to imagine another act from the late 1980s which could be cited with relative intelligibility in a scene in a novel, as Jive Bunny was in the third of Roddy Doyle's Barrytown novels, *The Van*. In fact, that little reference speaks accurate volumes about the appeal of the Bunny: the paterfamilias, Elvis-loving Jimmy Rabitte Sr., dances round the dining table pretending to be Jive Bunny to amuse his toddler granddaughter. The nostalgic middle-aged and infants – there was Jive Bunny's constituency in a nutshell.

The constituency certainly voted enthusiastically, with the result that Jive Bunny and the Mastermixers entered the record books of UK chart statistics alongside Gerry and the Pacemakers and Frankie Goes to Hollywood, as only the third act to reach Number 1 with their first three releases. The hat-trick was achieved with more style than either of the other groups. 'Let's Party', the Jive Bunny Christmas single, entered the charts at Number 1, although the release of the Band Aid II charity single the following week made it inevitable that the Bunny would be the first to record a less impressive UK chart statistic in becoming the first act to enter the chart at the top and stay there for only a single week (a feat emulated, to date, by Queen and U2). When the fourth Jive Bunny single was released the following March, chart statisticians and anyone with the slightest interest in pop music waited with bated breath for the record books to be rewritten. The relief when the fourth Bunny single transformed Jive Bunny into Jive Turkey at a single stroke was almost audible.

Coming in the age of sampling technology, the Jive Bunny singles are on the one hand a terrible example of how low the whole process can sink. They're the ultimate proof that something with revolutionary potential if used properly can be bent to producing the least challenging results. The technology in use, and the whole DJ connection, apparently linked 'Swing the Mood', 'That's What I Like' and 'Let's Party' to Bomb the Bass, Coldcut or S-Express. Those acts may have turned out to be disappointments, but it's scarcely fair to draw direct comparisons between them and what they set out to do and Jive Bunny. Because really the Jive Bunny phenomenon was at root a throwback to 1981, to 'Stars on 45'.

But such high-handed, highbrow moaning coupled with the 1981 parallel really won't do. The Jive Bunny singles throw an interesting light on British popular culture, on a facet of it which is always present somewhere, and deserves consideration as such. For the baby–grandparent constituency referred to above, Jive Bunny was their first, perhaps their only brush with the technology which had got those of us with more intellectual ambitions for popular music so excited over the preceding two or three years. The nerve which the Bunny so precisely hit was similar, but much more vital than that struck by the handclap craze of 1981.

The medley singles of 1981 had been, for the most part, specially recorded discs. With samplers around such effort was no longer technically necessary, although the intransigence of one record company meant that a re-recording of 'I Wish it Could Be Christmas Every Day' was needed for 'Let's Party'. As with the 1981 medley boom, the Jive Bunny records were designed to exude an air of partying and good times, of enjoyment provoked by an earlier, more innocent golden age. The apparent crassness was perhaps part of the point. No one ever got a platinum disc trying to appeal to the self-appointed discerning pundits. The appeal was strikingly similar to that of the endless stream of TV situation comedies co-written by David Croft – *Dad's Army*, *It Ain't Half Hot, Mum*, *Hi-de-Hi*, *'Allo, 'Allo* and *You Rang, M'Lord*. Apart from the seaside-postcard humour and complete lack of intention to use comedy as social critique, each of these programmes struck at least part of its chord with the public by being set in some previous time whose memory could be easily stylized. For all the comic bumbling of the buffoons in the Home Guard, *Dad's Army* (a programme which still draws a respectable audience when episodes are rerun almost twenty years after their original transmission) reinforces the decent, safe values of the Second World War when Britons 'all pulled together' and enjoyed 'their finest hour'. Even though historians have proved with relish and authority that this image is almost certainly a myth, that the threat of invasion was as much a Government-propagated myth as a real danger, that looting was rife in the blitz, that morale almost collapsed in 1940 and again in London in 1944 – for all this, the image purveyed by *Dad's Army* is the one that most people will recognize as real, even those people who were there at the time and might be thought to know different. In all these childish programmes set back in time, even in the dubious *'Allo, 'Allo* with its comic Gestapo officers, there is a reinforcement of innocence, of good old-fashioned values. The Croft collaboration most like the Jive Bunny records is *Hi-de-Hi*, a threnody to the old-style holiday camps and set around the turn of the 1950s to the 1960s – the good old days of rock 'n' roll before the liberal 1960s let things get completely out of hand, and when the height of people's aspirations for relaxation was to spend two weeks imprisoned in an organization run along the lines of the average 'civilized' POW camp.

Such nostalgia has always exercised a very real fascination upon the British, and it has always manifested itself very strongly in the records which the public takes to its heart. Before the advent of house music and the boom of the 'new' dance music in 1987 and 1988, as we've seen, there was a tendency for the charts to be clogged up with elderly reissues, whose reason for succeeding was sometimes evident (the great power of the annual Levi's adverts had propelled at least four singles into the Top 10 by March 1987) and sometimes mystifying (good record though it be, there seemed no earthly reason why record buyers should be seized with a sudden hunger for Jackie Wilson's 'Reet Petite', even at Christmas). Although the supremacy of Stock, Aitken and Waterman on the one hand and the apparent appetite for the new dance music and for sample-based records gave the superficial impression that this trend receded at least a little in 1988 and 1989, the evidence in fact points the other way completely. Take the Top 10 singles for 1988. Leading the pack, out-selling everything else that year in only five weeks (and that's a significant comment on sales over the rest of the year) was Cliff Richard, himself essentially a nostalgic article, peddling in 'Mistletoe and Wine' an image of Christmas as inauthentic as a Hollywood cockney accent; second was, admittedly, a Coldcut production, Yazz's 'The Only Way is Up', but this was simply a remake of a 1960s song; third was 'I Should Be So Lucky', a classic of tacky SAW pop but inevitably boosted by Kylie Minogue's status as TV soap star (as many of her later hits weren't, to be fair); fourth was the inevitable duet of Ms Minogue and her on-screen paramour Jason Donovan, a syrupy affair by anyone's standards and whose sole *raison d'être* was to allow SAW to cash in on the viewing figures for the Charlene–Scott nuptials in *Neighbours*; fifth came Tiffany's 'I Think We're Alone Now', another upbeat revamping of a 1960s number; sixth, Glenn Medeiros, teen heart-throb for a moment that summer, whose entire looks, personal style and image wouldn't have looked out of place in The Osmonds circa 1974 (while his hit, 'Nothing's Gonna Change My Love for You', made the average Barry Manilow song sound as wilfully avant-garde as Stockhausen); seventh, Phil Collins's remake of another 1960s song, 'A Groovy Kind of Love' (itself a tune culled from a classical piano piece), the love theme from Mr Collins's first major film, *Buster*, a nostalgic, heartwarming story of train robbery in the days when villains were cuddly like those nice Kray Brothers; eighth, The Hollies' 'He Ain't Heavy, He's My Brother', originally a hit in 1969, and reissued to coincide with its use in a TV lager advert; ninth, Wet Wet Wet's charity revamp (designed to sound identical to the original) of The Beatles' 'With a Little Help from My

Friends'. The Top 10 was completed by Womack and Womack's 'Teardrops', far and away the best single of the ten, and the only one belonging almost entirely in 1988 (even though the Womacks themselves were among the oldest of these acts). Given that the next two on the list were Kylie Minogue's assault on the 1962 track 'The Loco-motion' and Robin Beck's 'First Time', the theme from a Coca-Cola advertisement designed to imply that Coke (the drink) is an essential adjunct to losing one's virginity, 'Teardrops' stood out like a beacon in the darkest night.

Except that while 'Teardrops' might in one (perhaps elitist) sense be described as the only one of those discs 'belonging entirely in 1988', in another sense all of them, 'Teardrops' least of all perhaps, are very representative of their time. Nostalgia and escapism in their various forms were taking a stronger and stronger grasp on the public imagination, so much so that no advertisement on small or large screen was considered effective without its nostalgia-provoking hit from yesteryear. Very often, over the top of the nostalgic sound would be placed an equally nostalgic image. All of the Levi's ads seemed to be set in some kind of 1950s American Deep South backwater. As the purpose of an advertisement is to sell a product and to communicate a message, and no firm would be inclined to throw too much money away on ineffective advertising however impressive it might look within the industry, the prevalence of this style (to date largely unbroken) must be assumed to have hit a rich vein in the public imagination. People want the past – provided that it's nicely conditioned and sanitized. For example, a long-running TV and cinema campaign for Southern Comfort depicted a charming story of a poor white boy, nicely dressed up, taking his attractive black girlfriend to an exclusively black bar in a small town somewhere (to judge from the paddle steamer in the closing shot of the ad's second version) along the Mississippi. The use of the 1950s hit 'Why do Fools Fall in

Love?' performed at its most doo-wop seemed to place the action somewhere in the good old days of the 1950s, although the principal actor had a very mid-1980s spiky haircut and the leading lady could have come straight out of *The Cosby Show*. The original ad had to be cleaned up a bit. The shot of the couple dancing and the young man's hands straying over his inamorata's buttocks was felt to be a bit strong, so instead they took a dawn walk down to the river to gaze lovingly at a paddle steamer while engaging in a chaste side-by-side embrace, altogether much more wholesome. But it was terribly cute and affecting, ignoring the simple fact that in the 1950s Deep South either the entire black community would have beaten the youth to pulp, or the white community would have lynched him and his girlfriend. Sanitized nostalgia, with a theme vaguely in keeping with the product.

It was this soap- and nostalgia-dominated world that the Jive Bunny singles managed to exploit so brilliantly. Compared even with Frankie Goes to Hollywood, the shelf life of the Bunny turned out to be extraordinarily brief, but the whole Jive Bunny campaign seemed designed to maximize its opportunities within a short lifespan. Of the three acts which have managed the hat-trick in their first three releases, Gerry and the Pacemakers achieved the feat in just over seven months ('How Do You Do It?' was released in March 1963 and their third hit, 'You'll Never Walk Alone' reached Number 1 at the end of October). They had three more substantial hits, their last being 'Ferry Across the Mersey' in January 1965. Frankie Goes to Hollywood took nearly eleven months to get the hat-trick, racking up fifteen weeks at Number 1 along the way, as well as one of the longest-running chart singles of the 1980s ('Relax' had in fact grovelled around the middle reach of the Top 75 for several weeks before it suddenly took off in New Year 1984.) Jive Bunny first entered the charts in mid-July 1989, and more or less exactly five months later 'Let's Party' hit the Number 1 spot. Between the beginning of August and the middle of December, only three other acts (Black Box, Lisa Stansfield and New Kids on the Block) had Number 1 singles. You don't manage that without tapping into the *Zeitgeist* fairly effectively.

It's important to understand the extent to which the public taste was dominated by nostalgia at this point. There's always the suspicion that when pop music is dominated by elderly records and songs it simply embodies the fact that there's nothing new under the sun and nothing left to be discovered and therefore the predominance of the old has nothing to do with what's going on in the popular consciousness or anything like it. The grip of soap opera had proved to be especially strong over UK audiences in the 1980s too and soap opera always represents a kind of nostalgia, even if it's simply nostalgia for a non-existent preferable present rather than a departed (and also probably non-existent) past. For the first part of the decade it was the glamorous American soaps with their high lifestyles, increasingly implausible plots and fabulous wardrobes which had held sway. *Dallas* and *Dynasty* had put power-dressing on the agenda, and their rich anti-heroes (or, in the case of Joan Collins's *Dynasty* character, anti-heroine) to some extent helped set the tone for the acquisitive 1980s. As these programmes fell from favour, the more 'realist' British and Australian soaps grabbed the viewers' attentions. *EastEnders* provided grit and controversy and then *Neighbours* attracted a whole new generation as its audience. Where the American programmes had provided a fairy-tale dream which palled when the plots became absurd – and, anyway, there was our own inimitable Royal Family to take over the role of glamour models (and the popular attitude towards certain members of that family tells its own story about changes in popular sentiment as the affluent 1980s turned sour) – the homegrown products offered idealized home lives where family was all important and where, whatever grisly events might occur, right would triumph in some form. The

East End was, apparently, filled with loyal, closely knit communities, as was that amorphous suburb of Salford/Manchester housing *Coronation Street*. The Australian soaps achieved their particular hold on their particular audience by writing peculiarly mundane plots around peculiarly mundane characters and especially concentrating on the teenage members of these idealized families. Actually, if you look at the comings and goings in most of these 'close-knit' families, you realize that they exhibit a lack of stability to unhinge the most phlegmatic of people, but that never seems to matter too much. The especial appeal of the cheap Australian artefacts (above all *Neighbours*, a programme immensely tedious to most people over the age of twenty-three) to the younger audience could be seen in the careers of Kylie and Jason as pop stars, careers amazingly long lived by the standards of the day.

All such theorizing goes some way towards explaining the immense and sudden success of Jive Bunny, but it can't tell the full story. Pre-packaged nostalgia has been an especial hallmark of British popular taste over the last half decade or so, but the Bunny singles lacked a great deal of the gloss of much of this advertising-inspired psychological direction. It seems that every so often a product grabs the attention of the market and holds it effectively, almost ruthlessly, and the Jive Bunny singles simply took hold the way that *EastEnders* did in late 1986, *Neighbours* in late 1988 (the time of the Charlene–Scott wedding featuring Kylie and Jason; one wonders how many of the viewers knew the difference between the fictional couple and their real life counterparts) and *The Darling Buds of May* in 1991. At the time of writing it's unsure how long the sensationalism surrounding *Darling Buds* will last, but its appeal, in so far as it can be analysed, seems very similar to that of Jive Bunny: it's set back in time; it depicts life as fun, jokes and laughter; it's an impossibly idealized kind of nostalgia for old days very few people ever enjoyed.

Will Pop Eat Itself?

Of course, with the late 1980s accustoming more and more people to taking life in 'sound bites', the Jive Bunny singles offered a whole new sound-bite approach to nostalgia. Crucial moments highlighted without the surrounding context, the hook lines and catch-phrases without any of the build-up – these are perhaps cynical ways to describe the 'sound bite'. The phrase attained particular prominence in Britain around the time of the 1987 General Election, a contextual setting for the word underlined by its crucial nature in the 1988 American Presidential Election. The sound bite was the ideal weapon of the image-maker, of the advertising slogan man. The sound bite is the thing that will stick, the thing that's much more important than logical or consistent argument. British politics had been heading that way from the mid-1970s onwards, as Margaret Thatcher realized the power of the photo-opportunity, indeed of proper advertising. The impact of advertising agency Saatchi and Saatchi on the British political scene has been much discussed and analysed. Suffice to say here that by 1987 photo-opportunities were a traditional part of the game which even the Labour Party was trying to play. Sound bites were the logical soundtrack to this kind of political 'debate'. Slogans have, of course, always been an important part of politics, but since the late 1970s and especially in the late 1980s the idea that there might be any intellectual or analytical content to a speech organized around a few good sloganizing sound bites disappeared from common currency. The British had always liked to sneer somewhat at this tendency in American Presidential campaigns. It's hard to imagine how contests involving intellectual titans like Gerald Ford or Ronald Reagan could involve too much detailed analysis of events, although Reagan's inability to speak coherently about anything whatsoever unless prepared with a pre-written script took the level of American debate to a new low – he was so incoherent in his first TV 'debate' with Walter Mondale in the 1984 campaign that rumours of senility began to fly around. But the image-makers, the High Priests of the sound bite and the photo-opportunity had ensured that this was to be the coin of British politics. It's hard to see this changing in the very near future.

So to a market inured to sound bites, along came Jive Bunny with sound-bite nostalgia. At about the same time there was a great vogue for 'Party' LPs which mixed together vast numbers of 1950s and 1960s hit singles – or, more accurately, the danceable and singalong bits – for consumption at parties. All your favourite old records without the boring bits; life in the sound-bite era; the high-tech medley records. Without the technology of sampling it wouldn't have been possible to recycle quite so much quite so quickly. The Bunny's full title as a group, Jive Bunny and the Mastermixers, gave a nod of acknowledgement in the direction of the technology. And, as we shall see, the Bunny gave the green light to a whole new breed of medley record – the euphemistically titled 'megamix', which might in several cases more accurately have been called 'flogging a dead horse'.

The Bunny sold a lot of singles (comparatively, by the scale of the market anyway) in 1989, but just missed out on having the year's best seller. In thus missing out, 'Swing the Mood' also narrowly missed a foothold in the Top 20 of the Decade (pop-music decades, of course, run inaccurately from 0 to 9). One place above 'Swing the Mood' at Number 20 in this list was the best-selling single of 1989, Black Box's 'Ride on Time'. In its way, this hypnotically simple disc (again the word 'song' seems inappropriate, not so much because of any fault in its structure, but because lyrical content was minimal even by comparison with the less-verbal sample-based hit records of 1988) has proved something of a watershed, something of a small trailblazer.

To begin with, 'Ride on Time' heralded the arrival of a new Italian sound in the centre of the UK market, and marked to an extent the beginning of a general European invasion which was still making its presence felt in 1991. In a way, this 'new' Italian house style was just a new way of clothing the old Eurobeat and high energy so popular in 1984 and 1985, and which had been enjoying a rather surprising renaissance in the shape of The London Boys (who were neither from London nor young enough to qualify as boys) and their Top 5 singles 'Requiem' and 'London Nights'. The Italian house music was (still is, in fact) characterized by an upbeat tempo over quite a complex musical arrangement. This contrasted with the next and perhaps more successful European import, the Belgian and Dutch dance music which grew from Technotronic in late 1989 to 2 Unlimited in 1991, more sparse in timbre and more electronically based in its sound. The Italian style, apart from its heavy(ish) arrangement, was also distinctive for the prominence it gave to the piano, something Madonna, always astute when it came to spotting a bandwagon to leap on, made use of in her 1990 single 'Vogue'.

The basic elements of these Italian dance records could be found in 'Ride on Time' and Black Box's two immediate follow-ups ('I Don't Know Anybody Else' and 'Everybody Everybody') as well as Starlight's 'Numero Uno', Gino Latino's 'Welcome' and other discs picking up on that format (The 49ers' 'Touch Me', The Mixmaster's 'Grand Piano', even FPI Project's revamp of Odyssey's 'Going Back to My Roots'), all releases between late summer in 1989 and spring 1990. What made 'Ride on Time' stand out from the rest wasn't just that it was the first to draw the public's attention to the formula. 'Numero Uno' was popular at exactly the same time, and The Beatmasters' collaboration with Betty Boo, 'Hey DJ I Can't Dance to That Music You're Playing', wasn't so far removed stylistically from the Italian sound with the old Martha and the Vandellas track 'I Can't Dance to that Music You're Playing', whose chorus formed the 'chorus' section of The Beatmasters' record, having a very full sound. It was the uncredited vocal sample which made the disc a success, the soaring vocal of Lolleatta Hollaway, as taken from a Dan Hartman single called 'Love Sensation'. That vocal, along with the first two Jive Bunny singles, formed the soundtrack of the latter end of 1991 (so much so that the 'You're right on time' hook which sort of gave the Black Box disc its title was used in a 1990 French and Saunders sketch in which a would-be trendy, rapidly fading hippy kept singing the line to try and impress her studious and organized daughter).

But things were being sampled so far and so fast and so frequently by this time that the Italian producers who consti-tuted Black Box (also masquerading as Starlight of aforemen-tioned 'Numero Uno' fame) found themselves participating not merely in a success, but in a farce. Ms Hollaway was less than pleased to discover herself appearing uncredited on a record which enjoyed international success, with no remuneration coming her way at all. By this stage of the game, the principle of paying off the 'samplee' for a fixed sum either before release or on the record's attaining some kind of success was already established. But when the producers were completely unaware of what they were actually sampling, it became somewhat difficult to get the agreement of the featured vocalist or to give her a credit. And this was the case with 'Ride on Time'. The producers had sampled a sample, unaware – until Lolleatta Hollaway's righteous (and justified) indignation was reported to them – that they were tangling with either Hollaway or Hart-man. As without her it's highly doubtful that 'Ride on Time' would have had quite the impact it did, her claim on the Italian outfit was unassailable. The situation was, as I've indicated, a farce; unwitting sampling of a sample, pop not merely eating itself, but endlessly regurgitating the same morsels. And, like the phrase 'Pump up the Volume', like '*Uno, dos, tres, quatro,*' like the deep-voiced 'Oh yeah' finding its way on to absolutely everything from critically respectable tracks like J. T. and the

Big Family's 'Moments in Soul' to the appalling Bombalurina, Lolleatta Hollaway would keep on coming back – although in future with the appropriate credit.

'Ride on Time' fell out of the Top 30 at the beginning of December 1989. Such was the decline in Black Box's fortunes and the need to exploit the following wind after their slight revival with a (pretty straightforward) remake of Earth, Wind and Fire's 'Fantasy' that almost exactly a year later, in January 1991, their single 'The Total Mix' hit its dizzy peak of Number 15 in the UK charts. This small success coincided with the last (to date) Jive Bunny Top 20 single, 'The Crazy Party Mixes'. If one can argue such tortuous comparisons, the Bunny single could be said to be the more 'original' of the two, even though it stuck to the tried-and-tested and now conspicuously less successful Jive Bunny formula. At least they were still stitching together other people's discs to create a 'good party atmosphere' (I can't detect any subtler purpose in 'The Crazy Party Mixes'). Black Box were already reduced to regurgitating their own material in techno-medley form, following the examples of Alexander O'Neal (who had been peddling material from his 1987 album *Hearsay* in one mix or another for over three years), Bobby Brown and Technotronic, and thus following the example from nine years earlier of The Hollies, Star Sound, Lobo and the Royal Philharmonic Orchestra.

This neo-medley bandwagon even attracted the Brixton-based Snap in March 1991, and here was rich pop irony. In mid-March 1990, the fourth Jive Bunny single (imaginatively entitled 'That Sounds Good to Me' and leaning heavily on The Blues Brothers' 'Everybody Needs Somebody to Love', thus inadvertently helping – along with the sell-through video release of the cult *The Blues Brothers* film – to give that song a somewhat belated boost in sales) entered the charts at Number 4; admittedly a less-impressive debut than the instant chart-topping of the Christmas 'Let's Party', but equalling the second Bunny release and thus giving the single the appearance of being poised to hit the top the following week. This would have rewritten chart history, and there was a surprising amount of heat generated in anticipation of the event. But, to quite a few people's surprise, it didn't happen. The next week, Beats International's 'Dub Be Good to Me', a rewrite of Jam and Lewis's 1984 S.O.S. Band's 'Just Be Good to Me', colliding the vocal line with the bass line of The Clash's 'The Guns of Brixton', stayed at the top and the Jive Bunny single didn't improve its position. That sealed its fate in any case, but leaping over it the next week came the first of Snap's singles, a good example of a powerful, contemporary sample-based dance track, 'The Power', made as distinctive by Jocelyn Brown's sampled vocal yelps of 'I've got the power' as 'Ride on Time' was by Lolleatta Holloway's originally less-acknowledged contribution. 'The Power' had come almost entirely though the clubs, through white-label versions eventually forcing an official release which made Number 1 in a mere fortnight. It was original, fresh, instantly memorable and had the added distinction (slightly erroneously ascribed if you look at the statistics) of having saved the UK from the terror of the Bunny. But a year and three Top 10 singles later it was megamix time – a sad reflection of the demands of business and the market.

Snap could hardly be said to have become completely clapped out by the time their megamix appeared, an accusation which could perhaps with more justification have been thrown at dead-horse floggers like Alexander O'Neal and Bobby Brown. Just as the quick decline in Black Box's career and the apparent fall-off in the sales and content of Technotronic singles could be said to justify a 'one last fling at the market and grab it' attitude. But the megamix mentality had got such an effective grip on the end of the market producing dance music that a megamix medley (greatest hits so far) seemed to have become *de rigueur* by early 1991.

And it wasn't just producers (or bands as some liked to pretend they were) recycling their own material in this new megamix boom. Discs such as 'The Brits 1990' and Latino Rave's 'Deep Heat '89' were merely in one form or another compilations of other people's recent hits. And the fact that people went out and bought these patchwork-quilt dance medleys meant simply that people wanted them. The Latino Rave single coincided with Christmas, which might explain its appeal, but 'The Brits' was a Top 3 hit in March. Perhaps its charitable purpose was partly responsible for its sales. But then the singles market has become increasingly mystifying as sales have declined. After all, despite all these technically proficient, dance-orientated megamixes, it was 'Unchained Melody', a twenty-five-year-old recording of a thirty-five-year-old song, sounding as creaky as its years (with not a handclap or a drum machine in sight), which outsold everything else in 1990. Which is hardly evidence of the rampant health of the pop single as a sales unit. Ripe and ripe, then rot and rot.

10 · And the Law Won (but the Jury is Still Out)

Sampling is theft. If you want to be a complete jurisprudential purist about it, that three-word sentence sums it up. Any piece of a recording, however small, belongs to the performer, to the songwriter and to the recording company that issued it. Most musicians and producers who've ever fed a break or a beat into a digital sampler without first obtaining permission from the record company's various representatives (lawyers and Artistes and Repertoire people) as well as from the songwriter and the performer have been breaking copyright law on at least two counts. Copyright subsists, to use the technical verb here, in both the song *qua* song – the copyright which the song's writer or writers own – and the recording *qua* mechanical object – the copyright owned by the record company that issued the disc in the first place. Obviously recording copyright extends to cover such media as film, video, television and radio. In 1991 a single called 'Rhondda Rant Rap' was strangled by a BBC injunction because of its unauthorized use of material owned by BBC Radio. There was additional spice in this case because the material, part of an interview for Radio Four's news programme *The World at One* hadn't been broadcast, consisting as it did of Labour Party leader Neil Kinnock completely losing his cool in the face of mild questioning from anchorman James Naughtie.

But such a fearsome weapon as the injunction is rare in the annals of legal history involving sampling. Doubtless even the BBC wouldn't have gone in with all guns blazing against

'Rhondda Rant Rap' if it hadn't been for the sensitivity of the material and the implicit suggestion that someone inside the building had leaked confidential material. Apart from this, the most notable attempt to block a sample by injunction is Stock, Aitken and Waterman's action against M/A/R/R/S in September 1987, after a radio edit of 'Pump up the Volume' incorporated a brief snatch of the SAW self-credited rare groove spoof 'Roadblock'. Dave Dorrell, one of the masterminds behind M/A/R/R/S, is on record as wondering whether or not SAW would have noticed this sample if it hadn't been unwisely boasted about. This attempt at an injunction ultimately failed, and to this day there are two schools of thought as to what the real purpose of this legal skirmish was. Stock, Aitken and Waterman have always maintained, doubtless will always maintain, that there was a point of principle at stake here, that samples should always be cleared with the owners of whatever copyright was being contravened before use. Cynics tend to point out, however, that SAW didn't bother seeking an injunction until 'Pump up the Volume' reached Number 2 in the charts and that the record at Number 1 just happened to be Rick Astley's 'Never Gonna Give You Up' – a record written and produced by Stock, Aitken and Waterman. Whether or not the attempted injunction was responsible for delaying the M/A/R/R/S single at Number 2 for a second week is debatable. The Rick Astley single was the best-seller of the year and therefore out-selling everything else by miles for most of its run at the top. In any event, the matter was settled out of court.

Actual court cases in which songwriters – of all genres – are accused of plagiarism are not at all uncommon. Some of the most celebrated involve Al Jolson versus the estate of Giacomo Puccini; Andrew Lloyd Webber and an obscure private songwriter convinced he had provided material for at least one of the successful Lloyd Webber musicals; George Harrison's 'My Sweet Lord' was adjudged – quite understandably – to owe quite a lot to The Chiffons' 'He's So Fine'. In a bizarre reversal of the way these things normally work, Neil Tennant and Chris Lowe won damages from Jonathan King and the News International Group (the Murdoch paper chain including the *Sun* where King's column appeared) when his assertion that The Pet Shop Boys' second Number 1, 'It's a Sin', was plagiarized from Cat Stevens's song 'Wild World' was deemed absolute nonsense by a jury. King tried to prove his point to an indifferent and far from wild world by re-recording the Stevens song in a Pet Shop Boys-style arrangement. In most cases like this the jury is asked a more complex question than it might at first appear: is there a difference between melodic similarity and plagiarism? 'It's a Sin' has lines of melody which do bear a resemblance when written down to parts of 'Wild World', but that doesn't necessarily mean that any 'cribbing' was going on at either a conscious or an unconscious level. Once again, context is deeply important, the context of musical texture and arrangement. The jury in the Tennant/Lowe v. King case must have been quite musically astute, given their sensible and sensitive verdict. There's a world – a galaxy – of difference between the spare paranoia of the Stevens song and the lush, hysterical, bare-faced, confessional, lapsed-Catholic guilt of the Tennant and Lowe composition.

There are countless cases involving plagiarism or alleged plagiarism that have actually come to court. Sampling is a different matter. To date no case of breach of copyright involving sampling has reached court in the UK. To date every case of breach of copyright involving sampling in the UK has been settled out of court. I was rather surprised to discover this fact, but it was certainly the state of affairs at the end of 1991. Indeed, in late 1991 even the case which had seemed most likely to reach court and thus produce some kind of definitive ruling – and perhaps some guideline about awards to be made in such cases, although this point was of secondary interest – failed to do so.

The particular interest in the case which failed to reach court and was settled 'to the mutual satisfaction' of the parties concerned was the brevity of the sample involved, a 'mere' eight notes from a Hyperion disc of compositions by the medieval religious composer Abbess Hildegard of Bingen (the disc being called, after a tribute paid to Hildegard, *A Feather on the Breath of God*). These eight notes had featured prominently in The Beloved's 1989 release 'The Sun Rising'. Doubtless Hyperion's case would have revolved around the contention that the contribution of their Hildegard of Bingen disc gave The Beloved's single its distinctive quality. The case to be put forward by East West, the WEA subsidiary, was that the sample was 'too brief to constitute a copyright issue'. The matter had got as far as a preliminary hearing, at which the judge, Hugh Laddie QC, indicated that he had 'some sympathy' with East West's viewpoint, although he was none the less 'prepared to allow the matter to go to full trial'. In the end, though, Hyperion backed down, aware that unsuccessful litigation – or even successful litigation which didn't come up with a large enough award and full payment of costs – might be cripplingly expensive. Hyperion is a small, Oxford-based record company specializing in classical music, especially in certain types of early music. Its reputation in its own field is extremely high, not least for its remarkable project with Graham Johnson, a thirty-six CD edition of the complete *lieder* of Franz Schubert, each disc using a different singer, the whole designed to be completed to coincide with the Schubert bicentenary in 1997. It had been thought that Hyperion's owner was unwilling to be bought off – as most plaintiffs in cases involving sampling have been – as he felt there was a serious principle at stake. In the end the prospect of taking on the might of WEA may have proved just too daunting, especially after the judge's intitial indication of 'sympathy'. Eventually the Schubert Edition will prove to be of more lasting significance to global culture than the poaching of eight notes by The Beloved. Indeed, the sample may even have won the Abbess Hildegard some new and unlikely admirers.

None the less, the failure of this case to come to court meant that no definitive UK legal precedent was set establishing whether size is or isn't important. Another matter which remains to be clearly defined is that of 'recognizability' – whether a defence can be made against breach of copyright by clear indication that the sample could not normally be recognized. Setting aside the question which would immediately strike someone who isn't an expert in the finer and more arcane points of law: how on earth do you recognize something which isn't recognizable in the first place? It has been claimed that there is a ruling that recognizability isn't an issue, that 'quantity and quality' are the more significant elements in this matter. Or, as one lawyer writing to the trade paper *Music Week* put it, 'whether the sample is a copy of a substantial part of the sound recording from which it is taken'. That word 'substantial' could mean several things in this instance. After all, however small a part of something you may wish to appropriate, the chances are that if it's worth using it is, in the context of the song (or other recorded piece), of 'substantial' importance.

A new and added urgency entered this argument in January 1992 when finally the first significant legal adjudication on sampling was made. A federal judge in the USA declared quite baldly that sampling was 'theft' when announcing a decision against Biz Markie and the entire Warner WEA organization concerning the use of a sample from Gilbert O'Sullivan's 'Alone Again (Naturally)' in a track on the album *I Need a Haircut*. The immediate flippant response that you shouldn't waste too much sympathy on anyone who wants to perpetuate Gilbert O'Sullivan's music in any way, shape or form should be dismissed. The same federal judge referred the case to the United States Attorney-General for consideration whether there should be subsequent criminal prosecution. That aspect immediately rang

alarm bells. Even in the wake of the potentially sampler-
athetic preliminaries to the Hyperion case, British record
producers and distributors saw the spectre of Section 107 of the
Copyright Act 1988 raised before their eyes. That section is the
tough one designed to tackle piracy. The prospect of sampling
being placed legally on a par with piracy could have disastrous
repercussions for many pop acts and producers.

Still, that adjudication hasn't been made yet in this country;
quite possibly it never will be. A lot of people would have a lot
to lose, and it's hard to think of a record company whose hands
are entirely 'clean' of sampling. Let he who is without sin cast
the first stone. And until the Biz Markie business, the industry
seemed to have got a fairly standard procedure sorted out.

It's fair to say that when sampling first started, both in its
digital form and in the more 'primitive' scratch mixing of rap
artists, that an awful lot of it went unnoticed, especially where
a beat or a bass line was well hidden by electronic distortion or
just clever manual manipulation. Slowed down, speeded up and
mixed in with a whole load of other effects, a brief snatch of
something might easily become unrecognizable.

Likewise in the early days of sampling and scratching, when
much of it was done on shoestring expenditure and resultant
recordings were made for small companies and distributed
through independent cartels, there was a tendency just to use
the samples, release the record and hope that the 'samplee' (or
their record company, agent or lawyer) simply wouldn't find
out. This was certainly the 'groove-raiding' attitude espoused
by The Justified Ancients of Mu Mu. 'Don't Take Five (Take
What You Want)' was, as we've seen, their motto. Their story,
already recounted here, was one of continual trouble, but the
publicity didn't do them any harm. It's worth emphasizing that
the Abba sample which led to the destruction of their *1987*
album was as much resented for its context in a radically political
song alongside The Sex Pistols' anarchy as for the simple fact of

its use. Context is important in these legal matters too.

The days when a record using a sample would simply be released on to the market in the hope that no one would notice are long gone. In the vast majority of cases now releases of records are delayed until all the samples have been cleared and some agreement reached between the artist and record company issuing and the artist and record company being sampled. Sometimes the delay can be quite lengthy, especially where the samples are many and obscure. The 1991 release of De La Soul's second album *De La Soul is Dead* had to be held back for several months as every sample was scrupulously and meticulously cleared for use (in such cases, you'll usually find that each sample is also scrupulously and meticulously credited in the accompanying details). I can't help feeling that that honourable delay didn't help the album's reception when it finally did appear. Only when you get to Jackson or Madonna proportions can delay be a positive advantage in the release of new material. The De La Soul iron had cooled distinctly by the time *De La Soul is Dead* reached the shops.

There are, broadly, four ways in which sampling artists and their record companies tend to settle with their 'victims'. The most common, especially when a sample is cleared in advance of release, tends to be a lump-sum payment. This can vary depending upon the length of the sample, the extent and 'consequence' of its use (is it an integral part of the new track?), and whether the track in which the sample occurs is a potential hit single or a track which will lie forever dormant on an album without much exposure (again varying according to how successful the album is likely to be). The advantage for the 'samplee' with this settlement is that it represents a definite payment, dependent in no way upon the actual subsequent performance of the disc when it reaches the shops. The single or album can be the monster turkey of all time, but the 'samplee' still profits from it.

The second way, with an obvious potential disadvantage, is to settle for an agreed royalty on the sale of the single or album. This option might be worth taking where it's obvious that there's a huge hit in the offing, or if the track using the sample has already proved to be a great success, but the compensation to the 'samplee' depends upon public taste. Settlement for royalty would clearly be of more use when attempting to reach agreement over the use of a sample released without clearance.

The third possibility at first sight seems quite similar to the second but is, in fact, more likely to prove profitable. This is to demand a percentage of the overall income from all sources (including sale of the video). Although still dependent to an extent upon popular success, this can prove quite lucrative because fairly steep percentages can be exacted for relatively small samples, especially where the sample forms a 'substantial' (that word again) part of the new song. Thus Johnny Marr got something around 25 per cent (exact figures are always undisclosed and a subject of speculation) of the income from Soho's Top 10 hit 'Hippy Chick' because of its appropriation of the distinctive guitar introduction to The Smiths' 'How Soon is Now?', while Vanilla Ice is said to have been forced into surrendering 50 per cent of the income from 'Ice Ice Baby' to Queen and David Bowie.

The fourth option isn't as extensively used as the other three, as it really caters only for artists whose careers are either dead, dying or were never alive in the first place. It has been known for 'samplees' to settle for a new recording contract of their own with the 'offending' company, offering the chance to release a record (or a series of records). It's not been uncommon for sampling to resuscitate interest in the back catalogues of sampled artists, but to resuscitate or kick-start an entire career would require something very special.

These four modes of settlement have always been reached 'out of court' as the newspaper jargon has it. Indeed even cases where the offending disc has been destroyed, as with The JAMs' *1987* and Biz Markie's *I Need a Haircut* have been 'settled out of court'. Despite the technical requirement to receive the artist's blessing on top of that of the recording and publishing companies holding the copyright of anything which is being sampled, not all such settlements necessarily involve the sampled artist(s) at any stage of the proceedings other than the cheque-receiving at the very end, although there are performers who like to retain a personal input in decisions about samples of their work. James Brown, for example, ever the astute self-managing businessman, retains a personal right of veto, which must have created a lot of extra work for him over the past few years (as well as generating him a healthy extra unlooked-for income). Samples of James Brown are so frequent that two members of Polydor's American legal department devote their entire life to no other pursuit than tracking down James Brown samples, offering their opinions on the 'substantiality' of the sample and seeking the great man's view on each one individually. This office is said to have worked out a sliding scale of fees for samples, depending mainly on length.

It's also not unknown for an artist to be happy about a sample only to find that the recording company blocks its use regardless of his or her view. When Jive Bunny decided to compile a Christmas single based around 1970s Christmas hits, their thoughts naturally turned to Wizzard's 1973 single 'I Wish it Could Be Christmas Every Day'. They approached Roy Wood, the mastermind behind Wizzard and the song's writer, arranger, producer and everything else, and he was more than happy for the extended sample to go ahead. EMI, for whom Wood/Wizzard had made the original recording, refused permission. In this case, the solution was relatively straightforward, and one that the Jive Bunny outfit had used before. Wood re-recorded the song to provide a version to which the question of mechanical copyright of the recording no longer pertained. The first

Jive Bunny single had resorted to a similar ruse to get around the problem of sampling Glenn Miller recordings. An Irish showband which specialized in reproducing the Glenn Miller sound re-recorded 'In the Mood' and the Mastermixers used that instead. This is the technique which the Stock, Aitken and Waterman organization PWL uses as well. If they hear anything they want to sample they simply record their own exact copy and throw that into the mix.

It was in early 1990 that the major record companies managed to impose the obligation on all recording artists to identify and clear all samples before release (although this shifting of the onus hasn't stopped the record companies being the subject of actions, as both the Hyperion and Biz Markie cases have shown). Most record companies now stipulate in their artists' contracts that if a recording is issued without copyright clearance and, as a result, money has to be paid out in compensation, then that money will be deducted entirely from the artists' royalties. It's fair to say now that it would be almost impossible for a sample to escape unnoticed if a record is successful, and for most artists it simply isn't worth the hassle of trying to get away with it. However, some still try and do just that, and taking samples from ever more unlikely and eclectic sources is one way of trying to 'get one over' the system. 808 State imagined that no one would care about their sample of the theme from the movie *The Big Country* on their 1990 hit with MC Tunes, 'The Only Rhyme that Bites'. They were, of course, wrong; the wrong assumption cost them 40 per cent of the discs's income. Despite this, the Mancunians weren't deterred from future sampling without clearance (where possible). 'We haven't used less samples, we've just used less popular ones' was their attitude as quoted in a 1991 interview. Even more surprising in view of the ever-developing ears of the record companies and their legal departments was the view articulated at around the same time (early 1991) by Paul and

Phil Hartnell, the brothers who make up Orbital. 'Often you may use a sample from a particular field of music where the person involved is never gonna be in a club so they're never gonna hear the track.' Orbital, like all the better sampling techno acts, are fairly eclectic in their range (ABC and The Butthole Surfers, unlikely soul-mates at the best of times, have both contributed to the Orbital *oeuvre*), but their quoted comment is doubly strange when the track which they're actually referring to is the eight-note sample from the Abbess Hildegard of Bingen which landed The Beloved and WEA in such trouble.

Sometimes sampled artists can react unpredictably. There's a story that when Dave Stewart of The Eurythmics heard a DJ's bootleg track in which 'Sweet Dreams (are Made of This)' was sampled, he sought out the DJ and signed him to the record label he was forming. Certainly Stewart showed a lenience towards samples of his work which is said to have differed markedly from that of Annie Lennox, his Eurythmics co-star. When in 1991 she wanted to take out an injunction against The Utah Saints because of their sample of part of her vocal from 'There Must Be an Angel (Playing with My Heart)', Stewart was reportedly so impressed with the single that it survived unscathed (and reached the UK Top 10).

There's also the case of Suzanne Vega, although she wasn't so much sampled as remixed by DNA. 'Tom's Diner' started life as a rather cute and arty a cappella track on an album. Bristol-based production team DNA took this unlikely basis and created a bootleg dance track from it. The 'official sources', including Vega, were so impressed that it was released through her record company, A & M. Reactions can by no means always be anticipated; the most unlikely people are happy to have their work mutilated (particularly if they're likely to get something out of the end result).

It was mildly surprising to some people that the 1988 Copyright Act made no specific reference to or provision for sampling. The Act was being debated and framed at a time when the potential scale of sampling was becoming clear, at the same point of legal history when Stock, Aitken and Waterman were locked into deadly combat with M/A/R/R/S. Obviously samplers would like to see something in law which actually protected the right to sample, but unfortunately British law doesn't tend to work like that (a subject there for lovers of jurisprudential debate). Again, quite a few people – especially the larger record companies and their lawyers – looked to the Hyperion v. WEA case to give some guidance as to where the law might conceivably stand (at least in theory) on the issue of sampling. The judgment from the Biz Markie case, though, has sent a chill – in a non-rap-jargon sense – down the spines of many musicians. If that trend is followed, if the US Attorney-General decides to press criminal charges successfully, and if a similar ruling is made in the UK, then an awful lot of people could be out of work, or, even worse, in prison. And while there are plenty of pop artists who for the past few years have been making criminally awful records, that would scarcely be fair. Sampling may be theft in some moral, philosophical sense, but it's hard to see who's genuinely hurt by it. After all, some samples are improved by their new context.

Pop music, though, has traditionally long been a litigious business. As one saying has it, 'where there's a hit, there's a writ'. At this level sampling has merely afforded the legal departments a thrilling new field day, ensuring that in the end it's really the lawyers who are the winners. Maybe there's something to be said for the Bill Drummond philosophy.

I ought perhaps to conclude this chapter by admitting that an awful lot of its information is anecdotal. Legal issues – particularly those where no clear-cut law is involved – are notoriously thorny subjects and tend to attract more rumours and whispers than almost any other area (except sex). Opinions derived from lawyers tend to differ according to who their clients are and what particular legal axe they're being paid to grind at any given moment. It's a great shame that there isn't a definitive statement which would encapsulate the whole matter neatly and lay out the issues clearly and precisely. However, the confusion is a price worth paying to avoid a ruling in the UK like that in the Biz Markie case. Drastic changes in pop music should start with musicians and not in the law courts.

11 · Justifiable or Just Ancient?

The use of sampling has been so intrinsically immersed in dance music that it's easy to forget that a lot of pop music is, in fact, rock music. Furthermore, rock has shown itself to be an exceptionally durable genre, particularly as the rest of the market has declined around it. Established acts like Phil Collins, U2, Simple Minds, more newly established ones like the phenomenally successful Guns 'n' Roses, Metallica and (especially in 1991) Bryan Adams, have all continued to fly the rock flag with some success. Guns 'n' Roses managed to defy all convention and achieve huge sales success with the simultaneous release of two double albums, picking up a surprising amount of critical acclaim along the way.

A lot of the more fêted new acts in 1990 and 1991 have, at heart, been rock bands too. The UK's Ned's Atomic Dustbin, the USA's Nirvana (to name two who have won some praise from the more self-styled trendy section of the music press) could not by any stretch of the imagination be called dance acts. Nor were their names just temporary pseudonyms adopted by producers or DJs to promote a new anonymous techno dance single. These were 'real' rock bands, with 'real' guitars. Although the public appetite for dance-music singles remained seemingly insatiable during 1991, soft rock has proved amazingly resilient as a sales force. Bryan Adams's *Robin Hood* theme is perhaps a phenomenon beyond generic definition (and explanation). More conventionally in this field, American rockers

Extreme have found a place in the market (helpful for them, anyway) for soft ballads like 'More than Words' and 'Hole Hearted', while Swedish group Roxette aren't doing too badly with a similar blend of rock guitar and soft, poppy vocal lines.

The swing of both the popular and the critical pendulums (which are by no means generally synchronized) back towards some acceptance of guitar-dominated rock was probably inevitable, particularly in view of the gradual dehumanization of the dance scene. The 'trendy' acts of 1990 – almost all in the UK emanating from North-West England – attempted a marriage of guitar rock and dance rhythms. Guitar bands signed to small independent record labels rushed lemming-like towards the drum samples of the dance scene, and the phrase used by several of the leaders of this rush became a rock-business comic catch-phrase: 'There's always been a dance element to our music.' In fact, the Mancunian leaders of this rush, The Happy Mondays, had the 'dance element' partially foisted upon them by their fashionable producers, Paul Oakenfold and, on some remixes, Nellee Hooper (both club DJs) and were quite open about the other main reason for their desire to break into the dance scene. 'The drugs were better', their lead singer and main public front man Shaun Ryder declared. But then Ryder wanted to get back to the idea of the pop/rock star as shocking, controversial and beyond the law, hence his proud boastings about his 'career' as a drug dealer.

The Mondays, like most of their imitators, were at least 50 per cent about attitude. And if the attitude wasn't shocking it wasn't working. At the start of the 1980s, pop/rock stars who didn't like what was going on in Governmental High Places joined Red Wedge and CND, promoted the Labour Party and tried to revive the social and political consciousness of the 1960s in a new generation whose public perceptions were dominated by the figure of Margaret Thatcher (with Ronald Reagan lurking somewhere in the background). At the end of the 1980s the Red

Wedge mob were a standing joke even with the sections of the music press that had once provided their cheerleaders, the same sections which had spouted wordy, dense analyses of the music their careers revolved around, influenced primarily by Jacques Derrida, Jacques Lacan, Michel Foucault and Julia Kristeva. That type of musician and that type of music journalist had given way to a more cynical, blasé, altogether sneering set, possessed of all the cynicism which Bill Drummond and Jimmy Cauty had used so brilliantly in 1987 to create a soundtrack (by misappropriation) for the age, but with a whole new drug infatuation laid on top. Instead of reviving the political consciousness of the 1960s, the 1980s woke the stimulant awareness of that over-rated decade.

The drugs-and-dance equation really came into being with the 1988 craze for acid house, a logical progression of house music which added some instrumental texture – mainly high-pitched electronic-keyboard sounds – to the minimalist upbeat house sound. Despite the more sophisticated instrumental texture, there seemed to be less room in acid house for dominant vocal performances (like 'Love Can't Turn Around'), although screaming and soaring female vocals did occasionally make an appearance. The Italian sound of Black Box/Starlight (and so on) was another logical progression from acid house.

However, the point of the music wasn't entirely supposed to be its content. It was its effect on the dance floor, its hypnotic influence on the dancer, which was designed to combine to interesting effect with whichever amphetamine derivative the dancer had taken. Although the term acid was used, the drug particularly in favour with the predominantly young (teenage and pre-twenty-five) clientele has tended, since 1988, to be an amphetamine derivative popularly known as ecstasy. Much media coverage has been given to the rise of the acid party, or the warehouse party, usually in a field somewhere off the M25, and the strenuous – if ultimately ineffectual – police attempts to halt them. Despite the waning of such coverage, the phenomenon has continued more or less unabated, and provides the musical soundtrack to the 'rave scene', as it has become known for convenient shorthand. This term runs a gamut from official, even local-authority run, large one-off discos with well-known club DJs, to illicit, black-market events which tend to be staged as often in the centre of cities as in fields in Surrey or Berkshire. But drugs are commonplace to both extremes and every variant in between, the main difference being that the official raves make some attempt to stem the sale of illegal stimulants, whereas the illicit events exist mainly for the purpose of promoting drug purchase and abuse. In late 1991 this musical soundtrack of hard-core upbeat 'techno' dance music began to dominate the best-seller lists. At one point in November, half the Top 10 consisted of more or less purely instrumental dance music aimed specifically at this one scene. This may have been an indication of how low the sales figure required to reach the Top 10 had become, and many of these discs proved to have remarkably short shelf lives in chart terms; but quite a few others during the course of 1991 had proved surprisingly durable, especially 'Charly' by The Prodigy and 'Get Ready for This' by 2 Unlimited.

The latter single was simply a piece of Benelux standard techno music, effective because simple and hypnotic, totally unremarkable to anyone not plugged into the dance music of the particular scene which gave it its *raison d'être*. Judged objectively as a piece of music it was a stunningly uninteresting upbeat instrumental, a kind of electronic counterpart to any boring pop instrumental of earlier decades (the surprisingly successful and equally unremarkable 'Groovin' with Mr Bloe' from 1970 springs to mind) with its repetitive melodic and rhythmic figure punctuated by cries of 'Y'all ready for this?'

Apart from the fact that the market wouldn't have existed, it could probably have been made ten years ago without sounding especially different.

'Charly' was a different matter, though – very much a child of the age of sampling. Interwoven with the deliberately tonally ambiguous, not quite hitting the note, electronic noise was a vocal sample lifted from an early 1970s public-information cartoon film aimed at young children and widely shown on TV and in schools. The actual film was also lifted for use in the video accompanying the single (there was little else of interest to be seen except the general kind of frenetic atmosphere of dancing and performing typical of the raves for which 'Charly' had been created and at which The Prodigy, an Essex-based group, were in mid-1991 a top-rated act). 'Charly says: always tell your Mummy before you go off somewhere' was the text which was sampled (along with a lot of not very convincing fake cat miaows, supposed to be the authentic voice of Charly himself). The film was designed to warn children against predatory strangers, and by an unpleasant quirk of coincidence (at least one hopes it was), 'Charly' made a remarkably high chart debut (Number 9) in mid-August, the week after a series of grisly child abductions and murders had figured in the headlines and newspapers had pontificated on the fact that the UK had the highest child-murder rate in the West. Irony upon irony, of course, and despite disingenuous claims by the brains behind The Prodigy that he'd used the Charly sample because he'd 'always liked the film when he was younger', it was a simple fact that 'Charly' was designed to be played at events which you couldn't really tell your Mummy about before you went off to them (not unless your Mummy was remarkably tolerant, anyway). And underlying it all was the basic slang use of 'Charly' as a synonym for heroin to one generation, and cocaine-based crack to a younger.

One can in some lights applaud this kind of thinking, if not the record itself, whose appeal and great success mystified me. However enjoyable people may find raves, it seems rather a forlorn hope to imagine that they can be recreated in the privacy of one's own home by the simple expedient of buying a few records. It's very much the subversive use of a sample for which I've applauded The Justified Ancients of Mu Mu – very like their Samantha Fox quotation. But by most standards it's a sad come-down for the irony and vitality and sheer critique of some of that early sampling. As a record, 'Charly' doesn't have the vitality or wit of Coco, Steel and Lovebomb's 'Love Puppy' (and one might ask in this context what a 'lovebomb' was, in any case). The use of the 'Charly' sample was simply a clever way of advertising what the raves at which the record was so heavily featured were really about. And so when a host of vocal samples on high-charting discs like Altern 8's 'Activ 8 (Come with Me)' promised to take the listener to 'ecstasy', or even more baldly the title of the disc and the lyric were simply 'Ekstacy' (*sic*), it was just a way of reminding the participants of the rave scene what was going on, of proclaiming the commercial purpose of it all. Sex and drugs and rock 'n' roll had always belonged together, even when rock stars joined in with heavily publicized campaigns advising 'Just say no', but not until the end of the 1980s and the beginning of the 1990s – never even in the old 'Lucy in the Sky with Diamonds' days of the 1960s when drugs were considered almost socially *de rigueur* – had the music's sole *raison d'être* been to promote the narcotic. In the old days, the artificial stimulant had just happened to be around the business, much as writers on the American scene, or actors everywhere, found drugs floating around. The rave scene, following the acid-house craze, had taken a musical form and turned it into a promotional campaign for the drug sellers. Speaking personally, I find this one of the saddest developments in popular music over the last half decade or so, sad because its social consequences could be disastrous. Although the amphetamine derivative which forms the basis of ecstasy has been in use medically (on a highly restricted basis) since 1914, the jury is still out on the after and side effects of continued regular usage of these stimulants for purely 'pleasurable' purposes. And the signs to date are that at least 40 per cent of such users experience abnormal paranoia.

It was as champions of this kind of lyrically minimal dance music that Bill Drummond and Jimmy Cauty proved the words of 'Past, Present and Future' emphatically wrong. They had been producing upbeat dance music which didn't rely on sophisticated dislocated collage since the middle days of the Mu Mu period, mainly under the guise of Disco 2000. Although there was some attempt to try to preserve a separate identity for these efforts at the time, all the variants of 'I Love Disco' appeared on *Shag Times* the 1988 compilation of KLF products to date, under titles like '120 bpm' in the half of the compilation nominally credited to The KLF.

After 'Doctorin' the Tardis', the identity of The KLF seemed more firmly established than any other – The JAMs were dead, at least until their miraculous resurrection in late 1991. The KLF didn't seem, over the years 1988 to 1990, particularly possessed of a clear direction. There was a persistently released and re-released dance single called 'What Time is Love?', which appeared in various mixes, but despite winning plaudits from the music press, none of the versions ever quite seemed to take with the public. In fact in October 1989 various versions were welded together on to the same disc, technically qualifying it as an album, under the title *The What Time is Love Story*. There was another unsuccessful KLF single, entitled 'Kylie Said to Jason'. Despite the promise of its title, this was not a cut-up or a pastiche of the works of Ms Minogue and Mr Donovan. It was a rather curious and effectively haunting ballad, along the lines of the two less-upbeat tracks on *Who Killed the JAMs?* (such as 'The Porpoise Song'). It didn't seem specifically aimed at a dance market, or indeed at any discernible section of the record-buying public (which doesn't prevent it from being a good single). Even less obvious in its aim were the two KLF albums of 1990: *Chill Out*, a forty-five minute exercise in continuous ambience purportedly depicting a journey somewhere in the American West, with some background country-music noises which sounded like rehearsals for various things that made their way into the texture of the slower, more atmospheric parts of *The White Room*, and *Space*, a collection of tracks named baldly and inexplicably after each of the planets of the solar system.

The most prominent release dates of 'What Time is Love?' had been in the Summer of 1988 and 1989, so despite the fact that the story was supposed to be complete, the summer of 1990 saw it back in the shops, in a version 'featuring The Children of the Revolution'. This working, with the rap and the beat carefully tailored to the emergent rave tastes cultivated by the fashionable DJ producers like Oakenfold and Hooper, succeeded where its predecessors had failed, and established the name The KLF with the public. It also established a style which could be associated with the name, one which managed to be half a step ahead of the time. 'What Time is Love?', in its 1990 incarnation, looks forward to such 1991 hits as Nomad's '(I Wanna Give You) Devotion'. But much more than giving any leads or clues as to what might come from other acts, 'What Time is Love?' proved to be an endless source to which Drummond and Cauty themselves could return. It's not too much of an exaggeration to say that most of what appeared on the album *The White Room* and the various remixed versions of tracks it spawned as singles was already there somewhere on 'What Time is Love?'

The next single, '3 a.m. Eternal', was an obvious answer to the question posed by its predecessor, and to some extent it sounded rather like the question but with fewer words. There were the same cries of 'Ancients of Mu Mu' and 'KLF is gonna

217

rock you' (advertisements for the outfit's past and its present), and a very similar chord sequence. Additionally there were a few rounds of machine-gun fire which radio sensitivity required be deleted during the Gulf War. The mixture of DJ rap, sung female vocals and straightforwardly simple dance instrumental was the same – with less rap – as that of 'What Time is Love?' In some ways '3 a.m. Eternal', good though it was, wasn't as good or as inventively memorable as 'What Time is Love?' But '3 a.m. Eternal' had one great advantage over its predecessor: it was in the shops in January 1991. January is often a time of appallingly low record sales. The unenviable all-time-low sales record for a Number 1 single was achieved in early January (by, as it happens, New Kids on the Block's 'Hangin' Tough'). Recently, record companies desperate for Number 1 singles have caught on to this fact, and in January 1991 EMI managed to achieve two instant Number 1s in a four-week period by astute promotion of singles with a guaranteed large first-week sale (Iron Maiden's wittily titled 'Bring Your Daughter . . . to the Slaughter' and Queen's 'Innuendo').

In fact, '3 a.m. Eternal' performed relatively well for a January hit, and turned out to be the biggest of the three KLF hits of 1991. To my ears, it remains the thinnest of the singles, although as a track on *The White Room* it seems possessed of more substance than either 'Last Train to Trancentral' or 'Justified and Ancient'. In both these latter cases, the 'padding' used to augment album track to single proved inspirational. 'Last Train' became a driving dance track, everything that other electro tracks aspired towards, but with an added excitement from the sheer density of the overlay of different elements. It came even closer than '3 a.m. Eternal' to being a 'pure' instrumental; verbally all 'Last Train' had to offer was rapper Ricardo (Richard Lyte)'s observation that 'this is what KLF are all about, also known as The JAMs furthermore known as The Justified

Ancients of Mu Mu'. Added to this was his persistent refrain of 'Back to the heavyweight jam' (a fairly obvious group history self-reference). There were more cries of 'KLF' (provided by 1960s soul singer P. P. Arnold) and 'Mu Mu' (no 'Ancients of' in this case) and crowd noises culled from a variety of live albums (all sources faithfully and legally, if almost sarcastically, quoted on the credits of *The White Room*). The beat was the thing with 'Last Train' and it certainly lived up to '3 a.m.''s promise that 'KLF is gonna rock you'.

Just before the appearance of 'Justified and Ancient' – unquestionably The KLF's finest moment to date – at the end of November 1991, Drummond and Cauty resurrected The Justified Ancients of Mu Mu with a track called 'It's Grim up North'. Although lacking the chaotic, multi-referential collage framework of previous JAMs tracks, you can see how this single needed another artist credit. It didn't fit into the unfolding saga of egoism which was emanating under The KLF aegis. Indeed, you could almost say that there was some vague political point to 'It's Grim' (it managed to annoy a Tory MP in a marginal Northern constituency) even though it consisted for the most part of an ambient dance-ish electro noise over the top of a recitation of names of Northern towns (not all by any means 'grim') sounding like a cross between a motorway sign and a roll call of the Third and Fourth Divisions of the Football League *circa* 1959/60 (an effect heightened by the inclusion of the word 'Stanley' after 'Accrington'). Occasionally the voice would intone 'It's grim up north', yet another KLF reference to the comedy of Harry Enfield. Adding something more in the way of comment and intensity to this rather dull and childish-sounding piece was the gradual emergence and domination of an electronic performance of Parry's setting of Blake's 'Jerusalem', the great revolutionary anti-industrial, anti-capitalist poem which has been so effectively hijacked by the very forces it was aimed against. The power of the KLF logo was such that this essentially uncommercial piece made the Top 10. But it didn't fit in any way into The KLF Story.

'Justified and Ancient', in its single incarnation, took up more or less at the point 'Last Train' left off, with the cries of 'All bound for Mu Mu Land' implying that transport was still very much involved. The beat was slower, and the melody was exactly that used on *1987* in 'Hey Hey We're Not The Monkees' and resuscitated on *The White Room*. On the 1991 album the singing fell to Black Steel, a male vocalist, and the lyrics wre simply about Drummond and Cauty's desire to do what they wanted, without any 'master-plan'. As an album track 'Justified and Ancient' was ethereal, wistful even, with no urgent beat, no backing voices (picking up on the vocal effects kicked out of the way at the album's very start, when 'What Time is Love?' gets into its stride). Obviously, to turn this into a single required a good deal of beefing (and beating) up, more density and more voices. But the master stroke was the choice of vocalist for the 'song' element of 'Justified and Ancient'.

The promotional video for 'Justified' made it clear that Drummond and Cauty possessed an enormous respect at least for the statistical achievements of Tammy Wynette. All her awards, all her successes, are listed in subtitle along the bottom of the screen, while Ms Wynette herself parades around dressed as a beauty queen (crown, train and all) lip-synching the revised words of the 'Justified and Ancient' song. 'Miss Tammy Wynette *is* the First Lady of Country' is the culmination of this visual recitation, and there is a sense in which the whole enterprise is a tribute to her undoubted ability as a singer. In fact, it would almost be possible to believe that Tammy Wynette is in on the joke here, so sweetly and sincerely does she enounce such lyrics as 'They're justified and they're ancient/And they drive an ice-cream van' (the ice-cream van held the position on the single's sleeve previously held by Ford Prefect for 'Doctorin'

the Tardis', and Drummond and Cauty's appearances to promote 'Justified' were all done swathed inside enormous latex
ice-cream cones designed by Fluck and Law, creators of TV's
Spitting Image). The production surrounding Tammy Wynette's
voice suggests that Drummond and Cauty could put together
rather an effective country track if they ever wanted to (picking
up some of the distant pedal steel noises used on the ambient
Chill Out) and the marriage of country with 1990s dance is
nothing short of amazing. The interpolated 'Just roll it from the
top's and 'Turn the beat back's effortlessly balance the supposedly hostile elements, and when Tammy disappears, the track's
push towards the more usual KLF sound (more cries of
'Ancients Of Mu Mu') doesn't seem in any way disjointed.
Indeed, the female chorus's repeated 'All bound for Mu Mu
Land' even has a pseudo-African feel in its harmonies. Again,
this element is perfectly integrated. The end result is the nearest
thing (in 1991) to a perfect pop/dance record. It seems a million
miles from the raucous, disjointed, socially commenting, utterly
cynical JAMs *oeuvre* of 1987. After all (and like most of *The
White Room* only more so) it could be described as 'a well-
crafted song'.

But in another sense this collaboration with such an unlikely
figure as Tammy Wynette and its resulting in such a perfect pop
product was the logical conclusion of the whole KLF enterprise.
Tammy Wynette, unquestionably a leading figure in the
country-music field, is thereby representative of the whole
tradition of country music (one of the two bases of pop music
as we know it, as Elvis Presley, without whom pop music as
we understand the term at the end of the twentieth century
might never quite have happened, was first and foremost a
country singer). And country music is about songs, usually
about songs which tell stories. Country music is about sincerity,
about love and sad stories. Tammy Wynette has in her career
produced two of the most famous of all country songs, both of

which represent a particular kind of country music. 'Stand by Your Man' is the ultimate female country song (country music, like heavy metal or The Happy Mondays or, indeed if one is brutally honest, the mainstream of the pop market, doesn't have a lot of room for feminism). 'D.I.V.O.R.C.E.', one of the most parodied of songs, is a classic sad country ballad. Admittedly, neither of these songs involves either a death or God (the other two staple diets of country music), but then you can't have everything. But what's undeniable is that 'Stand by Your Man' and 'D.I.V.O.R.C.E.', like more or less every song which Tammy Wynette has ever performed, are songs 'about' something, made more plangent by the singer's evident sincerity.

So when such a sincere and clear voice commits itself to a (more or less) nonsensical lyric about a couple of maverick musicians, with references unintelligible to anyone who hasn't heard their previous output ('The last train left an hour ago/ They were singing "all aboard"'), what is going on? What is more anti-song than a song without meaning? And how better to make that meaninglessness effective than to get a sweet, pure, sincere singer who also happens to be a senior figure in one of the most conservative parts of the music business to deliver that pointless lyric? Admittedly a lot of black rap groups tend to produce endless self-referential lyrics, even the supposedly less egomaniacal outfits like De La Soul, PM Dawn and Definition of Sound. But they don't get in other people from other genres to do the lyrics for them. Of course, as a by-blow, Drummond and Cauty managed to cap one of the pop trends which dated – like the entire KLF enterprise – from round about 1987, the taste for unlikely and bizarre (and on occasion desperate) collaborations across pop genres. Even Yello and Shirley Bassey looked pretty orthodox next to The KLF and Tammy Wynette. Although I should say that there's every sign that the Drummond and Cauty approach to the country singer was every bit as sincerely motivated as The Pet Shop Boys' to Dusty Springfield and Liza Minnelli (both of which look pretty logical in hindsight, as The PSBs have showed themselves to be as interested in the question of stage presentation as in what could be achieved within the confines of the studio). And the result of this collaboration was infinitely more satisfying than that between, say, Coldcut and Mark E. Smith of The Fall, or The Art of Noise and Tom Jones.

And if 'Justified and Ancient' was meaningless as a song outside the limited sphere of The KLF's own history, then its constituent elements – the history of the song itself, in fact – was even more self-referential. The very title took you back to the origins of Drummond and Cauty's partnership. Every little choric interpolation referred to something else. In any case, the song was a revamp of an album track already available for almost twelve months, and that track was itself a reworking of an older track from another (now illegal) album. And although the arrangement of the song was different from the preceding singles, the basic musical material wasn't. After all, the whole of *The White Room* formed a kind of circular piece, with tracks interweaving and occasionally becoming confused with one another (the dread phrase 'concept album' might almost spring to mind). As an act of creation, 'Justified and Ancient' was rather like raiding the fridge in desperation and managing to make something remarkable out of the leftovers by the judicious and imaginative addition of only one or two extraneous ingredients. Having pretended that they'd 'never be allowed to get away with it again', Drummond and Cauty spent 1991 'getting away with it' time after time, to better and better effect. When they'd been The JAMs, in order to understand them properly, you had to have a fairly wide-ranging knowledge of pop-music history as well as being conversant with what was going on in the world. As The KLF they have managed to create a myth which is self-propagating, self-sufficient, self-consuming and self-recreating. It's probably clear from the foregoing that in my opinion 'Justified and Ancient' was the pop/rock/dance/any other sub-genre you care to mention masterpiece of 1991. It was difficult to imagine how they'd follow it, but the announcement in early 1992 that a new version of 'What Time is Love?' featuring at least one performer from one of the earliest, most-imitated heavy-metal bands, Deep Purple, came as both an amusing surprise and no surprise at all. Spotting the critical trend back to rock, Drummond and Cauty can't resist another double-edged joke. Just who the joke is on isn't quite clear. But evidently they don't feel the need to write any new material – and why should they? As long as they're getting away with it, there's no problem. Imaginatively – and sales-wise – they're still way ahead of the competition. If it is all a con trick, no one cares at the moment, least of all The KLF themselves. I wonder how much they enjoyed the coincidence (if it was only a coincidence) which emerged from the longest trial in British legal history, the fraud trial which concluded in the first week of February 1992. Peter Kellard was convicted on nineteen counts of fraud relating to a company he founded which was supposed to create a massive theme park in Derbyshire. The company was called KLF.

The KLF collaboration with Deep Purple serves as a reminder that their origins are in rock rather than dance. They may have advised everyone to throw away their musical instruments and may (almost) have done it themselves, if the instrumental credits on *The White Room* are to believed, but they could still play them if they had to. In fact, *The White Room* drew, from more than one source, comparison with a good old-fashioned rock album, whatever its apparent dance pretensions. And the days of techno-dance music may be limited – at least if the music press in late 1991 has its way. The return of rock as a 'respectable' musical genre may force a wry smile or two from some acts – not least that whose name suggested this book's title, the act who provided the point from which I started.

Pop Will Eat Itself were, to begin with, an old-style 'grebo' rock act originally called Wild and Wandering, who in 1987 crashed into the wonderful world of sampling and collage with their album *Box Frenzy*. The name 'Pop Will Eat Itself' came, so they say, from a phrase uttered in an *NME* interview (oddly with Jamie Wednesday, half of whom subsequently became Carter USM) by rock journalist David Quantick. In one of those stories which sounds suspiciously 'after the event' the group claim that they sent the same demo tape to three different record companies, using a different name with each (the other names employed were 'The Pop Tarts' and 'Grrr'), intending to adopt the name used for the demo which proved successful. I can't believe any band, however devoted to the cult of naffness, would willingly place themselves before the public under the title 'Grrr'. From their patchy – but brilliant where good – debut, PWEI, or The Poppies (both abbreviations are equally liberally applied, the former seeming somehow more in keeping with the high-tech theory which allowed the group's output, the latter having a deliberately down-market 'retro' sound) managed to establish themselves as a 'significant' and certainly much-loved and much-praised band, until critical opinion started to go lukewarm on them somewhere in late 1990 (round about the same time that PWEI came more into mainstream public favour with an established record sale). Pop Will Eat Itself have remained much closer to their original output and self-imposed brief than The JAMs/KLF, who are their obvious point of comparison, and while this, inevitably involving the use of the beat box, took them into the dance genre, there has been no sign as yet that PWEI are quite as drawn to producing music which would pass muster on the rave circuit. For one thing, they're too much in love with their own verbal inventiveness and tend to produce rap (or rapp-ish) lyrics of some density, packed with punning references across a wide referential frame of popular culture. This doesn't do too well with the dance-music record buyers these days, and Drummond and Cauty have always known, as they point out in *The Manual*, that too many words are counter-productive if you want to grab public affection. Obscenity can be quite common in PWEI's material, too, and they're not frightened of reverting to 'grebo' type in their attitude towards women. Not every politically right-on music journalist was happy about a title like 'Beaver Patrol'.

But The Poppies – and this aspect of their image has always been very much The Poppies rather than the high-tech PWEI – managed to make this primitive politically not-quite-so-correct way of disporting themselves part of their good-time, 'grebo' lager and curries and breaking wind package. Their visual style was deliberately retro, more so than the later 'style-less' dress adopted by other Midlands bands like Ned's Atomic Dustbin and The Wonder Stuff. 'Very much like scruffy pigs to look at' said the Johnny Morris sample at the beginning of *Box Frenzy* and that was the visual style they espoused. In fact, by the time they came to have their first (and, to date at the time of writing, only) Top 20 single in January 1991, the whirligig of time had brought their stylelessness to the forefront of fashion, and there wasn't much to choose from between The Poppies, Jesus Jones and The Happy Mondays to look at (although a greater clothes fad seemed to surround The Mondays – Mancunians were ever more neurotic about style than Midlanders) and The Poppies' brand of anarchic, sexist and slobbish behaviour was positively fashionable.

'Beaver Patrol' aside, though, there's a lot about PWEI that could easily qualify as 'politically correct' in left-wing terms. Like The JAMs, their music starts from a point which is half in love with and half appalled by the consumer society that they're necessarily part of. The average PWEI song uses a far greater number of samples than even The JAMs' early output, and does so in a more obvious, more neurotic manner. The music press, expressing disappointment at the 1990 album *Cure for Sanity*, complained that the humour of earlier offerings like *Box Frenzy* and *This is the Day . . . This is the Hour . . . This is This!* had been lost. This, I think, overstates the humour on these albums while ignoring the tense, frenetic, again I come back to the word neurotic, juxtapositions which are funny, yet manage to be quietly disturbing. There's much more pure and simple humour in a *Cure for Sanity* track like 'Touched by the Hand of Cicciolina' (indeed at seven minutes-plus the joke begins to wear a bit thin), the PWEI alternative 1990 World Cup anthem using a New Order track and title ('Touched by the Hand of God') as its basis, thus poking fun at New Order's bizarre collaboration with the England Squad on the 'official' release 'World in Motion' (further proof that John Barnes can't rap). 'Touched by the Hand . . .' is, I'd argue, much more humorous than the consumerist nuclear nightmare of 'Def Con One' (a title referring to an early stage of nuclear warfare alert), one of PWEI's greatest and most potent collages on *This is the Day . . .*

'Def Con One' – the point where we came in – collides the famous Holland–Dozier–Holland Motown drumroll (as heard on The Isley Brothers' 'This Old Heart of Mine'), a short breathy intonation of the title of 'Right Now' by The Creatures (Siouxsie and Budgie from Siouxsie and the Banshees), the synthesizer passage from Lipps Inc's original version of 'Funkytown' (a great, unintentionally humorous pop record, and arguably Giorgio Moroder's finest moment away from Donna Summer), the synthesized keyboard squeals from The Osmonds' first major UK hit 'Crazy Horses' and the theme from *The Twilight Zone*. And those are only the immediately noticeable samples. Over the top is a sort of rap (except there's some attempt from time to time at singing it) using Muhammad Ali-like shortly spaced rhymes – 'How sick is Dick? How gone is Ron?' – thus, I suppose, taking rap back to one of its origins, while advertising fast food ('Give me Big Mac, fries to go') and namedropping a few prominent American politicians of the late 1980s (Dick

Cheney, the US Defence Secretary and Ronald Reagan, the former President). The remarkable thing is that all the discrete elements which make up this track are perfectly detectable, but the whole still homogenizes into a 'song' and a pretty devastating song comparing the superpower war machine to a fast-food outlet, and seeing the nuclear arms obsession as part of late 1980s consumerism. The sampling here is not the kind of sampling you find in the work of a lot of the British rock bands who made their names around 1989 and 1990, bands such as Jesus Jones (for whom PWEI apparently felt a certain amount of resentment), EMF (for whom Jesus Jones felt a certain amount of resentment) or Carter The Unstoppable Sex Machine. These are rock bands who incorporate samples very much the way most dance acts do now – sampled bass lines, sampled guitar breaks, samples that aren't really there to draw attention to the fact they're sampled, but simply augment or amplify whatever noise the band want to make with something they think has been done the way they'd like to hear it done before they ever thought of it themselves. PWEI's sampling neurotically, obsessively, draws attention to itself, even at the risk of attracting lawsuits.

The music press were probably right to see *Cure for Sanity* as a less impressive release than *This is the Day*, but I still find their arguments baffling, and I find it baffling that PWEI went along with a lot of the theory about the 'humour' having disappeared. Another truism was that *Cure for Sanity* was more of a mainstream house dance-music album. It draws more on that area for its sources, certainly, particularly for its beats and bass lines, but its style and preoccupations (particularly its verbal and lyrical preoccupations) are very much those of its predecessor. And it still has a capacity for surprise you don't find in most dance music (the appearance of Erik Satie, for instance). There is, perhaps, a more subdued, less frenetic sound to *Cure for Sanity* (ironically, given the title) and nothing with the sheer foul-mouthed, upbeat attack of 'Not Now, James, We're Busy', or any double-edged consumerism like 'Can U Dig It?' or 'Def Con One'. But perhaps the slightly more laid-back, less-engaged sound is what, for some critics, puts the album more into the mainstream of 1990s dance music. The personality seems to be ebbing away from most dance music as the hard-core masters take over.

The future for Pop Will Eat Itself, like that of The KLF, is at the time of writing anyone's guess. Perhaps they'll all head back to 'authentic' old-fashioned rock, if it really is in the process of becoming fashionable once again. There are enough guitar noises on *Cure for Sanity* to suggest the group have kept at least part of a hand in this area. But then, predicting what genuine originals will do next is more or less like predicting where popular taste will head off. A lot of paper was devoted in 1990 and 1991 to an attempt to ascertain some *Zeitgeist* 'defining' the new decade, a decade about which there seems to be a more particular obsessive fascination than many other isolated ten-year units. It's not hard to understand why this should be; it's the final decade of the century, and to some extent it was the sense of a definite *Zeitgeist* in the 1890s – the vogue for aestheticism, decadence (the Naughty Nineties), the rise of 'newness' as especially evidenced in such a phenomenon as the 'New Women', who slightly pre-dated the active attention-grabbing women's suffrage movement (and who was, indeed, a necessary prerequisite for the emergence of the suffragette as we came to understand the term) – that first made the concept of the 'decade' noticeable in cultural life. So one hundred years later we have expectations about the second 'defined' Nineties. But these aren't just any old Nineties, this isn't just any old turn of the century – this is the millennium. It's the millennium, at any rate, in the Western calendar. As we get excited about defining the new spirit of the Caring Nineties, as various journalists desperately tried to label them, it's worth remembering that the vast majority of people currently alive on the planet operate by a calendar which places them in no such predicament.

Will Pop Eat Itself?

The Caring Nineties, epitomized by the New Man (enjoying his vogue more or less on the centenary of the New Woman), don't seem to have had any correlation in the music world. Quite the opposite, in fact, if the ascendancy of many of the blatantly sexist rave and rap acts is anything to go by. The reaction to the 1980s seemed to come in the conscious rejection of 'sharp' style, epitomized in the vogue for bagginess in clothes. Of course, the relationship between pop music and dress being what it always has been, the supposed rejection of style became as much a style tyranny as the previous obsession with it. In the world of rap and dance music, the 'new' attitude was supposedly embodied in acts like De La Soul, A Tribe Called Quest, The Dream Warriors and – subsequently – PM Dawn. The last act actually found the subtlety of their style almost counter-productive, although coming out of a dance/rap background, with all of those influences, their music is possessed of a softness, a reflective quality, which doesn't help it catch on in the clubs – particularly not in a club scene where 2 Unlimited and The Prodigy can make the running. Although all the acts I've just mentioned have achieved singles success (and rave reviews for their debut albums), it's ironic that in each case greatest success has been achieved with a track where an obtrusive, easily definable sample could be heard. Why is this 'ironic?' Because all these acts are seeking and largely succeeding to create a new, personal, 'different' sound. They may all owe something to each other, but they all have separate and distinctive styles. Yet to the public A Tribe Called Quest are tied forever to Lou Reed's 'Walk on the Wild Side' (omnipresent in 'Can I Kick It?'), The Dream Warriors to Quincy Jones and Count Basie (providers of the essential breaks in 'My Definition of a Boombastic Jazz Style' and 'Wash Your Face in My Sink'), and PM Dawn to Spandau Ballet's 'True' (the 'hook-break' which helped to sell 'Set Adrift on Memory Bliss').

In the case of PM Dawn, there's even further irony (if that

isn't overloading a dangerously over-used word). As spiritual successors to De La Soul and despite a distinct visual image espoused by Prince B, PM Dawn stand against the conventional world of 'style' and fashion, and that their greatest success to date relied on Spandau Ballet who were, with all due respect, almost all style with very little musical or any other substance, does seem to merit the term 'irony'. For any listener who remembers 'True' first time in its original incarnation, those unmistakable opening chords summon up images of sharp lapels, suits and ties, pretty boys posturing in a self-conscious manner far removed from the laid-back, loose aesthetic of PM Dawn. Not that this will have worried the rap duo. As far as they were concerned, 'True' was just another record with a nifty break. Evidently, though, the record company didn't quite think this way. 'Set Adrift on Memory Bliss' was promoted in part by a poster campaign featuring old publicity shots of Spandau Ballet. PM Dawn seem, at the time of writing, talented enough to go on to greater triumphs; but pop shelf life gets shorter and shorter and, as the example of De La Soul (among many others) shows, the tide is all too easy to miss. In which case PM Dawn will go down in pop history yoked forever to the less than apposite Spandau Ballet. By their samples shall ye *not* know them in this case. But then, the converse of this is that as pop always returns to its own entrails, nobody need necessarily be dead for ever.

Which brings me back to the point that predicting the future in popular music is more perilous than any other form of pretended ESP. When, at turns of the year, newspaper columnists in both the mainstream and music press offer their prognostications for 'Who will be Big in Whatever Year It Happens to be Next', usually their opinions are led, to a greater or lesser extent, by what the recording companies have told them will be on offer over the first few months of the coming year. The Piers Morgans can write in the tabloid press about the scheduled batch of new heart-throbs; the 'serious' music press will know which of their long-trumpeted and largely unrecorded bands is due to make the transition to cassette and CD. No one ever successfully predicts what is really going to sell – the result which, in the end, matters the most – and some of the predictions are about as likely as *News of the World* astrologer Mystic Meg's confident assertion that 1991 would see a big hit single based on the secret music of the planets (unless there's something Bryan Adams hasn't told the world). For all the hype surrounding Michael Jackson's *Dangerous* and U2's *Achtung Baby* in 1991, both albums were easily and quietly outsold by Simply Red's *Stars*, which continued to dominate album sales through the busiest time of the year after the Jackson and U2 hype had died away. Not that that need worry either Michael Jackson or U2; their offerings weren't exactly popular failures.

The future of the sampler is more certain. As I've suggested in Chapter 6, it's certainly here to stay, although perhaps as a more conventional production tool than its headline use has hitherto suggested. The kind of samples employed by groups like Carter USM and EMF are more the way things seem to be heading: discreet samples, chosen to blend in with a distinctive product on a pre-created song, rather than the element which dictates the creation of the song. The song chooses the sample; the sample doesn't create the 'song'. This goes back, of course, to the manner in which Jazzie B used samples in creating the Soul II Soul sound which spawned a thousand imitators, perhaps even to the way that original rappers like Grandmaster Flash and Melle Mel used samples – the samples weren't there to draw attention to themselves. Indeed that samples used by artists like (MC) Hammer and Vanilla Ice did draw such attention to themselves seems to me an inherent weakness in their material. My reservations about Hammer have already been given a sufficiently extensive airing and, to my mind, next to Vanilla Ice he appears a daring, controversial genius. Neither Hammer nor Ice were at all clever with what they did with their backing tracks, and their choice of breaks and beats tended simply to suggest that their record collections weren't all that large or all that original. But then if one sample is going to dominate your record to the extent that tends to be the case with each Hammer or Ice track, why take a risk on something unknown, why not go with a proven hit like 'Under Pressure' or 'When Doves Cry'? Nobody expects Dick Francis to write a book which isn't a thriller set in the world of horse racing, so why expect Hammer or Vanilla Ice to stretch themselves musically? I can't imagine that their bank manager would, not at any rate on the basis of their success in the US (although Ice's near-instant demise in the UK may signal something worth worrying about).

The sampler as production tool has actually crept quite a way into rock music in the more conventional sense of the term. When producing the 'indie' guitar-orientated group Wire, Pascal Gabriel found it more convenient to feed everything recorded through a sampler and mix it all by adjustment within the machine rather than asking the band to do endless retakes of the same material. Partly this was because Wire's songs tend to be very harmonically intricate and dense, and splicing together different takes from within the same song would be getting on for a nightmare – but also it was the way of the future, truth be told. It's the way, for instance, that Jim Steinman tends to produce material by archetypal Goth band The Sisters of Mercy (not the first group you'd think of when considering the use of samplers). Pascal Gabriel swore that he was going to avoid sampling when producing an album by Manchester guitar-based, Stone Roses near sound-alikes The Inspiral Carpets, but whether he can manage this will be interesting. After all, Pascal Gabriel was using a sampler probably before The Carpets could manage guitars, and despite Gabriel's evident loss of interest in a dehumanized dance-music scene, can the leopard change its spots quite so casually?

Will Pop Eat Itself?

Popular music, like all popular culture, goes on, and finding a point at which to draw a full stop when considering any aspect of any part of it is difficult. It continues around me as I write, around you as you read. It's the nature of any book like this that many of the views in it will seem hopelessly out-moded by the time you read them. Several have become out-moded as I've been writing them. But all writing about popular culture, like popular culture itself, is at least partly a snapshot of a particular moment, a freeze-frame of an attitude appropriate to one point of time. Great popular culture (whether there *is* any great writing or analysis of popular culture is a highly debatable matter) has the ability to package that moment, make it desirable – essential even – and sell it to a mass market. 'Give me Big Mac, fries to go', as PWEI put it, knowing that for any British person that simple order thrusts them straight into the latter part of the 1980s, the time at which the McDonald's culture could be found even in nicely discreet, architecturally acceptable outlets in historic towns like York as well as any London suburban high street, in Cardiff as in Edinburgh – in Moscow as in Rome, even.

If I conclude by saying that pop music is an elaborate form of 'Big Mac, fries to go', that's not meant to be ultimately derogatory. There are times when only a Big Mac will do. And will pop eat itself? To be truthful, pop has been eating itself ever since it began. The sampler was just a new way, a more up-front, apparently dadaist way for it to do this. 'Pop will eat itself because it can', an *NME* reviewer once said. True in a way, but, more than this, pop will eat itself because it must. Popular culture, like all culture, feeds on itself endlessly and having eaten itself, produces not waste but another dish for the paying consumer.

Epilogue: End of the Road?

1992 was probably the first year which led me to feel disenchanted with, or uninterested in, most mainstream pop music. An article by Mark Edwards in the *Sunday Times* on 8 December might suggest that this is merely a function of age, that the good music of the rock/pop/dance scene is and ought to be hidden from anyone over thirty. I'd have found his argument more convincing if any of the albums he named as proof that 'music isn't dead' had been either surprising or brand new. Instead he trotted out obvious candidates such as Nirvana, Primal Scream and Arrested Development. They've all produced excellent albums in the last couple of years, but a few swallows scarcely make a summer. And, with all respect, none could be said to be creating anything remarkably 'new'.

The sampler-based music, of which I wrote so lovingly, eventually found its termination in the dance music of the rave scene. No rave record of late 1992 is remarkably different from or much of a development on a commercial rave success of 1991, such as The Prodigy's 'Charly'. Rave music has its little fads. The summer of 1992 saw the great influx of 'Toytown Techno', rave tracks sampling children's TV themes, the great commercial cross-overs here being 'Sesame's Treet' and 'A Trip to Trumpton'. There's been a little craze for ragga, too, most publicly attested to in SL2's 'On a Ragga Tip' and The Prodigy's 'Out of Space'. Yet the most notable thing about the development of rave music hasn't been any increased sophistication, any developing wit in its choice of samples or breaks – simply that it goes on getting faster. There must come a point where no one – not even under the influence of Ecstasy, speed or anything else – can dance any faster, but the music speeds up and up, leaving discs like The KLF's 'Last Train to Trancentral' and Nomad's '(I Wanna Give You) Devotion' sounding a bit andante moderato. The *Melody Maker* review of The Prodigy's *Experience* album suggested that if the music tried to go any faster it would disappear up its own orifice. Perhaps the rave scene will do exactly that.

In any case, by late summer of 1992, the rave music you could hear on the radio and in the charts bore less and less resemblance to what you'd actually hear at a rave. Various bands, producers and session musicians caught on to the idea that there was a commercial market for old songs 'raved up', a sort of 'rave karaoke' effect. Hence the appearance of KWS, with three hits based on 1970s soul songs against a 'rave-ish' beat, and the egregious Undercover, meting out the same treatment to two hits of 1978. It has occurred to me that Undercover are in fact working to a hidden agenda with the aim of producing identical-sounding versions of all the Top 10 hits of April 1978. In which case, look out for 'Wuthering Heights', the tribute song to L. S. Lowry, 'Matchstalk Men and Matchstalk Cats and Dogs', and, most surreal of all, the Scottish World Cup novelty song 'Ally's Tartan Army'. At least such a hidden agenda would prove a sense of humour; I'm sure Bill Drummond and Jimmy Cauty would do it. Most pathetic of all these rave cash-ins, though, must surely be Slipstream's 'We Are Raving', a rewrite of 'Sailing' so embarrassing that I'm surprised Gavin Sutherland allowed it. There's the obligatory references to 'unity' and, of course, 'ecstasy' and the whole thing sounds like a corporate attempt to cash in. At the time of writing, this lamentable piece had struggled into the UK Top 20.

These 'rave' records, especially the latter, are aimed at people who've probably never been anywhere near a real rave and wouldn't recognize Ecstasy if it jumped up and bit them. Far and away the cleverest exploitation of this market was that achieved by The Shamen. At one time great favourites of John Peel, they crossed into mainstream success with their 1991 hit 'Move Any Mountain', but became one of the most consistent chart acts in the UK in 1992 by a combination of commercial and catchy electronically based music and carefully cultivated controversy. All Shamen songs have a nagging, anthemic chorus calculated to follow you around for days. But their great coup was the 'dangerous' Number 1 single 'Ebeneezer Goode', which revolved around the hook-line 'Eezer Goode' (i.e., 'Es are good'). Radio One very sensibly ignored the calls for this record to be banned on the grounds that it was an incitement to take drugs. Frankly, anyone so feeble-minded that they base their habits – be they drugs, drink, sex or violence – on what they hear in a pop lyric is probably beyond help. The whole point of 'Ebeneezer Goode', from the viewpoint of the teenagers who bought it, was to try to convince their parents and friends that they were somehow involved in the rave lifestyle. No genuine raver I've met would touch it with a barge-pole, and it's hard to imagine such a poppy, singable, lightweight (in the best sense of the word) track fitting in easily with the hard-core, bass-line-driven, anti-melodic, rhythmically heavy music that was popular in raves and fashionable venues at the time 'Ebeneezer Goode' was at the top of the charts. No, this song, like most of the *Boss Drum* album, was a clever, slightly cynical stroke by a band keener on shifting units than retaining the critical kudos they'd enjoyed for some time. Bill Drummond and Jimmy Cauty would have approved the motivation if not, perhaps, the product.

Of course, the Drummond/Cauty/KLF story is easily concluded. After the heavy metal-ized 'America: What Time is

Love?', complete with screaming camp video, and their outrageous Extreme Noise performance at the 1992 'Brits' UK record-industry jamboree, it was announced that KLF was dissolved and their entire back catalogue was immediately deleted. This was a splendid solution to the perennial problem faced by acts in Chapters 8 and 9 of this book, the problem of 'what next?' It even conferred a certain extra value on all existing KLF products. I have no doubt that Drummond and Cauty will resurface, probably in the least likely guise, but this splendid full stop was somehow a much more fitting end to KLF than a string of singles and albums yielding diminishing returns.

The anti-pop-star trend which they began has maintained its fashion. Indeed, the concept of 'pop star' in the old-fashioned sense has rather died the death. Madonna and Michael Jackson continued to prove throughout 1992 that music is only a portion of their concerns. In fact, Madonna's generally under-rated *Erotica* album was only a very small part of the campaign surrounding her ludicrously hyped book *Sex*. Michael Jackson's 'Dangerous' tour proved to be so calculated a piece of staged theatre that the management could give assurances to parents about its exact finishing time. This is scarcely the stuff of spontaneous, 'dangerous' popular music, be it rock, pop, soul, or whatever.

1993 offers a new chance to assess the shelf life of teen heart-throbs in the UK. My own belief is that most of the little girls so enthusiastic about their Take That 1993 calendars on 1 January will have difficulty remembering which of this very indifferent group is which by July, but I may be wrong. After all, Curiosity Killed the Cat did almost come back to life for a brief moment. The success of Take That (rather limited in record-sales terms as yet, compared even with Bros and New Kids on the Block) is almost welcome as it has finally provided Ian Levine with the kind of mainstream success he enjoyed on the 1980s gay circuit with Seventh Avenue. And let us not forget that for the two years or so during which they failed to make any real impact on the music scene, Take That found a useful means of support on the same gay scene. But any group which derives its biggest hit from a Barry Manilow song, even one stolen from a Chopin prelude, has to be treading on thin, insubstantial ice.

No, despite the efforts of marketing men, who have laboured long and hard with Take That, I'd contend that the last great pop album by the last great pop star was released in the UK on 24 August 1992. Kylie Minogue was the last star to use pop music, or to be used by the creators of her pop music (and I think it was, ultimately, a two-way process), to make a whole integral package. Like the early Madonna, like the Jackson Five, there was a perceptible Kylie sound and song, slightly distinctive even from all the other Stock, Aitken and Waterman acts. There was never a coherent, definable Jason Donovan 'package' in the same way, and consequently Jason's pop career was that much shorter. (His success in *Joseph* gave it an artificial extension in 1991.) The down-trodden, ill-treated, patient, slightly tacky Kylie image was perfectly judged, so much so that the *Greatest Hits* album almost manages to tell a story. Songs like 'Je ne sais pas pourquoi', 'Hand on Your Heart' and 'Better the Devil You Know' are memorable, singable and go right to the heart of anayone who's ever had a crush, especially an unrequited crush. Kylie's greatest hits are all set in the real province and domain of good pop music, the world where all you need is 'your baby' and where love is the thing that matters. The majority of good, memorable popular music is about love and sex (love more than sex, I'd contend) and not about drugs or, with all respect to Tasmin Archer, the tragic abandonment of the NASA space-exploration programme.

I don't think the market would currently allow for another pop star in the old mould, the mould that Kylie more or less broke. Claims are made for figures like Vanessa Paradis (no real pop star was ever French, either; French pop stars don't travel and, looking at Johnny Halliday, one must utter a sigh of '*Merci, Dieu*') and the various Garies, Marks, Robbies of Take That. I wonder if a Take That fan could tell which member of the group was singing lead vocals at any given moment. And I don't think anyone apart from a Take That fan would care very much.

Of course, part of the reason for the decline of the old-fashioned pop star is the decline of the single. Clearly the old vinyl seven-inch is well on the way out, swamped by multiple formats, and a great deal of print has been devoted to analysing this phenomenon. 1992 was generally a lousy year for record sales across the board – hardly surprising in the middle of the biggest recession for sixty years – and at various moments the single looked to be completely out for the count. It was said that Right Said Fred's 'Deeply Dippy' managed to arrive at Number 1 in April on a weekly sale of less than 30,000; and the longevity in the top spot of Shakespears Sister's camply dramatic 'Stay' from February to April had little to do with vastly escalating sales. Oddly, the effect on the singles chart of low sales is rather similar to that of enormous sales: movement at the top end of the chart becomes sluggish. The only real difference is the frequency with which records enter the charts at extremely high positions and then crash down immediately. The first half of 1992 saw myriad examples of this phenomenon, involving indie bands like Ride (whose 'Leave Them All Behind' debuted at Number 9, falling to Number 29 the next week), heavy-metal stalwarts such as Iron Maiden ('Be Quick or Be Dead' dropped immediately from 2 to 13) and rave records (Shut Up and Dance's 'Raving I'm Raving' also entered at Number 2 and outdid Iron Maiden by plummeting to 15). A fairly useful indicator of singles sales for the first full week of each month was the new release by the indie group The Wedding Present. As a gesture of faith in the old seven-inch format, they had expressed the intention of releasing a new single on the first Monday of every month through 1992. Record-company economics, however, demanded that the release be restricted to a limited edition of 10,000. The Wedding Present, like many indie bands of any longevity, has a dedicated following of more than that number, so it was inevitable that each single would quickly sell out. Following these releases we can detect a curve in the year's sales pattern – the highest chart entries were around May and June, when one single actually managed a Top 10 position on the strength of its 10,000 sales.

Actually, the UK still sells more singles per capita than any other country, and the year ended on something of an upbeat note for record sales, especially for singles sales, with Whitney Houston achieving only the second million-selling single in the UK since 1985. For Ms Houston it was a spectacular return to form both in the UK and in the US, where there hasn't been a simultaneous Christmas chart-topper since the heyday of The Beatles. Houston's success, though, meant that for the third year running the year's best seller was taken from the soundtrack of a movie, and its existence is as much a signal of her intention to make the Madonna move and relegate the importance of singing in her career. The sucess of 'I Will Always Love You' was achieved, of course, by attracting many consumers who wouldn't normally buy singles, and this was managed by deliberately turning away from any overtly modern technical devices. The appeal was of a good old-fashioned ballad written by a country and western singer (Dolly Parton), dealing with the fundamentals of life (true love) and strongly sung to an arrangement which could have been made at any time since the 1940s.

In fact, all the strongest singles of the latter part of the year, both here and in the US, showed a determined taste for retrospection. Autumn 1992 saw the longest ever occupancy of the American Number 1 spot since rock 'n' roll began – a thirteen-week run by Motown group Boyz II Men's 'End of the Road' (another movie soundtrack extract). This was also one of the dominant singles of the last quarter of the year in Britain, giving Motown its first chart-topper here since Stevie Wonder in 1984. A slow close-harmony ballad, 'End of the Road' owed more to the Platters or the Mills Brothers or the Ink Spots than even the soul music of the 1960s, let alone anything that's been happening since the sampler was first put on display. And there was a small irony that Motown's first UK Number 1 should have been displaced by Charles and Eddie's 'Would I Lie to You?', a song whose inspiration seemed to lie almost exclusively with the old Holland–Dozier–Holland team (with a touch of Little Anthony and the Imperials thrown in for good measure), and whose production was designed to sound like something from the 1960s or early 1970s. What with the Abba revival happening alongside all this, as well as cover versions of songs like 'The Impossible Dream', 'As Time Goes By' and 'She' turning up around every corner, the music business gave the impression of having thrown itself desperately into reverse.

The single will, I think, stagger on for a little while longer, if only because the Top 40 singles chart still remains the easiest way to break new material on to the public consciousness. The album charts, especially in the UK, have become more and more the closely guarded preserve of a small number of acts, and only a small elite has managed to break through to the kind of permanent residency bands like Simply Red, Genesis, Simple Minds and U2 seem capable of achieving with each new release. It's highly pleasing that one of this small number is the excellent R.E.M., whose *Automatic for the People* was undoubtedly the single most imaginative piece of work in the rock/pop world in 1992. It's also quite pleasing that albums by rave acts don't quite make the impact record companies might hope for them. If people want rave on albums, they buy compilations. The Shamen's *Boss Drum* has sold tolerably well to date, but, as I've already said at length, I think The Shamen are something of a special case. But these days, crossing over from the singles chart to the albums is more difficult; it's easier to do what Nirvana did and travel the other way.

And the successful albums of 1992, R.E.M. apart, have given the same impression as the singles – one of a music business going into reverse. Perhaps the most dreadful event was the relative success of *Tubular Bells II*, the arrival of which made it seem as though punk had never happened. Indeed, when a single, 'Sentinel', was extracted from the *opus*, it entered the charts in the same week as the re-released 'Anarchy in the UK' – twenty-one places higher. The very idea of re-releasing a Sex Pistols single was perhaps proof that punk achieved little in the long run, but it surely rubbed salt into the wound that the great rallying cry of the movement designed to smash the old musical farts into oblivion was ridiculously out-performed by Mike Oldfield.

When I first set out to write this book in 1990, I regarded the new technology of music as a dynamic force. Despite the careers of Bomb the Bass and S-Express, despite Jive Bunny, I thought there was a great deal of wit and excitement in the work of PWEI, The JAMs/KLF and even Snap. KLF did the decent and clever thing and got out. PWEI's 1992 album *The Looks or the Lifestyle*, although greatly loved in some quarters, seemed a very depressed, subdued, rockist piece of work; the black humour may have been in keeping with the times, but the level of invention had flagged completely. And Snap turned out to be not a radical set-up based in Brixton, but a couple of German producers. 'Rhythm is a Dancer' and 'Exterminate!' are both passable dance tracks, but they're scarcely earth-shattering (even if 'Rhythm is a Dancer' does possess 1992's most ludicrous rhyming couplet, about being 'serious as cancer' concerning the fact that 'rhythm is a dancer'). Rave music is fine if you're on drugs; and I have to admit that a lot of the reservations I expressed about that drug scene in Chapter 11 were based on instinctual fears rather than hard fact. In the time since I wrote that chapter I've probably done more damage to myself with alcohol than the average raver has with Ecstasy. But I still feel that a musical scene which exists courtesy of a drug has got its priorities wrong. Rap seems to have dug itself into a hole, in that to be successful in the US you must be more and more a preacher of violence, like Ice Cube. And while there's much to enjoy in Arrested Development's debut album, *3 Years, 5 Months and 2 Days in the Life of . . .* , it's scarcely radically different from what De La Soul were doing in 1989, or A Tribe Called Quest in 1990, and it's equally possible that Arrested Development are something of a dictatorship, dominated by front-man Speech. I hope I'm wrong.

And, of course, the old dinosaurs grind on – Genesis, U2, Simple Minds – joined by slightly younger dinosaurs like Guns 'n' Roses and Extreme. The American album scene is dominated by rappers like Ice Cube and the astonishingly old-fashioned country singer Garth Brooks, as well as the usual leavening of soundtrack albums.

For the first time I can remember, pop music – to use that broad, nebulous term again – is going round in an ever-decreasing circle which remains unchallenged. Pop is always eating itself, but it seems to be producing the inevitable kind of waste as a result. Perhaps Mark Edwards is right; perhaps I am getting old. After all, I haven't mentioned Suede, or Curve, or a whole load of indie bands whose names dominate the British music press; I've scarcely discussed the endless looping puns of Carter the Unstoppable Sex Machine, who appropriate language and lyrical reference the way that Drummond and Cauty once appropriated others' recordings; and I haven't mentioned any of these because they all seem caught in the same interminable rut as rave music, Genesis and Guns 'n' Roses. Perhaps pop finally has eaten itself; perhaps the success of 'End of the Road' was a message; perhaps Take That will save the world; or perhaps I should just shut up and dance, at the same time joining Abba in the cry of 'Thank You for the Music'.

London, January 1993

Discography

This Discography is far from definitive, and is meant to serve mainly as a starting point for the curious. Inclusion of any disc here most emphatically does *not* mean that a disc has my personal seal of approval; usually context in the main text will make my own attitude clear.

The order is dictated by appearance in the main text.

Introduction

POP WILL EAT ITSELF: *This is the Day . . . This is the Hour . . . This is This!* (LP) [PWEI Product, BMG Records, 1989]

MARTIKA: 'Toy Soldiers' (Single) [CBS, 1989 – can you detect any 'meaning' in the lyric?]

1: Things Fall Apart

VARIOUS: *The Sound of Music* (Soundtrack LP) [RCA, 1965]

RIGHTEOUS BROTHERS: 'Unchained Melody' (Single) [London, 1965; Verve/Polydor, 1990]

2: Bricks in the Wall of Sound

LUDWIG SUTHAUS, KIRSTEN FLAGSTAD, WILHELM FURTWÄNGLER: *Tristan und Isolde* [EMI, 1951]

VARIOUS, SIR GEORG SOLTI: *Wagner's Ring Cycle* [Decca, 1959–65

– not the Ring Cycle I'd personally recommend, but a major event in the history of recording]

VARIOUS: *Back to Mono* (a 2-CD Phil Spector Greatest Hits collection) [EMI, 1991]

VARIOUS: *A Christmas Gift to You* (Phil Spector's Christmas LP) [EMI, 1991]

THE BEACH BOYS: *Pet Sounds* (LP) [Capitol, 1966]; the singles can be found on any Beach Boys compilation; the most recent was Summer Dreams [Capitol, 1990]

THE BEATLES: *Rubber Soul* (LP) [Parlophone, 1965]; *Revolver* (LP) [Parlophone, 1966]; *Sergeant Pepper's Lonely Hearts Club Band* (LP) [Parlophone, 1967 – possibly the most over-rated album of all time]

HOLLAND–DOZIER–HOLLAND: Any compilation of 1960s Motown singles, especially the Motown Chartbusters series, will contain a fair sample of HDH material. Their work is probably best illustrated by a FOUR TOPS compilation.

ARETHA FRANKLIN: *I Never Loved a Man (the Way I Love You)* (LP) [Atlantic, 1967]; *20 Greatest Hits* [Atlantic, 1987]

DARYL HALL AND JOHN OATES: *Abandoned Luncheonette* (LP) [Atlantic, 1974]

THE SWEET: *Blockbusters* (Greatest Hits LP) [RCA, 1989]

BLONDIE: *Parallel Lines* (LP) [Chrysalis, 1978]; *The Best of Blondie* [Chrysalis, 1981]

FRANKIE GOES TO HOLLYWOOD: *Welcome to the Pleasuredome* (LP) [ZTT, 1984]

DEAD OR ALIVE: 'You Spin Me Round (Like a Record)' (Single) [Epic, 1985]

RICK ASTLEY: *Whenever You Need Somebody* (LP) [RCA, 1987]

KYLIE MINOGUE: *Kylie* (LP) [PWL, 1988]

BANANARAMA: *The Greatest Hits Collection* (LP) [London, 1988]

SCOTT STRYKER: 'Less than Lovers, More than Friends' (Single) [Nightmare, 1987]

3: Stars on 45

SEX PISTOLS: *Never Mind the Bollocks, Here's the Sex Pistols* (LP) [Virgin, 1977]

YES: *Tales from Topographic Oceans* (LP) [Atlantic, 1974 – the worst excess of 'progressive' rock?]

TALKING HEADS: *Fear of Music* (LP) [Sire, 1979]; *Remain in Light* (LP) [Sire, 1980]

STAR SOUND: 'Stars on 45' (Single) [CBS, 1981]; 'Stars on 45 Volume 2' (Single) [CBS, 1981] etc. . . .

ROYAL PHILHARMONIC ORCHESTRA: 'Hooked on Classics' (Single) [RCA, 1981]

LOBO: 'The Caribbean Disco Show' (Single) [Polydor, 1981]

MICHAEL JACKSON: *Off the Wall* (LP) [Epic, 1979]; *Thriller* (LP) [Epic, 1982]; *Bad* (LP) [Epic, 1987]; *Dangerous* (LP) [Epic, 1991]

MADONNA: *The Immaculate Collection* (LP) [Sire, 1990]

STEVE 'SILK' HURLEY: 'Jack Your Body' (Single) [London, 1986]

4: Scratching Where It Itches

JAMES BROWN: *Star Time* (4-CD compilation) [Polydor, 1991]

FUNKADELIC: *Funkadelic* (LP) [Westbound, 1970]; 'One Nation Under a Groove' (Single) [Warners, 1978]

PARLIAMENT: *Mothership Connection* (LP) [Casablanca, 1975]

GEORGE CLINTON: *Computer Games* (LP) [Capitol, 1981]

PIGMEAT MARKHAM: 'Here Comes the Judge' (Single) [Chess, 1968]

SUGARHILL GANG: 'Rapper's Delight' (Single) [Sugarhill, 1979]

ISAAC HAYES: *Hot Buttered Soul* (LP) [Stax, 1969]; *Black Moses* (LP) [Stax, 1970]; 'Theme from *Shaft*' (Single) [Stax, 1971]

AFRIKA BAMBAATAA: *Planet Rock* (LP) [Tommy Boy, 1982]

GRANDMASTER FLASH AND THE FURIOUS FIVE: 'The Message' (Single) [Sugarhill, 1982]

MALCOLM MCLAREN: *Duck Rock* (LP) [Charisma, 1983]

GARY BYRD AND THE GB EXPERIENCE: 'The Crown' (Single) [Motown, 1983]

THE BEASTIE BOYS: *Licensed to Ill* (LP) [Def Jam, 1987]

ERIC B AND RAKIM: *Paid in Full* (LP) [4th & Broadway, 1987]; 'Paid in Full – Coldcut Remix' (Single) [4th & Broadway, 1987]

PUBLIC ENEMY: *Yo! Bum Rush the Show* (LP) [Def Jam, 1987]; *It Takes a Nation of Millions to Hold Us Back* (LP) [Def Jam/CBS, 1988]

5: Kick out The Jams

This is a bit of a poser, as in 1992 the whole KLF label back catalogue was instantaneously deleted. Thus the only way of finding any of the recordings by The Justified Ancients of Mu Mu discussed in this chapter is by rummaging around second-hand shops. The best bargain would be the Greatest Hits collection, *Shag Times* [KLF Communications, 1988]

6: Hitting the High-tech Groove (Not Entirely Legally)

THE SINGING DOGS: 'Singing Dogs' (Medley) (Single) [Nixa, 1955]

BETTY BOO: *Boo-Mania* (LP) [Rhythm King, 1990 – an example of Rex Brough's work as half of King John]

DEFINITION OF SOUND: *Love and Life: a Journey with the Chameleons* (LP) [Circa, 1991 – Rex as the Red King]

Sadly, *Psychoporridge* has yet to be released.

7: Pump up the Volume

M/A/R/R/S: 'Pump up the Volume/Anitina' (Single) [4AD, 1987]

GEORGE MICHAEL: *Listen Without Prejudice Vol. 1* (LP) [Epic, 1990]

MC HAMMER: *Please Hammer, Don't Hurt 'Em* (LP) [Capitol, 1990]; 'Addams' Groove' (Single) [Capitol, 1991]

8: Dirty Cash

BOMB THE BASS: 'Beat Dis' (Single) [Mister-Ron/Rhythm King/ Mute, 1988]; 'Don't Make Me Wait' (Single) [Rhythm King/ Mute, 1988]; 'I Say a Little Prayer' (Single) [Rhythm King/ Mute, 1988]

COLDCUT: 'Doctorin' the House' (Single) [Ahead of our time, 1988]

S-EXPRESS: 'Theme from S-Express' (Single) [Rhythm King/ Mute, 1988]; 'Superfly Guy' (Single) [Rhythm King/Mute, 1988]; 'Hey Music Lover' (Single) [Rhythm King/Mute, 1989]

COCO, STEEL AND LOVEBOMB: 'Love Puppy' (Single) [Red Rhino Cartel, 1987]

9: Mix-omatosis

JIVE BUNNY AND THE MASTERMIXERS: *Jive Bunny – the Album* (LP) [Telstar, 1989 – this contains all three Number 1 hit singles]

BLACK BOX: 'Ride on Time' (Single) [deConstruction/RCA, 1989]; 'The Total Mix' (Single) [deConstruction, 1990]

ALEXANDER O'NEAL: 'Hitmix (Official Bootleg Mega-Mix)' (Single) [Tabu, 1989]

BOBBY BROWN: 'The Free Style Mega-Mix' (Single) [MCA, 1990]

TECHNOTRONIC: 'Megamix' (Single) [Swanyard, 1990]

SNAP: 'The Power' (Single) [Arista, 1990]; 'Megamix' (Single) [Arista, 1991]

10: And the Law Won (but the Jury is Still Out)

GOTHIC VOICES: *A Feather on the Breath of God: Sequences and Hymns by the Abbess Hildegard of Bingen* (LP) [Hyperion, 1984]

THE BELOVED: 'The Sun Rising' (Single) [East West, 1989]
ORBITAL: 'Chime' (Single) [ffrr, 1990]; 'III' (LP) [ffrr, 1991]

11: Justifiable or Just Ancient?

NIRVANA: *Nevermind* (LP) [Geffen, 1991]
HAPPY MONDAYS: *Pills 'n' Thrills and Bellyaches* (LP) [Factory, 1990]
THE PRODIGY: 'Charly' (Single) [XL, 1991]
THE KLF: *The White Room* (LP) [KLF Communications, 1991]
THE KLF featuring TAMMY WYNETTE: 'Justified and Ancient' (Single) [KLF Communications, 1991 – see Chapter 5 above]
POP WILL EAT ITSELF: *Box Frenzy* (LP) [Chapter 22, 1987]; *Cure for Sanity* (LP) [RCA, 1990]

Epilogue: End of the Road?

PRIMAL SCREAM: *Screamadelica* (LP) [Creation/EMI, 1991]
ARRESTED DEVELOPMENT: *3 Years, 5 Months and 2 Days in the Life of . . .* (LP) [Cooltempo, 1992]
THE PRODIGY: *The Prodigy Experience* (LP) [XL, 1992]
THE SHAMEN: *Boss Drum* (LP) [One Little Indian, 1992]
TAKE THAT: *Take That and Party* (LP) [RCA, 1992]
KYLIE MINOGUE: *Kylie's Greatest Hits* (LP) [PWL, 1992]
WHITNEY HOUSTON: 'I Will Always Love You' (Single) [Arista, 1992]
BOYZ II MEN: 'End of the Road' (Single) [Motown, 1992]
CHARLES AND EDDIE: 'Would I Lie to You?' (Single) [Capitol, 1992]
R.E.M.: *Automatic for the People* (LP) [Warner Brothers, 1992]
SNAP: *The Madman Returns* (LP) [Arista, 1992]
POP WILL EAT ITSELF: *The Looks or the Lifestyle* (LP) [RCA, 1992]
CARTER USM: *30-Something* (LP) [Rough Trade, 1991]; *1992 – the Love Album* (LP) [Chrysalis, 1992]

Index